GREENING VERMONT

GREENING VERMONT

The Search for a Sustainable State

By Elizabeth Courtney and Eric Zencey

Foreword by Tom Slayton, consulting editor

Afterword by Bill McKibben

VERMONT NATURAL RESOURCES COUNCIL

THISTLE HILL PUBLICATIONS

Also by Eric Zencey:
Panama (a novel)
Virgin Forest: Meditations on History, Ecology, and Culture
The Other Road to Serfdom and the Path to Sustainable Democracy

——

Greening Vermont

By Elizabeth Courtney and Eric Zencey

Foreword by Tom Slayton

Afterword by Bill McKibben

Published by Thistle Hill Publications and the Vermont Natural Resources Council

Copyright ©2012 by Elizabeth Courtney and Eric Zencey

Distribution: VNRC (vnrc.org) and Enfield Publications (enfieldbooks.com)

Design: Laughing Bear Associates, Montpelier, Vermont

Printing: Villanti, Milton, Vermont

ISBN: 978-0-9705511-5-3

Library of Congress Contol Number: 2012941457

Thistle Hill Publications

P.O. Box 307
North Pomfret, Vermont 05053
802.457.2050
thistlehillpub.com

9 Bailey Avenue
Montpelier, Vermont 05602
802.223.2328
vnrc.org

ACKNOWLEDGMENTS

The authors wish to express their gratitude to Dot Hines, Cathleen Miller and Kinny Perot for their support for this project and for their generous contributions to ensure a healthy VNRC—and a beautiful Vermont—far into the future. Thanks also go to Lynne and Al Kammerer for their support and encouragement. We also appreciate Barbara's generosity and respect her desire for anonymity.

The VNRC Legacy Committee and the VNRC Board of Directors shared our vision for this book and provided the support to make it a reality. Special thanks go to Legacy Committee Co-Chairs Judy Geer and Susan Ritz, VNRC Board Chair Kinny Perot and VNRC Treasurer Susan Atwood-Stone. We are also thankful for the reviewing and helpful suggestions offered by a variety of environmentalists with first-hand and other experience, a list that includes many of the staff of the VNRC, especially Jake Brown, Jamey Fidel, Kim Greenwood, Kate McCarthy, and Johanna Miller. Virginia Farley, Beth Humstone, Meg Ostrum, Gerry Tarrant, Scott Reilly, Susan Ritz, Bill Roper and Gus Seelig read portions of the manuscript and offered insight and advice, helping the book become clearer, more accurate and more detailed. State Archivist Greg Sanford was particularly helpful in finding photographs of key moments and other appropriate illustrations for the book, and also read portions with an eye for accuracy and clarity. We thank Brian Shupe, representing the VNRC, and Jack Crowl of Thistle Hill Publications whose support for and continued faith in the book was crucial. Thanks are also due to Steve Holmes and James Sharp for their outstanding job of collating research materials from past *Vermont Environmental Reports*, contemporary news accounts and other sources. Jake Claro provided quick and efficient emergency research that got us through some rough passages. Thanks to those who graciously consented to be interviewed (and to have their pictures taken) for the book—and to Curtis Johnson, photographer extraordinaire. Mason Singer of Laughing Bear Associates not only contributed all design and production services, but also deserves acknowledgement for keeping his good humor and for having a geologically-scaled patience with a process that involved much tinkering and many many (many) very very (very) late changes.

Most of all the authors wish to express their gratitude to Tino O'Brien and Kathryn Davis for their patience, forbearance, clear opinions (solicited or not) and their unwavering support and encouragement as they watched us wrestle this book into being.

Of course, the authors bear sole responsibility for any errors and mistakes that remain. We want especially to note that the uncredited opinions, interpretations and arguments offered by the book are ours and ours alone, and do not reflect the opinions or positions of the VNRC, its Board of Directors, or its staff.

Elizabeth Courtney and Eric Zencey
Montpelier, 2012

CONTENTS

FOREWORD

Vermont Environmentalism

by Tom Slayton

Greening Vermont
sees Vermont
environmentalism
as a continuing saga,
one that will not
be completed in
our lifetime.

This book, *Greening Vermont*, looks both back in time and forward.

First, it looks back to tell the story of a half-century of environmental activism in Vermont. This was a time, starting in the late 1960s, that saw the establishment of the state's strong body of environmental law and other major conservation successes, even as dairy farms were going out of business by the hundreds and unplanned development threatened to transform the state forever. This is a tale of environmental victories, defeats, and, perhaps most significantly, collaborations and compromises that have put Vermont at the forefront of the national environmental movement.

The book also looks to the years ahead, when that movement will face even greater challenges. It asks whether Vermont can become environmentally stable—that is, sustainable. And what will that "sustainable state" look like?

Greening Vermont, in short, sees Vermont environmentalism as a continuing saga, one that will not be completed in our lifetime. It is an unfinished, ongoing story, one that ultimately embodies a call to personal action.

The authors of this book rightly see the arrival of the interstate highway system in Vermont in 1958 as the spark that ignited Vermont's contemporary environmental movement. That event, as well as the accompanying proliferation of electronic media, catapulted the "most rural state in the nation" into the twentieth century and set off a wave of population growth and development that continues here today.

Among the legislation that eventually resulted was Act 250, Vermont's basic development-control law, which raised the curtain on a decade of environmental activism and controversy.

But isolated events— even those as important as the coming of the interstate and the passage of Act 250—do not a movement make. To truly understand the ground from which Vermont's environmental movement grew, we need to turn the clock back more than 150 years and visit a farm on the outskirts of Woodstock.

The Vermont environmental movement can trace its roots to Vermonters like Woodstock's Frederick Billings (above), the well-travelled George Perkins Marsh (right), and Middlebury's Joseph Battell, a passionate advocate for our forests and mountains.

There, a young boy named George Perkins Marsh listened carefully as his father, a lawyer and farmer, explained to him how natural watersheds worked and what soil erosion was. The young Marsh saw nearby streams overflow and the shape of nearby Mount Tom change after heavy rains; he learned that the mountain had been clear-cut—stripped bare of trees—and was eroding away. He observed and considered.

Marsh went on to a distinguished career as a congressman and diplomat, but he never forgot his Vermont upbringing or his early experiences of environmental devastation. His travels around the Mediterranean and the Middle East helped him augment those first insights, convincing him that deforestation and soil erosion had ravaged natural systems and left deserts in place of fertile land throughout the world.

Even more fundamentally, Marsh was the first to argue that human actions could seriously damage natural systems. He went beyond the life sciences of his day and showed how human social systems interacted with natural systems and compromised them. It was this insight that made Marsh the first ecologist.

In 1864, he authored *Man and Nature*, a massive tome that warned of the dangers of human environmental degradation and noted the effects of deforestation and soil erosion on watersheds, flora, fauna, and humankind worldwide. It is considered the first environmental manifesto.

"Man is everywhere a disturbing agent," Marsh wrote. "Wherever he plants his foot, the harmonies of nature are turned to discords."

Man and Nature also contained the following passage: "Man has too long forgotten that the earth was given to him for usufruct [fruitful use] alone, not for consumption, still less for profligate waste."

This, written more than a century before the passage of Act 250, is a succinct statement of Vermont's environmental ethic—an ethic that encompasses human activities like farming and logging yet counsels care and nurturing of natural systems. It was Marsh's traditional Vermont farming experience that helped prepare him for environmental advocacy.

Not every Vermont farmer is an environmentalist, to be sure. Many have opposed the regulation that Act 250 and other environmental statutes enacted. Nevertheless, Vermont's strong farming traditions, as well as the closeness to the land and weather that they have fostered, are some of the threads from which this state's environmental legacies have been woven.

Another thread is the love that Vermonters bear for their state's natural beauty. Vermont's pastoral beauty is, to a large extent, a product of farming. Journalist Neal Peirce, in his 1976 book, *The New England States*, subtitled his chapter on Vermont "The Much-Loved State." That long-standing affection lives on in today's Vermont and is another wellspring of the state's strong environmentalism. Vermonters' love of nature and their state's quiet beauty has been expressed many times and in many ways, in paintings, poetry, songs, and stories. And it is not always tied to the useful beauty of productive agriculture.

Long before terms like "environmentalism" entered the public vocabulary, Vermonters were protecting large portions of the landscape. Joseph Battell, an eccentric millionaire who lived in

Vermont's strong farming traditions, as well as the closeness to the land and weather that they have fostered, are some of the threads from which this state's environmental legacies have been woven.

Middlebury and Ripton in the late nineteenth and early twentieth centuries, became a passionate advocate for Vermont's forests and mountains.

Battell saw the threat that indiscriminate logging posed in that era, and so he began purchasing huge tracts of land, including entire mountains, in order to protect them. He became the largest landholder in Vermont and at one point wrote, concerning his activities: "People go to Europe and pay $10,000 for a painting and hang it up in their home where none but their friends can see it; I buy a mountain for that money and it is hung up where everyone can see and enjoy it."

Joseph Battell fought long and hard in the Vermont legislature for forest conservation and mountaintop protections. The fact that Camel's Hump, Lincoln Mountain, and many other high peaks in the central Green Mountains are now protected areas is the direct result of his love of those high, remote places and his actions on their behalf. And there have been many others. In a similar action, the owners of Vermont's highest peak, Mount Mansfield, gave all the land above timberline to the University of Vermont for safekeeping.

> Vermont was no longer a place apart. It was suddenly within a day's drive of millions of people, many thousands of whom wanted what Vermont had to offer.

However, despite many Vermonters' love of the natural world, by the late nineteenth century, the thoughtless clearing of woodlands and other misguided agricultural and forest practices had left much of upland Vermont environmentally ravaged, the land barren and forests stunted. These were, of course, the very practices that men such as Marsh and Battell opposed.

In 1903 and 1904, a series of forest fires across northern New England and upstate New York had brought new urgency to Vermont's growing conservation movement. Shortly after that, the

Forestry Association of Vermont was formed to protect forests.

Rapacious logging was a national problem as well as a Vermont problem, and finding a solution resulted in the first wave of American environmentalism. The Weeks Act of 1911 allowed for the creation of national forests east of the Mississippi. (It was in this same year that Joseph Battell donated Camel's Hump to the state, with the stipulation that its forests be protected.)

Nationally, the work of Marsh and his successor, Frederick Billings, helped convince powerful men, including President Theodore Roosevelt, that forest conservation was necessary. Billings, a Vermonter who was president of the Northern Pacific Railroad from 1879 to 1881, became concerned about the deforestation of Vermont and devoted himself to promoting and practicing sound forestry on the property that Marsh had owned and that Billings bought and expanded.

The Green Mountain Club was later formed, in 1910, "to make the Vermont mountains play a greater part in the life of the people." Although the club's focus was primarily outdoor recreation and the building of the Long Trail across the state's highest mountaintops, the club also became a strong voice on behalf of the environment.

All of which brings us to Vermont in the mid-twentieth century, as the interstate highway system approached and the state's first television station, WCAX in Burlington, was sending out its first not-too-crisp black-and-white signal. As the authors of this book note

in detail in Chapter One, it was those events that began the transformation of Vermont and led, ultimately, to the environmental activism of the 1960s and 1970s.

Vermont was no longer a place apart. It was suddenly within a day's drive of millions of people, many thousands of whom wanted what Vermont had to offer: open land, beautiful vistas, and a lot of unspoiled nature in which to get away from the confusion and hustle of city life.

Those forces would transform the state in the decades that followed the opening of the interstate. And yet, even as that reshaping continues today, there remains an underpinning of stability and constancy in the Vermont experience that has helped the state receive the enormous changes of the last fifty years with some measure of grace. Vermont's farming traditions and the affection in which Vermonters hold their state are elements in that constancy. They are the ground out of which Vermont's environmental activism grew. And they remain a vital force in the Vermont of today, a part of every Vermonter's intellectual and spiritual heritage.

As the authors of *Greening Vermont* show, the passage of Act 250 and other environmental legislation in the 1970s was far from the end of the environmental story in Vermont. This book traces the ensuing history through five decades of struggle, compromise, and gradual, sometimes halting, but continual progress.

Vermont has, through all its changes and despite great social and

Joseph Battell's love for high, remote places helped protect Camel's Hump, Lincoln Mountain, and many other peaks in the Green Mountains.

economic pressures, managed to hold onto much of its natural beauty, environmental integrity, and gritty, innovative character. Yet now it finds itself facing a greater threat than ever—global climate change. Can this small state actually mount any significant opposition to such a monstrous impending catastrophe?

Characteristically, the answer from Vermont has been a resounding yes. Vermonters have declared that they will do what they can.

Consequently, this book's final chapter looks at several initiatives that offer hope and the possibility of creating what the authors term "a sustainable state" in this rural corner of America.

The patterns of history tend to repeat themselves, and environmental history is no exception. Just as the 1960s saw new infrastructure—the interstate highway system and television—bringing unexpected pressures to bear on the Vermont countryside, so the new challenges of the twenty-first century—global warming

and the exponential growth of the information highway—have brought a new set of problems and challenges to the Vermont environment of today.

Can Vermont find a creative, positive response to these new challenges? The authors of *Greening Vermont* believe so.

Their hope leads us to the opening of a new chapter in the environmental history of Vermont—and the nation.

INTRODUCTION

What Exactly Is a Sustainable State?

Our system is unsustainable, and unsustainable systems do not last. Clearly, we need to change our economy and its relationship to the planet.

As the global economic system begins its slide down the back slope of peak oil, more and more of us have begun to see that we need to wean ourselves from this energy source that can't last forever. But human energy use is only part of the environmental problem we face; everywhere you look, planetary systems have been taxed to their limits and beyond. The atmosphere can't absorb any more greenhouse gas emissions without giving us dramatic changes in climate and weather. Globally, freshwater is being used faster than the solar-powered hydrological cycle can replenish it, and much of our agriculture uses fossil fuels to subsidize its capture of daily solar income while also extracting the fertility of the soil, meaning that each harvest season leaves the planet less able to produce sustenance for us in the future. The species that compete with humans for a place in nature are being driven into extinction at a rate the planet hasn't seen since a meteor crashed into the Yucatan and ended the Cretaceous Era. We are living in the era of peak water, peak agriculture, peak carbon, peak extinction, peak footprint: peak everything, as Richard Heinberg put it in a book title.

Our system is unsustainable, and unsustainable systems do not last. Clearly, we need to change our economy and its relationship to the planet if we are to maintain anything like the levels of comfort and material security that have long seemed our birthright. The goal is and must be to create a form of human civilization that doesn't take more from nature than nature can sustainably give, a society that preserves its foundation in healthy ecosystems.

Vermont is not now a sustainable state, but in the effort to achieve that goal, it has a head start. How this came to be is the story we have aimed to tell in this book.

And what, exactly, is a sustainable state? As with any longed-for object, distance and anticipation shape our expectation, making the destination seem a completely marvelous place. We'll recognize the sustainable state as a place where economic and environmental interests are identical, because we've shaped the economy to the limits that the planet gives to us and learned our hard lessons about what is and isn't possible. We'll know it by its lush and life-filled forests, its clean waters, its stable climate, its productive and well-farmed fields capable of feeding us forever. It will be a place where living an environmentally friendly life is as easy as breathing—a matter of simple, unconscious, natural habit, with no special effort required. In that sustainable state,

In the sustainable state, our lives and work, our economy and its environment, our selves and our social relations in communities and families will all be in balance.

the normal course of our lives and work and play won't shortchange our children or our children's children, depriving them of the resources and wherewithal they'll need to live lives like the ones that we enjoy. We'll thrive in strong neighborhoods and walkable communities, where we'll know not just material comfort and security but also the satisfactions that come with better physical and psychic health. In the sustainable state, our lives and work, our economy and its environment, ourselves and our social relations in communities and families will all be in balance.

That's the romance—the vision—that sustainability has to offer. More practically, a concrete definition would

be useful. As a simple matter of logic, a sustainable state is one that doesn't undercut its own preconditions for existence. Specifically, a sustainable state preserves the ability of humans to live good lives in healthy communities in healthy ecosystems indefinitely into the future. To do this, it lives on current income—resources that can be renewed. It doesn't borrow against its environmental future. It doesn't cash out its resource base or the healthy communities that have been bequeathed to us by the past. Like a climax ecosystem, a sustainable state is one of dynamic balance, not stasis.

While the term "sustainable" is of relatively recent origin, achieving this state has been the goal, implicitly or explicitly, of the Vermont environmental movement throughout its history.

While neither of us was living in Vermont in 1958, where our story begins, on the movement's recent history we can speak from personal experience. One of us—Elizabeth Courtney—is a Harvard Loeb Fellow, a former Act 250 Environmental board member and chair and, with fourteen years in the position, the longest-serving executive director of the Vermont Natural Resources Council. The other—Eric Zencey—has been writing, thinking, and teaching about the subject for more than thirty years, twenty-eight of them in Vermont, where he currently is a Fellow of the Gund Institute for Ecological Economics at the University of Vermont. Neither of us can claim native status in our adopted home, but as long-term residents, we've witnessed change—both sweeping and

incremental—in the environmental policies and the physical landscape of the Green Mountain State. Some of those changes have been positive; some have not. The positive changes wrought in Vermont are, we think, sufficient enough that the answer to the question "Can humans achieve a sustainable balance with nature in Vermont?" is a hopeful, if cautious, yes. We have work to do, but we have a relatively solid foundation on which to build.

That's because, by and large, Vermont has managed to hang on to its natural and social character, despite the enormous pressures brought to bear upon it by the kind of rampant, fossil-fuel-driven development that transformed other parts of the country and much of the world. As a matter of geography, economics, and cultural predisposition, in Vermont the Hydrocarbon Revolution—that phase of the Industrial Revolution that was kicked off by the rapid drawdown of the antique solar energy stored in fossil fuels—arrived rather late in the game. With no sources of coal or oil of its own, and far from the seaports and transportation hubs through which such energy sources might have been imported in large quantities, Vermont remained, through the early days of the Age of Oil, what it had been long before: an agricultural society that subsisted on the solar and renewable energies offered by its own forests and fields and rivers. For the most part, its economy was fueled by wood for burning, fodder for draft animals, and hydropower to run its mills and machining industries.

This difference in its history helped to make Vermont a place apart. To a degree unmatched by most places in the country, Vermont retained its historic settlement pattern: compact town centers surrounded by working farms and forests. The landscape holds not just humans and their works but also pristine streams and lakes, verdant wetlands, deep forests, and broad meadows. The forces of oil and coal didn't spin apart the natural and social character of Vermont as thoroughly as they remade other states and landscapes in the country.

But the conservation of Vermont's working landscape into the twenty-first century was neither automatic nor accidental. Vision, hard work, difficult compromise, and some truly notable successes on the part of the state's conservation, historic preservation, and environmental movements—movements built by thousands and thousands of Vermonters—played a role too. Their work helped the state retain the landscape and built environment that support its enduring Yankee values, including the tradition of face-to-face democracy in its town meetings; the principles of civil equality and mutual neighborly respect on which that democracy is built and to which it contributes; and its habit of frugal self-reliance, which had its origins in the necessity of getting along with what could be made, had, and kept in good repair within its local economies.

Even if it seems that the Green Mountain State is on a path toward doing its part to achieve a sustain-

AN UNSUSTAINABLE CLIMATE

Sustainability is an either-or goal—you either achieve it or you don't. And Nature decides what is and isn't sustainable; it always has and it always will. We humans, with our limited vision, have to make our best guess as to what the limits imposed by nature must mean for us.

There is disagreement about those limits, naturally enough. As a matter of logic, not every voice in the conversation can be right, and as a matter of probability, any particular voice is likely to be wrong. Indeed, all the voices could be wrong; there may be limits and constraints that we fail to see until their consequences are unavoidable. Such was almost the case with the ozone layer, until an enormous, concerted, and historically unprecedented act of cooperation led to the banning of the chlorinated fluorocarbons that were degrading it and causing it to shrink. That whole movement—from chemical theory to observed confirmation to international ban in 1987—took just fourteen years. We've known about climate change for a good deal longer (an understanding of the chemistry dates as far back as 1908), but so far we've been unable to take coordinated, effective action. Why the difference? Unlike a particular commercial refrigerant, fossil fuel has no close substitutes, and use of it is embedded in every part of our economy. And oil has stronger, more powerful political muscle behind it. But unlike the case of the ozone layer, which repaired itself, processes are now underway (the shrinking of the ice caps, the emission of methane—a significant greenhouse gas—from thawing permafrost) that will reinforce global warming long after humans stop using the carbon fuel that set it in motion.

able state, clearly there is still work to be done, both in the state and beyond. Sprawl has come to the Green Mountains and continues to be a problem, as it takes established farmland and ecosystems out of production and degrades the commercial viability of town and village centers. Landscapes that look lush and appealing to the human eye can be troubled by ecological problems. Some crucial ecosystems stand as isolated oases that are too small to maintain the populations of flora and fauna within them, and roads and other aspects of the built environment deprive them of interconnection.

And to a degree that Vermonters couldn't have foreseen half a century ago, other threats to the continued existence of a vibrant, healthy, and wealthy human culture in Vermont arise from outside the state's borders. Climate change, resource scarcity, deforestation, and desertification, a burgeoning global population, the withdrawal symptoms that a world-spanning economy will experience as it is forced to give up its reliance on cheap oil—these global-scale problems are gathering into an unprecedented planetary crisis that can't be solved by any one state or nation acting alone. But Vermont can and must (and we think will) do its part to implement the policies and solutions that will be required to achieve a sustainable human culture in Vermont. Vermonters have always been a self-reliant breed, disinclined to wait for others to fix things or tell them what to do, and this characteristic will continue to serve them well.

One aspect of a sustainable Vermont is clear: the only sustainable energy foundation for human society is the planet's current solar income. We need to live on that, not on an inheritance of fossil fuels, not by delivering a bill to the future in the form of radioactive wastes that need to be stored and isolated for millennia.

The transition won't be easy. And with that change will come others, some of them impossible to predict. But this, too, is clear: we will achieve sustainability either through conscious decision or the condition of sustainability will be thrust upon us by system breakdown, incremental collapse, and frantic patching. The first path gives us more of what we want; the second leads to a great deal of human pain and suffering that could otherwise be avoided. Either way, change will come—even as strong forces and strong voices insist that such change is neither needed, nor wanted, nor likely to happen.

Which is to say: Vermonters haven't been immune to the maladies of the larger nation, including overconsumption, the denial of ecological reality, an addiction to fossil fuel, and the continuation of irrational, piecemeal development that imposes unnecessary harms and damage on our communities and ecosystems. The state's working landscape is still being compromised, still in danger of dying the death of a thousand cuts. Farms and forests are becoming fragmented, falling to scattered, incoherent development in which big-picture limits—the constraints that nature imposes on culture—can find little or no way to be represented.

How, and to what degree, have Vermonters acknowledged the existence of environmental limits? How has Vermont's environmental movement helped to prevent or forestall the degradation of the state's natural and social landscape? How have that movement and its challenges evolved? These are the issues and questions this book explores.

The transition won't be easy. And with that change will come others, some of them impossible to predict.

But this book is more than an exploration. By looking at where the environmental movement in Vermont has been, we hope to help point it toward what must lie ahead: effective advocacy for, and constructive and intentional movement toward, a sustainable state. In pursuit of this, we interviewed some of the key people in Vermont's environmental movement, asking them to reflect on their work and look to the future. As one of them noted, the work is not so much a marathon as a relay race in which the baton is passed from citizen to citizen, organization to organization, generation to generation. In its way, this book is intended to be a record of part of the race so far, and a call to run and run hard for the goal that must be achieved.

We begin our story a little more than fifty years ago, when Vermont had very few statewide environmental groups. There was the Green Mountain Club, a group of outdoor enthusiasts formed to build trails (the Long Trail, the Vermont portion of the Appalachian Trail) and to promote and support outdoor recreation. The state hosted regional offices of some national organizations—the National Wildlife Federation, The Nature Conservancy. The formation of the Vermont Natural Resources Council (VNRC), the Conservation Law Foundation (CLF), and the Vermont Public Interest Research Group (VPIRG) were yet to come. Since that time, Vermont has seen the development of more than thirty statewide, non-profit environmental and conservation-oriented organizations. Some have not survived and have either merged with other groups or simply closed up shop. A much larger number of local groups have formed, as concerned citizens organized to protect a watershed, to preserve particular landscapes and habitats, to deal with particular problems or affect particular decisions about energy use, land use, housing patterns, or the siting of a mall or a waste dump. Much like the abundant variety of creatures that Darwin found in the Galapagos, each of these organizations filled a niche within a larger complex system, lending vigor and purpose to the life of the whole. United by a common goal of protecting the quality of the environment, they are as diverse in their methods and manifestations as the beaks of Darwin's finches, and like those adaptations, their structure and

work were shaped by the demands of their specialized tasks.

It would take a much longer book than this to tell the story of them all. What we offer is a selection, a few threads picked from a very large, very complex tapestry. By focusing on selected passages in the history of Vermont's environmental movement, we want to illustrate a central idea: the movement has implicitly (and sometimes explicitly) worked to establish in Vermont a sustainable balance between humans and nature, between our culture and its physical home on the planet.

Even within that purpose there is, of course, room for choices to be made. One strong strand in the history of the environmental movement in Vermont is Act 250, Vermont's premiere land use control law, and we've placed it near the center of our story. No doubt other threads would have proved equally useful. A similar book could have been produced that focused more directly on Vermont's complicated experience with land use planning, or the work of land trusts and conservation organizations, or its long tradition of citizen activism and town-based governance, or its tradition of concern for social justice in political,

economic, and environmental matters, or the history of its energy use or carbon footprint. Each of these connective threads would have had us trace a similar-but-different path through the tapestry of the complex whole. We think that our focus communicates its essential feature: in Vermont, culture and nature are not as dramatically imbalanced as elsewhere, which means the state has a good start in meeting the challenges of becoming fully sustainable.

There are many Vermonters who worked to give Vermont that head start. They researched, organized, agitated, legislated, and educated; they wrote, spoke, testified, argued, and collaborated; they demonstrated, built, imagined, advocated, lobbied, persuaded, and invented. In dozens of ways, they contributed to the high purpose of fitting economic life into its proper ecological and social context so that Vermonters could continue to enjoy a healthy environment and vital communities indefinitely. While our story is in part about some of those people and the tools that they developed and honed over time, our focus is primarily on the collective result—the evolution of the movement that gave Vermont its leg up on the difficult task of establishing a sustainable society. Tracing that story should yield useful insight into how Vermont might, in the future, achieve the sustainable state that we know is clearly necessary. And possibly, by doing so, Vermont can create a model for a nation in need.

That is our hope for this book.

CHAPTER 1

The 1960s

Conservation

Vermont is opened to the larger world by the arrival of the Interstate, and its modern environmental movement is launched.

On a brisk Saturday morning in November of 1958, a few hundred citizens and officials gathered at the edge of the town of Guilford, Vermont, on the imaginary line that separates Vermont from Massachusetts. They were there to mark an important moment in the state's environmental history—though it's doubtful that any of the participants would have described what they were doing in those terms. They had gathered to listen to speeches, witness a bit of ceremony, and then climb in their cars to take an inaugural drive on Vermont's first stretch of Interstate highway.

Running a scant six miles from the Massachusetts border and not quite reaching Brattleboro, the road was a major work of engineering, built to a design that's familiar to every American: four wide lanes, limited access, an ambitiously sculpted right-of-way, and gentle curves that could be taken at speed. To the Vermonters who gathered in Guilford, the new highway was a marvel. There was no other road like it in the state.

During the ceremony, the highway's official certificate of completion was handed from the contractor to the state highway commissioner and then to Governor Joe Johnson, who made brief remarks ("one of the greatest accomplishments in the annals of state history"). In a program that would likely be challenged today for its blending of church and state, the Reverend Fred H. Miller from All Souls Church in Brattleboro offered an invocation, and after some music from a high school band, another minister pronounced a benediction. Once the ribbon was cut, the motorcade began: about a hundred cars drove north, with open roadsters from the twenties and thirties leading the way, their occupants bundled against the chill. When the procession reached the end of the highway, the official party made their way on to Brattleboro, where they retired for lunch at the Hotel Brooks.

VERMONT BY THE NUMBERS:

1960

- Population: 389,881
- Percent born in state: 76.7
- Cows: 258,000
- Farms: 9,400
- Total farm acreage: 2,624,371
- Registered motor vehicles: 151,976
- Seasonal homes: 18,171

"Like it or not...the fact remains that adequate roads are the lifeblood of Vermont's economy and the heart of our hopes for growth."– *Rutland Herald* **editorial**

That first section of Interstate was impressive, but as a portent of dramatic and far-reaching change it was easy to underestimate. It offered a few scant minutes of motoring. Along much of its length, it paralleled old Route 5, the sinuous road it was designed to supplant, and in places lay a mere 200 yards from it. It was an upgrade— an impressive one—but still nothing more complicated than a road.

But change in form sometimes brings about a change in function. The opening of those first few miles of modern roadway signaled the opening, also, of an era of rapid and far-reaching

change for the state of Vermont, which had been until then a lightly populated, rural mountain fastness. Many of the hallmarks of modern life—television, telephones, even electricity—were not yet fully present in the state. The engines of twentieth-century progress had largely passed the state by. It was too remote, its population too sparse, its towns and villages too small to draw much attention. With the arrival of the Interstate that was about to change very quickly, for the world that held Vermont in a remote and distant corner had suddenly become much smaller. As one state official put it years later,

the highway "took us out of the sticks and put us within a day's drive of eighty million people."

Quite a few of those 80 million were ready to make the trip. Vermont had long marketed itself as a tourist destination. In the nineteenth century, "flatlanders" arrived by train to enjoy the state's mountain scenery, its lakes and rivers and hiking trails, and to immerse themselves in the slower pace of life in its villages and towns. A state program dating to the early twentieth century encouraged farmers to add to their income by offering guest rooms to urbanites looking for pastoral escape and a restorative rural experience. Beginning in 1948, a state-published magazine, *Vermont Life*, touted "our beautiful countryside, the friendliness of our people, and the 'Vermont way of life'" to visitors, aiming to sell the tranquil pleasures of its bucolic countryside —and, somewhat paradoxically, the glamour and excitement of America's fastest-growing outdoor sport, downhill skiing. (The enthusiasm that one of those skiers had for the state would have a very large effect on its economy and landscape; International Business Machines chief executive officer Thomas Watson Jr., decided to locate a manufacturing plant in the state in part because of the ready access he would have to his favored sport.) With the progress of the Interstate, an increased traffic of outsiders—"leaf peepers" and hunters in the fall, urban exiles in the summer, and, increasingly, skiers in the winter—would bring commerce and trade and the opportunity for Vermonters to work and make money.

The opportunity was widely appreciated; in 1950 per capita income in Vermont was just three-fourths the national average, and the percentage of Vermonters living in poverty (23.5 percent in 1959) compared unfavorably to the bordering states of New Hampshire, Massachusetts, and New York (14.9, 12.2, and 14.2, respectively). Vermont was, in many ways, an underdeveloped land in a wealthy country, and the arrival of the outside world via the highway was expected to change that. To any Vermonters skeptical of the cost and the likely effects of the new high-

Guilford, Vermont, 1958: an important moment in the state's environmental history.

way system, the *Rutland Herald* offered an editorial admonition: "Like it or not, desire to raise the required money or not, the fact remains that adequate roads are the lifeblood of Vermont's economy and the heart of our hopes for growth and expansion."

Growth and expansion—the easily foreseeable result of the Interstate—were widely embraced. If change meant jobs, a path out of rural poverty, and lives like those whose images had begun to flicker in (some) Vermont homes through the wonder of television, then change was good. What wasn't so easily foreseen was how thoroughly those changes would

shape the state, testing its ability to preserve its landscape, its communities, and its character.

There were signs available to those who cared to read them. In his autobiographical account of his years in Vermont as an Associated Press reporter, Chris Graff tells the story of Romaine Tenney, a farmer who worked his land in Ascutney the way his father and grandfather had worked it before him, plowing with horses and laying in his hay with a pitchfork. Tenney refused to vacate his land to make way for the Interstate. "I was born here and I'll die here," he vowed. Matters came to a head when

If the Interstate itself was unstoppable, so too seemed the changes it brought in its train. Dover and Wilmington, due west of Brattleboro and containing the Carinthia and Haystack ski areas, were hardest hit. Both saw an explosion of new home construction—some for workers drawn by the economic opportunities, most for visitors looking for accommodations or a second home. With the skiers and construction came roads, restaurants, shops, bars.

As they competed for skier visits and expanded their facilities to handle the increased traffic, many ski area owners were no longer content with the mountains as natural processes had made them. Entrepreneurs like Fred Pabst Jr., brewing mogul and owner of Big Bromley ski area, used heavy equipment, dynamite, and countless thousands of man-hours to carve new trails and mold the mountain slopes into skier-friendly terrain. "Although Nature provides the basic ingredients, her unaided efforts are not quite enough," was the judgment of one *Vermont Life* article.

Before the arrival of the Interstate, Vermonters made do with what could be made, had, and repaired locally. For many Vermonters, splitting wood still is an annual chore.

bulldozers and work crews arrived in his pastures. Eventually, a sheriff arrived with a court order and a cohort of deputies, who set to work dispossessing the old man from the family farm. They moved tools and harnesses from the outbuildings, working until sunset, intending to return the next morning to finish. They never got the chance. That night Tenney's house and buildings burned to the ground, with him inside. He had fulfilled his vow.

Not just the mountains but ski towns and the quality of life Vermonters could live within them were remodeled as well. Downhill skiing in the 1930s and 1940s had been a clubby sport. Practitioners were hardy types who hiked up the mountains they then skied down. They'd get in one or two runs before nightfall, and then repair to the local general-store-cum-equipment shop for a debriefing, a cup of hot chocolate, and maybe a shot or two of something stronger. Skiers from "away" mingled with locals and were readily absorbed into the camaraderie that comes from shared dedication to a difficult and challenging practice. They didn't change the "Vermont way of life"— that nebulous-but-real phenomenon that *Vermont Life* would come to brand in the future.

The installation of Vermont's first rope tow in Woodstock, in 1934, had already begun to change that. With the ongoing development of lift technology —T-bars, chairlifts—skiers no longer needed to be mountaineers and, for the first time, could spend more time going downhill than up. The application of ingenuity and fossil fuels broadened the demographic appeal of the sport, and with the Interstate, its geographic reach was extended as well. Ski towns began to fill with transients and strangers who came for the day or week and were gone before you could get to know them.

Thus, Vermont's traditional, face-to-face "handshake" culture was gradually displaced by a modernizing society, one reliant on exchanges between strangers that had to be structured (and, when need be, enforced) by law rather than by custom or the social and family ties that bound Vermonters one to another. The social cost of that change is difficult to calculate, but a direct measure of its scale can be made in dollars. In the late 1940s, skiers spent about five million annually in the state. By the early 1960s, that figure had risen to well over thirty million, a sixfold increase in a decade and a half. In ensuing years, the

A HANDSHAKE CULTURE

The "Vermont way of life": Is there— was there—such a thing? Most assuredly. It was formed by a host of influences: the state's rural and agricultural land-scape; its citizens' participation in a predominantly local commerce and culture; a deep-seated egalitarianism and tradition of civil respect, which was rooted in the direct democracy of its town meetings; and a sturdy stock of old-fashioned Yankee values—honesty, thrift, forbearance, and a reverence for time-tested values and habits that, like the land itself, had been handed from generation to generation.

The social character of Vermont was also shaped by the considerable effect of the Vermont winter, which fell, then as now, on everyone alike. In the 1960s, most Vermonters met winter as their ancestors had, with wood and wool and woodstoves and, in general, the limited resources available in a preindustrial, undeveloped American society. In her mountain villages, Vermont's January nights regularly hit ten below, and during cold snaps, the daytime temperature might never rise much above that number for a week or two at a time. From childhood, every Vermonter knew that in winter a body was only one bad choice or one stroke of bad luck away from misfortune, pain, or death. This common sense of shared vulnerability to nature and its winter was an unspoken foundation of rural and village life.

Another obvious and frequently remarked foundation was the inter-lacing of communities and families through blood ties and neighborly familiarity. With little immigration in the late nineteenth and early twentieth centuries, Vermont was peopled by folks who were known to each other, or who knew someone who knew just about anyone you cared to name. It was a handshake culture, given to doing business on promise and honor rather than contract and law.

new roadways—the Interstate and the upgraded state routes that were built to connect them to ski areas—redoubled that pace of change.

Skiers spent money on lift tickets and equipment, of course, but also on food and lodging and entertainment, giving rise to a hospitality industry whose hotels, motels, restaurants, bars, and parking lots were an unprecedented presence in the state's formerly remote and deeply forested mountains. With few mechanisms of control, many a select board found itself powerless to halt the changes. "Thus it came to pass," wrote the popular Vermont historian Ralph Nading Hill, "that at the foot of the ski tows were constructed great parking lots for the cars that brought the people to engage in their struggle against gravity…. And around the ski tows grew clusters of buildings to feed and amuse these people, and on the roads near these tows arose lounges, chalets, A-frame cottages and every manner of structure." He might have added that the roads leading into them were increasingly banked with signs and billboards encouraging visitors to favor this or that restaurant, hotel, motel, bar, or ski area. Together, the signs and homes and businesses made a distinctive pattern of development: linear rural sprawl, a marked contrast to the state's compact village centers with their clear edges against the forested or open countryside. Nearby cities began sprawling too, as they felt the effects of secondary growth stimulated by the ski areas.

To many, what mattered wasn't just the visual dissonance of the new land

By the early 1960s, skiers were spending $30 million annually in the state, a number that would grow exponentially in the years to come.

use pattern, but the damage it did to the ecosystems of the mountains, and the burden of new expense it put on towns too small to absorb it. To those inclined to see development in its broader context, the skiing boom in Vermont in the 1960s brought jobs and commerce, yes, but also exemplified a troubling dynamic: developers took private profit and imposed very public costs in their wake, as roads needed maintenance and plowing, houses needed fire and police protection, towns needed sewage treatment plants, schools needed classroom space and new bus routes. Some developers

simply bought land, subdivided it into housing parcels, and resold it at a profit. Others didn't actually develop anything but speculated, buying low, holding for a while, selling high. The rising property values that resulted put a burden on Vermonters, as town expenses and property taxes rose with them; farmers and holders of family homesteads found themselves needing to sell off land to pay the bills. That practice simply accelerated and spread the troubling dynamic that prompted it.

Clearly, something had to be done.

MAJOR MOMENTS IN LAND USE PLANNING IN VERMONT

1957

Thomas Watson Jr., CEO of IBM, decides to locate a manufacturing plant in Essex Junction, initiating unprecedented growth in Chittenden County. Eventually employing 8,000 workers, the company will become and remain the state's largest private employer.

1958

The Interstate Highway arrives in Guilford, opening Vermont to tourism, population growth, and development.

1960

The U.S. Census shows that for the first time people outnumber cattle in the state of Vermont.

1962

Vermont governor Phil Hoff establishes the Central Planning Office and charges it to organize state, regional, and local efforts to manage growth.

1964

The legislature creates the Interagency Committee on Natural Resources, which has some planning functions. Governor Hoff creates the Scenery Preservation Council that promotes a billboard ban and the regulation of junkyards and municipal dumps.

1965

The legislature authorizes the creation of eleven regional planning commissions (covering the entire state), which will use grants from the federal Department of Housing and Urban Development to write comprehensive regional plans.

1967

Governor Hoff forms and chairs the Vermont Planning Council. Its report, *Vision and Choice,* defines goals and patterns of development that would "preserve and protect, cultivate and promote the human and natural resources and attributes of the state in the interest of all the citizens of the state and on their terms."

1967

The Vermont legislature passes the Municipal and Regional Planning and Development Act, which serves as a model planning law for other states.

1969

Governor Deane Davis tours southern Vermont with Windham regional planning director Bill Schmidt and sees the effects of unplanned development. He reaches a handshake agreement with International Paper CEO Ed Hinman to abandon plans to build 1,400 vacation homes in the town of Stratton (pop. 104). He convenes the Governor's Conference on Natural Resources and forms the Governor's Commission on Environmental Control, chaired by state representative Art Gibb.

FOUR VARIETIES OF CAPITAL

The Vermont that saw the arrival of the Interstate in 1958 may have been an agrarian state that hadn't yet felt the full force of the Hydrocarbon Revolution that was transforming the country at large, but it was by no means a fully sustainable society. A sustainable society doesn't degrade or eliminate any of the preconditions for its own existence. An emergent school of thought in economics—Ecological Economics—offers one way to further define sustainability: a sustainable society doesn't draw down any of the capital stocks on which its operation depends.

These capital stocks come in four varieties: built (or economic) capital, natural capital, social capital, and cultural capital. Every business owner knows that you can't stay in business if you don't set aside some part of your income to replace your capital equipment as it wears out and ages; your built capital has to be preserved, or your business isn't sustainable. The same applies to the other forms of capital. "Natural capital" can be defined as "healthy ecosystems understood as providers of economically valuable services to humans." Those services include the flood control services that forests provide, which George Perkins Marsh was the first to write about in 1864. The list includes climate moderation and stability, nutrient recycling, water purification and delivery, maintenance of soil fertility, habitat for wildlife, and the opportunity for aesthetic, spiritual, recreational, and educational experiences. The benefits we get from sturdy social and cultural capital may be less concrete, but they are no less real. Social capital can be defined as "the stock of mutual trust, shared understanding, and publicly held knowledge that allows for a satisfying life in society." Concern for the Vermont way of life is a concern for the state's stock of social and cultural capital.

A sustainable society doesn't draw down any of the capital stocks on which its operation depends.

Three Streams and a Confluence in Plainfield

One other event, five years and 125 miles from the ribbon cutting in Guilford, was an equally consequential moment in the modern environmental history of the state. In February of 1963, Goddard College in Plainfield hosted a two-day conference called "Natural Resources in Transition"—the transition being the one wrought by development pressures, including especially the changes brought by the advancing Interstate. By then the road from Guilford reached twenty-eight miles into the state, and a section had been opened between the capital, Montpelier, and the town of Bolton, half the distance to Burlington, the state's largest city. This meeting in Plainfield was the first-ever statewide gathering of officials, educators, and knowledgeable citizens dedicated to thinking about the future of the state's natural resources.

Presentations included an inventory of those resources, with reports by the state geologist and the commissioners of agriculture, forests and parks, and water resources. Panels discussed how agriculture and transportation were being transformed by technology (the fossil-fueled machinery that many Vermont farmers, like Tenney, had declined to adopt). Other panels discussed the need for coherent planning to balance development with preservation of Vermont's landscape and natural heritage.

In taking up these subjects, the group that met in Plainfield didn't have to start from scratch. They, and the nascent Vermont environmental movement they represented, drew on the conservation ethic that had developed in the United States in the late nineteenth century, as exemplified in the writings and life projects of men like George Perkins Marsh, Gifford Pinchot, John Muir, and others. What many Americans understood to be a coherent conservation movement was, in fact, a confluence of several distinct streams that arose from different sources. These streams mingled and seemed to be drawn, as a river is drawn by gravity, toward a common end; but the different waters retained something of the character—the flavor—of their origin.

For Gifford Pinchot, a forester, conservation meant using resources "for the greatest good for the greatest number over the greatest period of time." In Europe, he learned the principles of sustained yield forestry and brought them back to the United States, rooting them in the Yale School of Forestry that he helped found. The commonsense ideas at the heart of sustained yield forestry—if you cut a tree, you ought to plant a tree; and you ought not to cut wood faster than the forest can grow it—were, in 1900, a novelty in the United States. The country had been used to an expanding frontier, and it seemed there would always be more of everything over the ext horizon. As the first chief of the U.S. Forest Service (1905–1910), Pinchot helped establish forestry as a professional discipline that brought scientific methods to the lumber industry and managed forests for the maximum benefit they could give to humans.

In 1900, though, the range of those benefits wasn't as broad as we see them now to be. Early conservationists generally thought of forests solely in terms of economic values, not ecological values. In that vision, woodlands give humans a sustainable flow of board feet of lumber, some recreational experiences, some watershed protection and not much else. For Pinchot, deadfall trees—trees that are left in the forest to rot, to play their natural role in the recycling of nutrients and energy in the forest—were "wasted," because they brought no economic value to humans. At one point, Pinchot declared that "this physical earth consists of just two things: humans and resources." The non-human world, clearly, was just potential economic value.

That view was completely at odds with the vision of John Muir, whose preservationism was another element in the environmental consciousness of Americans. Muir wrote of the sublime vistas of the Sierras, calling us to appreciate the opportunities nature offers for transcendence—for spiritual experience or (if you're not particularly spiritually minded) for deep aesthetic experience and psychic grounding, for the re-creation of the self that is possible in an encounter with nature as an immense and glorious other.

Theodore Roosevelt worked with both men and both visions. For a time, the two different visions seemed capable of being good bedfellows, united in their dedication to the wise use of resources.

In 1963, Goddard College hosted the first-ever statewide gathering of officials, educators, and knowledgeable citizens dedicated to thinking about the future of the state's natural resources.

Muir called on us to appreciate the opportunity nature offers for serene and aesthetic experience.

Tom Slayton, Alec Webb, Megan Camp, and Bob Klein

IT'S A RELAY RACE

Bob, Tom, Alec, and Megan talk about the childhood roots of their engagement with conservation issues, as well as the challenges facing the movement today.

Bob Klein's professional life spans thirty years, but his first attempt at environmental conservation goes back further than that, to when he was a young boy. Near his home along the east coast of Florida, bull-dozers were knocking down and scraping away the forest where Bob and his friends explored and adventured. Developers were about to build hundreds of vacation homes overlooking the Atlantic Ocean, in what Bob considered to be his woods. What Bob did next shows the kind of initiative he'd always be capable of: he found the blueprints for the project and hid them from the contractors. He was frustrated to find that his bit of boyish direct action didn't slow the project at all.

The realization that special places are vulnerable to economic forces and that forests have a reality that paper can't always protect guided Bob's choices for years to come. By 1985, after studying botany and forestry in college and graduate school, Bob was living in Vermont and working with Hub Vogelmann to conserve natural areas through both the Vermont Natural Resource Council (VNRC) and the Vermont Chapter of The Nature Conservancy, which he has headed since the early 1980s. With fifty-four natural areas to its credit, and its other contributions to the protection of federal, state, and municipal lands, The Nature Conservancy has an established conserved landscape in every county of Vermont. More than one hundred of these places are open to the public. Like that forest that Bob knew and loved as a child, they too will offer generations to come the opportunity to find and lose themselves in the exploration and experience of nature.

Tom Slayton, editor emeritus of *Vermont Life* magazine, also traces his conservation ethic to childhood roots, in his case to the family farm in Duxbury and to his experiences hiking on Mount Mansfield in Stowe in the 1950s. "These were magical places for me then," he says, "but sadly the farm has been lost to a dying rural lifestyle, and Mansfield's mountain wilderness has been compromised by ski development and a booming resort economy."

Prior to his twenty-one-year association with *Vermont Life,* Tom was a reporter and editor for Vermont newspapers for twenty years. His book, *Searching for Thoreau: On the Trails and Shores of Wild New England*, was published in 2007 and, in 2008, received the gold medal for creative non-fiction from the Independent Publisher Book Awards. It also won an honorable mention by *Foreword* magazine as one of their top ten nonfiction books of the year. With several more books to his name, Tom is now a VPR commentator and freelance writer and editor.

Experience of nature, especially in youth, is crucial, Tom believes. "You can't convince people to preserve something if they don't know it's valuable … getting that message out there"—and getting people out there, into the landscapes of the state—"plays an important role in helping to maintain Vermont's beauty." If they've had that primary experience, Tom says, then the work of the conservation movement is a great deal easier; it consists not so much of hectoring and lecturing but of "reminding people" that the integrity of Vermont's landscape is essential to our values and our quality of life.

As president and vice president, respectively, of Shelburne Farms, Alec Webb and Megan Camp oversee an organization whose mission is to cultivate a conservation ethic for a sustainable future. Shelburne Farms does that through educational programming and through its long-standing commitment to preserving and encouraging rural land uses that are environmentally, economically, and culturally sustainable.

Alec grew up on Shelburne Farms and was happily influenced by several farmhands who possessed "admirable skills not taught" to the young men in Alec's preparatory school in Massachusetts. As a boy, Alec learned hands-on dairying from his father. In 1972, he became a conscientious objector during the Vietnam War and was assigned to work at the Vermont Arts and Crafts Service in the Department of Education. Interest in promoting local arts and crafts led directly to his work collaborating with Marilyn Neagley to organize the first farmers' market in Burlington in 1974. Alec was among the first in Vermont to see, and to act on, the connection between land use, farm preservation, community development, and strong markets for fresh, locally produced food.

Megan's early memories are of Washington, D.C., where her parents were active in the Johnson administration's War on Poverty. "I thought every family marched on the weekends," she laughs. The

Above: (l. to r.) Megan Camp, Alec Webb, Bob Klein, and Tom Slayton

activism of her parents taught her that "you can make a difference in the world." Her connection to an agrarian landscape came when her family moved to north central Massachusetts, where the beauty of the orchards and fields and a Fredrick Law Olmstead park gave her a foretaste of what she'd come to know in Vermont. In 2001, when Vermont public schools adopted new curriculum standards in sustainability, it was in part because of Megan's dedication to providing every Vermont child with the opportunity to experience nature and to develop the skills and knowledge needed to live in the twenty-first century.

Several themes emerge from their conversation. One is the long-term value of education. "The secret to conserving a place is to make sure that it is loved," Megan says. It's a sentiment the others share. Shelburne Farms, under Alec and Megan's leadership, and the Vermont Chapter of The Nature Conservancy under Bob's, have invited thousands of visitors to know, to learn from, and to love the landscapes they've conserved. The National Wildlife Federation, the Vermont Land Trust, the Green Mountain Club, the Lake Champlain Committee, the Vermont River Conservancy, the Preservation Trust

of Vermont, other advocacy organizations, and the many local land trusts, watershed groups, and outdoor schools—"all of them understand that a personal relationship with nature is essential to its protection," Bob reimnds us. It's the product of a kind of education, which, done well, combines theory and practice—cultivating a love of place by getting young people outdoors, helping them understand their home territory, and letting them see the role of energy use in society, the value of local agriculture, and the difference between finite and renewable natural resources.

Is Vermont still "a place apart"? The group agrees that Vermont clearly changed with the arrival of television and the Interstate. The extent to which Vermont has managed to hang on to its ethos and its working landscape despite those changes is impressive. The state's agricultural economy and heritage has played a large role in supporting environmental awareness, even among non-farmers in the state.

"Conservation work needs to be sustained over time—generations, in fact. Vermont is our hope for the future," says Bob. "You can't think of it as a sprint," Alec says. "And it's not a marathon, either; it's a relay race." The movement needs the continual entry of fresh energy, fresh legs, if it's to conserve the natural and social capital on which our state depends.

But long-simmering and fundamental differences in the two visions came to a head early in the twentieth century over the fate of a wilderness valley located on federal land—Hetch Hetchy, in Yosemite National Park in California. To Muir, it was one of the most ravishingly beautiful landscapes the American West had to offer, "one of nature's rarest and most precious mountain temples." To Pinchot, it was an excellent site for hydroelectric development that could supply electricity and water to San Francisco, which was then rebuilding after the earthquake of 1906. As Pinchot saw things, a river running wild in its natural course—not dammed for electricity and recreation and irrigation—was a river whose resource potential was being wasted.

Pinchot testified to Congress while Muir made his case in the 1912 book *The Yosemite*. Muir lost; in the end, Congress voted to allow the dam in the valley.

The episode showed that preservation and conservation could be united in common cause when the land is broad and accommodating, but when population presses against the limits of ecosystems, the alliance is strained and often the two must part company.

By the time of the gathering in Plainfield, the divergence of preservation and conservation was becoming increasingly visible in the country at large but had yet to become so obvious in Vermont, with its smaller population and very nearly preindustrial way

As they competed for skier visits and expanded their facilities to handle the increased traffic, many ski area owners were no longer content with the mountains as natural processes had made them.

of life. As Vermont's population grew in the second half of the century, its demands on the landscape increased. Today, the old conservation-versus-preservation rift has emerged as a controversy over the development of ridgeline wind power in the Green Mountain State, a controversy that has (as we shall see) divided environmentalists. It's Pinchot versus Muir, updated, in twenty-first-century Vermont.

A third stream is present in the confluence of ideas that shaped the environmental movement in Vermont, and it, too, is present in the controversy over ridgeline wind development as well as other renewable energy sources in Vermont. It points to the civilization-sustaining natural services that some economic development often threatens: water quality, forest integrity, and the contiguity of habitat for wildlife, among others. This stream of thought had its origin within the Green Mountain State—although the man associated with it, George Perkins Marsh, achieved his key insights as a result of travels he made far from his native Woodstock. In 1864, Marsh published *Man and Nature, or Physical Geography as Modified by Human Action*; it was the first book to argue (and to document with historical examples) the completely novel premise that nature was not an unchanging entity lying wholly outside culture, but was instead a set of complex systems that could be damaged and degraded by human action. Sometimes the damage was so severe that civilizations lost their base in nature and could no longer exist. (In this, Marsh was the intellectual progenitor of Jared Diamond, whose *Collapse: How Societies Choose to Fail or Succeed*, makes the same case).

Marsh was a renaissance intellect. He spoke half a dozen languages, worked at translating biblical passages from the original Greek, had a hand in designing Vermont's current statehouse, was a railroad entrepreneur, and built the first mills on the Winooski in the town of that name. In 1861, Abraham Lincoln selected him to be his ambassa-dor to Italy. Marsh took the opportunity of travelling to Europe and the Middle East to visit some of the places he'd read about in his Bible studies and was led to ruminate on what he found. The ancient "land of milk and honey" had become dry and stony desert. Marsh's genius was that he connected this observation with his own experience in Woodstock, where he had noticed that the spring freshets of the Ottauquechee River that ran near the family homestead had steadily grown over the years. Marsh's early years encompassed the era of rapid forest exploitation in Vermont, as woodland was cleared for agriculture, sheep grazing, timber, fuel, and potash. During this time, Vermont went from nearly fully forested to 80 percent deforested by 1850. Marsh surmised that clear-cutting on the uplands around the village of Woodstock played a role in the behavior of the river; he was among the first to make the connection between deforestation and flooding. On his travels in the (formerly) Fertile Crescent, he saw a landscape that had lost its forests—the cedars of Lebanon were long gone, cut for fuel and construction of houses and ships. His book argued that this change, as well as the salinization of soils from irrigated agriculture, lay behind the transformation of the broader landscape. These changes rendered the land incapable of supporting the storied civilizations of antiquity. In modern terms, we would say that Marsh began pointing us to an appreciation of ecosystem services that were unaccounted for in the visions of Muir and Pinchot.

More than a century after Marsh wrote, in February of 1962—just five months before the conference in Plainfield—Rachel Carson published *Silent Spring*, her penetrating account of the ecological damage brought about by widespread pesticide use in the United States. The book, a *New York Times* bestseller and a Book-of-the-Month Club selection, would have been known to all who attended the meeting. It helped galvanize a movement that led to the first Earth Day observance in 1970 and the landmark national environmental legislation of that era: the Clean Air Act of 1970, and the Water Pollution Control Act of 1972,

The hills above the Capitol, like much of Vermont were deforested in the 19th Century.

Hub Vogelmann

THE MAN ON THE MOUNTAIN

Hub Vogelmann, professor emeritus and former chair of the Botany Department at the University of Vermont (UVM), was instrumental in putting a key provision into Act 250. Hub's multidecade study of forest growth on Camel's Hump showed Vermonters the importance and fragility of these ecosystems and also gave the state incontrovertible evidence of the effects of acid rain and climate change on the most iconic of mountains in the state.

Hub was a founding member of the VNRC and served on its board in the 1960s and 1970s and again from 2004 to 2010. In the late 1950s, as a brand-new faculty member at UVM, he was asked by Dr. James Marvin, chair of the Botany Department, to help found the Vermont chapter of The Nature Conservancy, which predated VNRC (and which helped midwife it into existence). Those early years were slow going, he remembers, with only a handful of people at the first meeting and a few more turning out for meetings in "bogs and marshes" around the state. With his brand-new doctorate in plant ecology from the University of Michigan completed, he toured Rotary and garden clubs around the state with a slide show about ecosystems and the ways that human culture was changing them. "They had to have a speaker every month," he laughs. "So I rode that wave."

Hub's love of botany is rooted in childhood experience, particularly a "special appreciation" for the honeybees he kept with his father in their backyard and later on the roof of their house. It seemed only natural for him to follow the bees into a lifelong interest in flowering plants, an interest that took him to collecting medicinal plants in Bogotá and studying cloud rain forests in the hills of Mexico. Fortunately for Vermonters, his career track had a firm rooting at UVM, where his ongoing study of alpine vegetation on Mount

Mansfield and Camel's Hump helped preserve these fragile ecosystems from development.

The future? "There's rightly a great deal of concern about climate change these days," says Hub. One effect that Vermonters will become increasingly aware of: "Climate change will lead to water scarcity," he predicts. If Vermont has a head start in dealing with the changes coming our way, Hub Vogelmann is prominent among those who have helped give the state that edge—through his vision, hard work, and generous community service.

the Endangered Species Act of 1973. Tutored by Pinchot, Muir, and Marsh, mindful of Carson and other contemporary warnings, many Vermonters had grown concerned about the transformation in the landscape that increased commerce was bringing. "There was a ferment in the state," Jim Wilkinson, a key figure in the early movement, recalled. Many thoughtful Vermonters were eager "to get some kind of organization going" to protect the character and resources of the state they loved.

As conference chairman Sam Ogden noted in a follow-up letter to participants later that summer, "the idea of a Resources Council was proposed early in the conference." It came up repeatedly for discussion, and before they adjourned, participants voted unanimously to create a small working group that would develop the idea. It had first been broached at the conference by Robert Fish Jr., a trustee of the Vermont chapter of The Nature Conservancy, who was well positioned to see both the strengths and the limits of his organization's efforts. The Vermont chapter, formed in October of 1960 by two University of Vermont botany professors, James Marvin and "Hub" Vogelmann, worked to protect environmentally sensitive (and, often, breathtakingly beautiful) land through outright purchase and preservation. In 1962, it made its first purchase, Molly Bog—thirty-five acres in Morristown for $500. (Eleven years

The arrival of the petroleum-fueled economy reshaped the landscape and culture of Vermont.

later this classic northeastern kettle hole bog was designated a National Natural Landmark, along with several other wetlands parcels protected by the Conservancy.)

The purchase-and-protect strategy had limited reach, since it was neither financially feasible nor especially desirable to preserve from every sort of development all the landscape that would benefit from being used wisely. What was needed, conference participants saw, was an additional mechanism—one that would take account of the ecological effects of development, one that would bring about conservation not through protection and outright prohibition of development but through regulation that secured wise and fair use of the land and its resources. This cause could best be advanced by a new organization, one that could identify and work to implement appropriate constraints on development in the state.

The six-member working group presented its proposal to another meeting at Goddard on June 27, 1963, and held an organizational meeting the following day in Burlington, on the campus of the University of Vermont. A press release issued the next day announced that "The Vermont Natural Resources Council was organized yesterday at Burlington." It gave the objectives of the council:

To educate the public in regard to the interrelationship of our soils, waters, plants, and animals, their effect on man and man's effect on them;

To promote wise use and preservation of natural resources to the benefit of Vermont citizens; and

To provide a means for representing all interested individuals and organizations, and to present their representations to the public.

Begun as an all-volunteer organization, with no staff or office, the VNRC aimed to influence policy from its inception. "We got our point of view across by inviting people to visit sites, writing newspaper articles, getting newspapers to review our projects, and buttonholing key people to explain to them what we thought—often in private," recalled Dick Brett, the VNRC's chair, news-letter editor, and financier from 1963 to 1967. "It was a very informal, seat-of-the-pants kind of thing." When the Army Corps of Engineers proposed a flood control dam that would have destroyed an important wetland in the town of Victory, a busload of VNRC members went to investigate the site. Their number included Lucy Bugbee, pioneer protector of the state's wild-flowers, whom Governor Phil Hoff later honored with the naming of the Lucy Mallary Bugbee Natural Area in Peacham and Danville. After their visit, VNRC members could speak with personal authority about what the dam would cost in terms of loss of rare wetlands flora; they were instrumental in organizing local opposition to the construction, and the project was shelved.

Vermonters came to accept that roadside advertising compromises one of the prime attractions that the state has to offer. With the passage of the state's billboard law, down they came.

The Billboard Law and the Viewshed as a Commons

While the VNRC, with its loose coalition of environmentally minded people, began shaping Vermont environmental policy and, through that, the landscape that Vermonters experience, one of the most effective pieces of landscape legislation in the 1960s was in very large measure the work of one man: Ted Riehle. He was, by all accounts, unusual. A lifelong Republican, a fan of both Barry Goldwater and the Grateful Dead, he was a well-connected politico who much preferred the solitude he got as the owner-operator-designer of an off-the-grid sheep farm on an island in Lake Champlain. "Jimmy Stewart meets John Wayne" is how his son once described him to a reporter. In 1968, Riehle convinced his Republican colleagues, who held a majority in the statehouse, to support a bold idea: a complete ban on roadside commercial advertising in the state. The idea had first surfaced in 1934, along with a proposal for a very different solution to the problem: the creation of a Green Mountain Parkway, like the Skyline Drive in Virginia, that would offer scenic views from a billboard-free roadway along the ridgeline of mountains that give the state its name.

Neither proposal won enough converts; automobiles stayed off the mountaintops and billboards continued to line some roadways. But in the ensuing years, tourism became an increasingly important part of the state economy, and in 1965 a court-mandated "one man, one vote" reapportionment balanced legislative representation with population, diluting the legislative power of rural districts whose farmers benefitted from the rental fees that roadside signage could command. With these changes, the idea of a billboard ban gained grudging support. Most business owners were at first dead set against it. Riehle helped them see the logic: while each of them might gain some small advantage from having roadside signs, the advantage would disappear when their competitors followed suit, and meanwhile one of the major attractions that drew tourists to the state—panoramic views of a scenic, working, preindustrial landscape—would be degraded, imposing losses on the tourist trade as a whole.

The available records don't show whether Riehle or anyone else made the connection, but this dynamic is the one that zoologist, systems theorist, and population biologist Garrett Hardin identified as "the tragedy of the commons" in his widely reprinted essay of that title. If you give individuals free access to benefit from the appropriation of a finite public good—to pasture more and more cows on a shared commons, or to raise more and more signs along a state's roadways—their individual self-interest will bring about the degradation of the resource for all.

U.S. Senator George Aiken
1941–1975: REPUBLICAN

Aiken was seventy-five when he ran for his last term in the Senate in 1968, but he was still so popular that, according to legend, he spent only $17 on his campaign. He finished his Senate career as an environmentalist. From the beginning, Aiken saw our natural resources as a common heritage that should not to be used to the sole advantage of special interests. In his last years in office, he hoped to create eastern wilderness areas so that citizens in the East, like those west of the Mississippi, would have the same opportunities to enjoy pristine forests close at hand. He had a passionate desire to open the Northeast Kingdom (a name he coined for the northeastern counties of Vermont) for recreational use, and in 1974 he sponsored the Eastern Wilderness Areas Act to create such a place in the heart of the Kingdom. He was an author as well as senator, and his publications track his early interest in environmental matters: *Pioneering with Wildflowers* (1933), *Pioneering with Fruits and Berries* (1936), *Speaking from Vermont* (1938), and *Aiken: Senate Diary, January 1972–January 1975* (1976). Throughout his life and work Aiken held to a sturdy vision of a "Vermont with a heritage of ideals that included the principles of loving liberty, of self-reliance, of thrift and liberalism."

It's a logic that applies to other common assets, not just town forests and pastures. Air quality and water quality are common assets, and so are the "sink" services —absorption capacities—of lakes and forests, wetlands, and farmlands. Another commons: the carbon-sink capacity of the planet, its ability to absorb greenhouse gases. No one owns it. It is currently overused by individuals acting in their own self-interest.

One solution to the tragedy of the commons is to enclose the commons by establishing property rights in it. That can work for a pasture but is impractical for some kinds of common assets, like the viewsheds that Reihle sought to restore and protect. The solution he supported is, by some accounts, the very definition of government: "mutual coercion mutually agreed upon in pursuit of the comon good." The logic of the billboard law lies behind much of what the Vermont environmental movement would seek to accomplish.

The scope and work of the Vermont environmental movement grew throughout the decade, even as it continued to draw largely on volunteer efforts. The VNRC didn't hire its first full-time employee until 1969—Justin Brande, as executive director, was contracted for just four months. "Further employment," his contract stipulated, "depends on raising sufficient funds to carry on the program." The VNRC got its first official office, two rooms upstairs at 97 State Street in Montpelier, in December of that year. Robert Klein, sole employee of the Vermont Chapter of The Nature Conservancy, worked in an attic office above.

Development had taken root in Vermont, and so too had an environmental movement prepared to shape policy and preserve the landscape and values of Vermont.

Thirty years after it was first proposed, Vermont's billboard law restored scenic views from its roads.

Attack that Pest, Attack and Fight

Attack the growing Billboard Blight

A Confident Synthesis, Forged and Strained

At its broadest, the story of Vermont's environmental movement is the story of how the citizens of Vermont shaped the relationship between humans and nature in the state. In terms an economist might use, it's the story of how Vermont came to set limits on developers' ability to take profit by imposing loss, cost, and damage on the public. It's appropriate to begin that story with the arrival of the Interstate and the founding of the Vermont Natural Resources Council because those two events illustrate the twinned dynamics that drive the tale: progress and protection, development and concern, the desire for improvement in the material conditions of life and the desire to ensure that the existing conditions of life wouldn't be degraded in the process. In the 1960s, from the vantage of both the ribbon-cutting in Guilford and the conference in Plainfield, Vermont seemed large enough to accommodate both.

No person embodied this confident synthesis more fully than Perry Merrill, first recording secretary of the VNRC. One-time state forester and a longtime commissioner of forests and parks, he is remembered as both "the father of the Vermont state parks" and "the patron saint of Vermont skiing." *Vermont Life*, listing him among the most influential Vermonters of the twentieth century, allowed that "Perry Merrill did more to shape the physical Vermont that exists today than any other single person."

He did this through his role as a founding board member of the VNRC and through his innovative support of the ski industry as commissioner of forests and parks. In that office, he engineered deals that allowed ski areas to expand into public lands and state forests and that gave them state-funded access roads to their mountains. He was an unflagging supporter and canny manager of the state forest system. In the 1930s, the federal government under President Franklin D. Roosevelt had come around to the idea that government spending, through such instruments as the Civilian Conservation Corps, could boost the country out of the Depression. Money was available for projects, money that Roosevelt wanted spent sooner rather than later. Merrill, as commissioner, had a long list of forestry and park projects planned and awaiting funding; in today's idiom, we'd say they were "shovel ready." First in the queue with his list, Merrill secured an outsized portion of the CCC's work budget, and the results are visible in almost every state park and forest in the Vermont—most noticeably in the beautiful and convenient structures that are sturdy, and serviceable and in design detract nothing from their rustic setting.

Longtime U.S. senator George Aiken offered this appraisal of Merrill's role: "It was in no small way due to his aiding and abetting, his cajoling and urging, that Vermont is now noted for its ski areas. His was one of the first cries in the wilderness for conservation." Aiken's judgment captures the straddle of conservation and development,

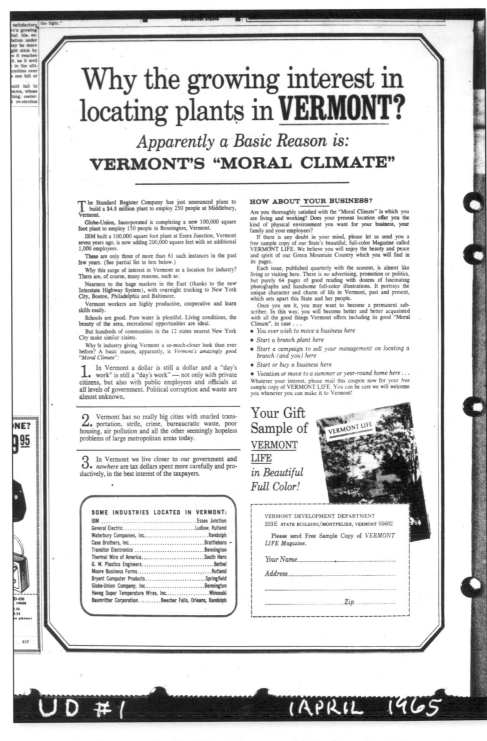

Vermont found that what we now call quality of life could be a commercial attraction as shown in this clipping of a newspaper advertisement promoting the state as saved in the state archives.

a pairing that seemed possible in Vermont long after it had been tested and strained in the country at large.

With the arrival of the Interstate, a flood of commercial ambition had been loosed upon the land; pent-up population and development pressure cascaded into the state from afar. In dealing with it, Vermonters could learn from the experience of other regions, other states, other landscapes. Just as development had leapfrogged the state in the early half of the twentieth century, Vermont could leapfrog half a century's worth of evolution in environmental regulation and jump straight to best practices. This it did, under pressure from a variety of citizens' groups and through the leadership of an unlikely environmental champion, Governor Deane C. Davis.

A country lawyer, Republican, and retired president of National Life Insurance, the wiry Davis didn't style

himself an environmentalist, though he might have allowed that he was an "outdoorsman" like the majority of his fellow Vermonters. He had fished since his boyhood in Barre and was a hunter —or had been, before professional duties made it increasingly difficult for him to take a rifle into the woods for a couple of weeks in the fall. An avid horseman, during his 1968 campaign the sixty-nine-year-old candidate made appearances on his Morgan, riding with a "posse" of supporters, in part to show that even in retirement he had the energy for the job—the first and only elective office he would hold. His governorship came at a crucial moment in the environmental history of Vermont, and he soon became one of the most effective figures in the state's environmental movement.

The changes arriving in Vermont had become obvious to Davis during

Tourists came to Vermont for many reasons, including simply to enjoy views of its working farms and preindustrial landscape.

his campaign. Especially as he worked the southern part of the state, he heard from Vermonters whose lives and towns had been affected by uncontrolled development.

In February of 1969, the newly installed governor received a letter from Justin Brande, chair of the six-year-old VNRC, urging Davis to create a commission to "study and advise the government and citizens of the state on the trends and directions of our use of the environment." While the term "sustainability" had yet to come into widespread use, clearly that's what Brande had in mind. The commission, he advised the governor, should be charged to "recommend what changes should be made to ensure reasonable prospects for the survival of the state and its citizens."

Two events would shape Davis's response to this prompting by Brande. First, soon after taking office he learned that the International Paper Company, owner of thousands of acres of forest in Vermont, had begun site work on its plan to build 1,400 vacation homes on its mountainside property in Stratton. The town was nearly all mountain; with just 104 residents, it held a ski resort and little else. And like most Vermont towns, it had no zoning regulations whatsoever. It had never had the need.

With no legal grounds on which to stop or even simply review the International Paper Company plan, Davis called up Ed Hinman, the president of the company. Reached at a remote Canadian village where he was on a fishing trip, Hinman agreed to come to Montpelier for a meeting. When they met, Davis reports in his autobiography, "I told him as courteously as possible but in no uncertain terms that Vermont would not stand for a development of this size in such a small town." Hinman consulted with a few aides and then, surprisingly, agreed to stop the work until and unless the plans were approved by the state. As Montpelier attorney Paul Gillies put it in his account, "In 1969 a little gubernatorial persuasion was enough. But everyone saw this as a close call." It was a last, powerful instance of handshake culture, the way things had been done in Vermont for ages. But clearly, Vermonters couldn't continue to rely on informal methods of control—appeals

to altruism, tradition, and common neighborly courtesy—to rein in developers whose plans would generate profit and economic benefits by imposing costs on the residents of Vermont.

The second episode that shaped his response to Brande's letter came at the invitation of Bill Schmidt, director of the Windham County Regional Planning and Development Commission. (Under the Municipal and Regional Planning and Development Act of 1967, this body was authorized to plan for the region and to assist towns in the development of local plans. The law "was an advanced piece of legislation nationally," writes Elizabeth Humstone, well-known Vermont planner and cofounder of the Vermont Forum on Sprawl. "It gave regions and towns authority to do what was then very innovative planning." But it neither created nor granted any regulatory authority to enforce the plans that were created.) Windham had been hit hard by development, and Davis toured parts of the county in the company of Schmidt. What Davis saw infuriated him. Jim Jeffords, who was Vermont's attorney general at the time, later wrote that Davis "saw raw sewage bubbling out the ground next to some quick-built ski chalets," and that "that was enough." Years later, Davis described his thinking in an interview with Joe Sherman, author of *Fast Lane on a Dirt Road: A Contemporary History of Vermont*. "I found these developments were being built on the most improper basis," Davis said. "I mean, on hillsides where there were very fragile soil[s].

The roads that they had to them were the kind of roads that you could never get a school bus around. And of course the history of second home development is that a lot of them do become permanent homes, and it becomes the responsibility of the town to educate the kids, and also to keep up the roads, to plow the roads." A town with a population in the hundreds scarcely had enough voting citizens to fill its unpaid civic offices—select board, school board, cemetery commission, dog catcher, viewer of fences, weigher of coal—let alone the resources to manage development. Davis saw that developers were profiting by imposing harm, loss, and expense on the land and people of Vermont; and this, he knew, was wrong.

Less obvious were the costs that development would cumulatively impose on Vermont agriculture—

Sally Laughlin

AN EARLY ENVIRONMENTAL EDUCATOR

Sally Laughlin became one of the founders of the Vermont Institute of Natural Science (VINS) after she and some fellow citizens took on the town of Woodstock in the first water quality litigation in the state in the early 1970s. They brought a suit to stop the discharge of raw sewage into the Ottauquechee River and they won. "A bit bruised from the public struggle," she says, she and David Laughlin, Rick Farrar, and June McKnight "pondered how to do things differently." They decided that battles like the one they'd just fought would be easier if more Vermonters understood the ecosystems that their lives depend on. Thus grew the idea for VINS, an environmental organization aimed at educating kids and conducting baseline environmental research. Sally served as its director for over eighteen years.

Through its Environmental Learning for the Future program, VINS trains parents and community volunteers to provide environmental education in Vermont schools. In its thirty years of existence, the program has reached tens of thousands of children and adults across the state, helping to build ecological literacy among Vermonters. Sally remembers that in the 1960s, "Well-educated people of Woodstock didn't know the word 'ecology.' It simply was not on the radar screen."

Sally has been a chair or vice chair of Vermont's Endangered Species Committee for thirty years. She was chair of the committee's Scientific Advisory Group on Birds for twenty-six years. She directed the project that produced *The Atlas of Breeding Birds in Vermont,* published in 1985 by the University Press of New England and the first such atlas published in North America. She has served on many boards, including the Association of Field Ornithologists and the North American Ornithological Atlas Committee, which she chaired for fourteen years. In 2010, she won the first CVPS-Zetterstrom Environmental Award for her outstanding environmental work in restoring endangered species of birds to Vermont.

As a "native Vermonter, born to native Vermonters" and as the recently retired director of development and alumni relations at Johnson State College, Sally has a clear-eyed understanding of the state and its people. "The tools we use to restore or maintain our ecological health," she cautions, "will not work if the public doesn't trust them." That's why building ecological literacy is crucial. To gain Vermonters' trust and support for protecting the natural environment, she says, "You've got to teach them the ecological facts of life."

especially its iconic dairy industry, whose rolling pastures and nineteenth-century barns and homes were a definitive part of the scenic, non-industrial landscape that Vermonters enjoyed and which drew vacationers to the state. In 1959, there were twelve thousand farms in Vermont. By 1969, that number had been nearly halved (while the size of the average farm grew only slightly, from 243 to 279 acres). It was a trend that would worsen with time, as first- and second-home construction spread, driving up land values and squeezing farmland into development—a competing, more "economic" use.

In 1967, Governor Hoff had set up a Central Planning Office. The first Democrat to be elected governor in 108 years, he was (as he himself proclaimed) "the first [Vermont] governor to believe in planning," though he also knew that "the word planning was anathema to most Vermonters." He had seen the problem before Davis took office and had done what he could to contain it: "If I could have taken the legislature to New Jersey for the weekend," he once remarked, "I could have come back and gotten all my legislation through." What he did get through were laws that established regional planning commissions and in other ways laid foundations for later developments. The Municipal and Regional Planning and Development Act that Hoff championed prescribed guidelines for the regional commissions and towns to use—but they were suggestions, not mandates. In an effort to stimulate interest in and acceptance of planning, in 1967 Hoff formed and chaired the

Vermont Planning Council, whose report, *Vision and Choice,* was issued in 1968: "The traditional rural scene in Vermont, characterized by concentrated settlement in villages and open countryside dotted with farms, is disappearing. The sharp distinction between village and countryside is blurring throughout the state. Highways between towns are becoming ribbons of residential and commercial development."

With Hoff's decision not to run for reelection in 1968 the task of moving the project ahead fell to his successor, Deane Davis. With an executive order in May of 1969, Davis put into effect VNRC director Brande's recommendation, creating a seventeen-member Governor's Commission on Environmental Control. Both the commission and its twenty-nine-member advisory committee included many members of the VNRC; the commission itself included future Republican governor Richard Snelling. As chair of the commission, Davis appointed Arthur Gibb—a retired banker, Republican state legislator from Addison County, and, like many a Vermonter, an avid outdoorsman. Stories have it that, on his commute to the statehouse in Montpelier, Gibb would stop for a bit of skiing while passing through the Appalachian Gap.

The Gibb Commission, as it came to be called, took testimony and solicited information and perspectives from citizens and experts, working with a speed to match the pace of the changes that were sweeping into Vermont. "We worked straight through the

summer," Gibb later recalled—a practice that was then novel for Vermont's agriculturally paced, part-time approach to legislative government. The Gibb Commission's report, issued in 1970, called for the adoption of a statewide land use plan and a system of permitting within it to ensure "development without destruction."

"We still have more unspoiled resources than do most parts of the Eastern United States," the report allowed, and it cautioned that only through systematic land use planning and permitting could "optimum use" of those resources be achieved. To preserve Vermont's landscape and communities—to conserve its ecological balance—the state would have to exercise bold and unprecedented authority.

This marked a major change in how Vermonters—the Vermonters on the Gibb Commission, at any rate—thought about government. But new challenges called for new solutions. The environmentally damaging growth, some Vermonters knew, couldn't go on forever. The Gibb Commission had felt the same chill wind that had led Brande to write; they saw that business as usual had the potential to destroy not just Vermont, but civilization itself. What was at stake, the Gibb Commission warned, wasn't just a way of life for a small rural corner of the United States, but nothing less than "the survival of mankind."

CHAPTER 2

The 1970s

Regulation

Strong national legislation begins to regulate pollution. In Vermont, the costs and damage of unregulated development lead to the adoption of the landmark Land Use Development law, Act 250.

In 1969, the year the Gibb Commission was convened, the United States was fighting a losing war in Vietnam; hundreds of thousands of young people gathered for three days of "love, peace, and music" at the Woodstock Festival in New York State; Neil Armstrong walked on the moon; and with the first tick of the clock past midnight on the last day of the year, the National Environmental Policy Act (NEPA) went into effect, mandating a process of environmental review and the preparation of Environmental Impact Statements (EIS) for all proposed actions by federal agencies.

The law didn't apply to states, or to individuals within states, but its passage marked a shift in collective understanding. NEPA was part of a comprehensive environmental legislative package put forth during the administration of Republican President Richard M. Nixon. With their support of the law, the majority of Americans acknowledged that human acts and works had environmental consequences that needed to be predicted, articulated, regulated, controlled.

That point of view had also informed the work of the Gibb Commission. Their 1970 report included a detailed proposal for legislation that was taken up immediately by the legislature and passed with strong support. Quickly signed by Governor Davis, Act 250, as it was known, was a landmark environmental law that was soon widely admired. "We knew we could not stop change," recalled Elbert "Al" Moulton, special assistant to the governor from 1969 to 1973, "and that was not our objective. But we can direct it, and we can ensure quality change, if we establish standards and criteria as guidelines for change. At the same time, it was absolutely critical that we strengthen our economy."

VERMONT BY THE NUMBERS:

1970

- Population: 444,330
- Percent born in state: 69.5
- Cows: 194,000
- Farms: 6,874
- Total farm acreage: 1,915,520
- Registered motor vehicles: 228,796
- Percent of seasonal homes: 15.3

Act 250 set out clear criteria by which proposed development would be judged and also tried to strike a balance between state authority and local control. Land use regulation would not be managed by bureaucrats in Montpelier. The new law would be administered through nine District Environmental Commissions, comprised of lay citizens and supported by a modest staff, with their decisions reviewable on appeal to an Environmental Board, also comprised of citizens. The original members of the board included a professor of natural science, an architect, a real estate agent, a community leader and homemaker, a county extension agent, a ski area operator, an engineer, a businessman, and a county sheriff.

While the administrative process enacted by the law has gone through several revisions—some of them politically motivated, as we shall see—the ten criteria by which permits were to be judged have remained sturdy and stable. They were first laid out in a memo written to Gibb in October 1969 by Walter Blucher, a resident of Arlington, Vermont, and former executive director of the American Society of Planning Officials. With their enactment into law, for the first time developers had to show that their proposed development:

1. Would not result in "undue water or air pollution," with specific attention paid to the development's effect on headwaters, wastewater, storm-water discharges, floodways, streams, shorelines, and wetlands;

2. Would have sufficient water for its needs;

3. Would not unreasonably burden any existing water supply;

4. Would not cause unreasonable soil erosion or affect the capacity of the land to hold water;

5. Would not cause unreasonably dangerous or congested conditions on roads or in other means of transportation;

6. Would not create an unreasonable burden on the educational facilities of the town or municipality;

7. Would not create an unreasonable burden on other town services;

8. Would not have an undue adverse effect on "aesthetics, scenic beauty, historic sites, or natural areas," and would not "imperil necessary wildlife habitat or endangered species in the immediate area";

9. Would conform to the Capability and Development Plan—the statewide inventory of land capacities that the law also authorized;

10. Would conform to any local or regional plan or capital facilities program.

Left, Governor Deane C. Davis signs Act 250. Above, an early meeting of the Vermont Natural Resources Council.

Act 250 embodied the best practices that the developing field of land use management had to offer, and in adopting it, Vermont benefited from the hard-won knowledge and insight of others. Vermont was not, by this time, a commercially blank slate, but its entry into the modern fossil-fueled economy had been recent. The law telescoped fifty years' worth of environmental experience into a few brief pages and brought the state's environmental regulation out of the nineteenth century and into the cutting edge of the twentieth.

Many understood that the law was revolutionary. Governor Davis himself noted that it went against a long-standing tradition in Vermont, the idea that

the foundation of civil freedom is the right every Vermonter has to use his or her own land as he or she sees fit. But Act 250 could equally be described as counterrevolutionary, since it sought to limit the harms and damage of the revolutionary change that had been loosed on the people and landscape of the state. Expectably enough, it drew immediate criticism. Still smarting from the cancellation of the fourteen-hundred-home subdivision proposed by the International Paper Company in Stratton, Frank Snyder, president of Stratton Mountain Corporation and head of the National Ski Areas Association, complained that Act 250 had stopped his company "dead in our tracks." Non-residential construction dropped 40 percent in 1971, the first full year of the law's implementation, and critics pointed to this as an unacceptable consequence of regulating

growth. (The drop was an entirely fore-seeable result of the law; with the addition of a new permitting process to the construction calendar, projects in the pipeline suddenly faced a longer pipeline, so of course there was a downturn.) Over time, the Act 250 review process has approved 98 percent of the permits that have come before it—though the vast majority of those permits were for projects whose design was amended and improved in the permitting process. The law didn't put a halt to development, but it gave the people of the state, through its processes and criteria, a strong voice in setting limits and conditions—just as was intended.

While the southern part of the state had borne the brunt of development pressures in the early 1960s, Burlington (the state's largest city) and the nearby communities of Essex and Colchester were also being affected. The 1957

Mark Schroeder

A PLANNER AND A DOER

Mark Schroeder graduated from the University of Vermont in 1958 with a degree in animal husbandry. After stints in Nepal (with the Peace Corps) and Ithaca, New York (to get a PhD in Agricultural Economics), he returned to the Green Mountains in 1969 to take a job in the newly created State Planning Office with Walter Blucher, an author of Act 250. Mark wrote and assembled the "Yellow Book," the economic justification for the state land use plan that Act 250 called for.

But a majority of Vermonters weren't interested in the economic justification of land use planning. Despite a carefully crafted process, including many public hearings, the state land use plan was perceived by many Vermonters as an instance of top-down governing, and it was never implemented. "Planning," Mark says now, with characteristic sarcasm and a chuckle, "it's just so 'un-American.' I can remember Governor Dean announcing 'I'm a doer, not a planner' frequently during his tenure." Without a plan, the Act 250 process couldn't help but be directionless and almost entirely reactive. Under pressure from corporate interests, including the real estate lobby, all mention of a state land use plan had been cut from Act 250 by the early 1980s.

Mark has worked in the field—an early job in Vermont was as a hand on a beef and poultry farm, and he went on to operate a small dairy farm. He also did field work as a world-travelling agricultural economist, as when he returned to Nepal to review its Community Forest Program for the United Nations and the World Bank. He also was a partner in a successful seed, feed, and fertilizer business. The common thread in his long and varied career has been a focus on the relationship between humans and their environment. He has given freely of his time to worthy causes; an emeritus trustee of Sterling College in Craftsbury, whose curriculum is built on

forestry and sustainability, Mark also served on the board of the VNRC from 1994 to 2000, shepherding the organization as it grew in membership, added staff, and expanded the scope of its activities.

When asked about the future, Mark's answer draws on both his training as an economist and his life experience. "I'm afraid there's a huge and growing disparity in income and quality of life in this country. You can't keep a democracy going for very long with that kind of inequity." Animal husbandry, land use planning, forestry, and the economic foundations of democracy: he has lived and worked and seen the integration of all of these. Lucky for Vermont, Mark Schroeder has been both a planner and a doer.

decision by IBM CEO Thomas Watson to site a manufacturing plant near the city had a rippling effect, and within a few years, IBM had become the state's largest private employer, with as many as 8,000 workers at its plant in Essex Junction. The population of the city and surrounding Chittenden County grew by one-third, from 74,000 to 99,000, in the following decade. The first important judicial test of Act 250 came there in the Presault case in 1972, concerning a large residential development proposed for the city. The developer was denied a permit by the district commission and appealed the denial to the Environmental Board. In the board's deliberations, adjoining property owners were denied standing to present evidence and arguments. The Vermont Supreme Court reversed the Environmental Board's decision, calling its interpretation unreasonable and clearly contrary to the intent of the legislature. Despite the long-standing tradition that embodied the infinite-planet idea that what you did with your property was nobody's business but your own, the court affirmed a modern reality: harms and damage from some kinds of development extend well beyond property lines, and those who might be affected ought to be able to give evidence in decisions that affect them.

The Presault case was but the first in a long line of cases in which the Environmental Board, and later the Environmental Court, tackled the crucial issue of standing—the legal right to be a party in a lawsuit—which continues to

MAJOR MOMENTS IN LAND USE PLANNING **IN VERMONT**

1970

The Gibb Commission issues its report proposing what would become Act 250, the state's primary land use regulation.

1970

Act 250 is passed, setting out criteria that proposed development must meet, empowering district commissions to review applications for development under those criteria, and providing for oversight and appeals through a nine-member environmental board. It also mandates the development of a state land use plan in three stages.

1970

The legislature ratifies water and sewage disposal regulations that have the effect of constraining growth and development in some areas. It enacts regulation of wastewater discharges; the permitting process will function as another planning tool, as will state acquisition of development rights on some land, also authorized by the law.

1973

The Land Gains Tax is enacted, discouraging short-term land speculation.

1975

Governor Thomas Salmon issues an executive order mandating that state-funded projects conform to the goals of Act 250 and promote growth in established growth centers whenever possible.

"We must establish control over any act which has an undue adverse effect on the public health and safety, or the right of people to enjoy an unpolluted environment."
—Art Gibb

be controversial today. Many environmental harms are subtle and diffuse, and some kinds of environmental damage have their most visible effects far in the future. On an increasingly developed and increasingly crowded landscape, who will be accorded standing? Ultimately, with a civilization built out to and then beyond the limits of what the planet can sustain, the incremental loss of healthy ecosystems will affect everyone in the region, maybe even the planet. Does that mean anyone and everyone should have standing to participate in development review processes? Practically, of course, the answer has to be no. But where do you draw the line?

Act 250 was conceived, passed, and took effect with great speed, supported by a broad consensus that the status quo was unacceptable. Critics argued (and continue to argue) that the process is lengthy, timeconsuming, and expensive. Defenders of the law point out that the length, time, and expense of the permitting process depend to a great degree on the quality of the initial proposal; development that meets Act 250 criteria from its inception does not generally incur additional design expense. Even so, critics say, the law imposes front-end design costs and then additional construction costs on the developer. Exactly, proponents say; these costs reflect a necessary accommodation of private interest to public good. A proposal that says, in essence, "I plan to make money by building a hundred housing units" will always be cheaper and easier to pull off than one that says "I plan to make money

by building a hundred housing units that will not damage the water supply, will not harm soils, will not threaten endangered species, and will not impose any unreasonable burden or expense on neighbors and the town in which it is sited." The former increases the developer's profit by allowing him or her—or, more often, a corporation— to impose costs on a community by cashing out natural and social capital for wholly private gain; the latter folds the social costs of development into the price of the project and protects the stock of social and natural capital held as a common asset and a public trust by Vermonters.

The most controversial aspect of Act 250 was its mandate for state land

Developers found that there was money to be made in selling "flatlanders" a piece of Vermont.

use planning in three distinct stages: a quickly drafted Interim Land Capability Plan to guide immediate decision making by the District Environmental Commissions, a more complete and detailed Capability and Development Plan, and a final Land Use Plan. Walter Blucher, the nationally prominent planner who helped shape the law, had cautioned that such an over-arching plan was indispensable to achieving its purposes. As anyone who has ever been lost in the woods or in a city knows, it's possible to make incrementally good decisions that in sum produce a completely undesirable result.

An accurate map—an overview that places each individual decision within its broader context—is the best proof against ending up where you don't want to be. The state Land Use Plan would be that map, literally. It called for all the land in Vermont to be categorized into one of seven usage types (urban, village, rural, natural resource, conservation, shoreline, roadside) with the resulting map a useful guide for the decisions of the District Environmental Commissions.

This part of Act 250 also tried to reconcile the need for big-picture conceptualization with the state's strong tradition of local control and citizen participation. Towns that had adopted permanent zoning bylaws and development regulations would regulate development in their jurisdictions according to the plan; towns that had no zoning or development regulations would have their land's allowable uses and minimum lot sizes be determined by the state classifications.

To those in the environmental movement, the development and passage of the plan was critically necessary to preserving Vermont's resource base in nature and its way of life, its natural and social capital. To the plan's opponents, it looked like something else entirely: an overreach by government and an unnecessary burden of regulation that would harm the public good and infringe on freedom by imposing a centrally administered master plan on all land use in Vermont.

The Interim Land Capability Plan was completed in 1971. In June of that year, the Vermont Natural Resources

The squeeze on farmers led to a sad joke: asked what he would do if he won a million dollars in the lottery, the Vermont dairy farmer replies, "Well, I guess I'd just keep farming until it was gone."

Council created an Environmental Planning and Information Center— EPIC for short—to stimulate public awareness of and participation in the other two components of the plan. Directed by Arthur Ristau, EPIC conducted a public opinion survey about the new environmental laws, sponsored several studies and conferences, and held countless meetings with select boards, legislators, and community leaders. It also produced public service announcements and public television programs, and a slide-tape show, *So Goes*

Vermont, in which the soundtrack of a dairy farm being auctioned off piece-by-piece plays beneath images and testimony of Vermonters whose lives and livelihoods had been damaged by unchecked development. All across the state, dairy farms suffered from the pinch of declining milk prices on the one side and rising land values—and with them property taxes—on the other. (The squeeze on farmers led to a sad joke: asked what he would do if he won a million dollars in the lottery, the Vermont dairy farmer replies, "Well, I guess I'd just keep farming until it was gone.")

The EPIC project helped secure passage of the state's Capability and Development Plan—not as such, but

Richard Cowart, April Hensel, Ernie Pomerleau, and Leonard Wilson

REGULATION, NECESSARY AND DESIRABLE

With its mix of regulators and the regulated, this group is well acquainted with the laws, policies, and administrative procedures that shape human impacts on the landscape of Vermont.

Richard Cowart was a young man when his cousin wondered if the fish in the family's farm pond were dying because of the pesticides, including Malathion, that had been applied to the cornfield nearby. For Rich, the answer—"well, most likely"—was a defining moment that gave a clear direction and focus to his professional life. He came to Vermont for the first time as a law student to serve as Darby Bradley's intern at VNRC. In those days, VNRC was working on phospahte pollution in Lake Champlain, alternatives to nuclear power, and trying to stop highway sprawl, issues on VNRC's agenda today. Inspired by Vermont, its growth challenges, and the processes it had in place to shape development, Rich resolved to come back to live in Vermont after completing his degrees in law and planning.

He served as executive officer of the Vermont Environmental Board under the leadership of Peg Garland and later Len Wilson. This provided an excellent background for his later work as commissioner of the Department of Public Service and then chair of the Public Service Board (PSB), positions he held for thirteen years. Influenced by the idea of "negawatts"—the concept that the cheapest electricity to produce is often the electricity customers save through investments in efficiency—Rich led the way to putting efficiency on the PSB docket. This work led eventually to the creation of Efficiency Vermont, a first-in-the-nation regulated utility that meets part of our demand for power not through generation but through efficiency and conservation. In 1999, Rich left the PSB and joined the founders of RAP, the Regulatory Assistance Project, a global non-profit organization that works with utilities and governments at all levels—across the United States and in more than twenty-five other countries—to design and implement clean energy policies using innovative regulatory approaches that rely on market incentives. The goal is to deliver consumer benefits and promote energy efficiency and renewable energy.

April Hensel, of Cavendish, has served as the District 2 environmental coordinator for the Vermont Environmental Board and the Vermont Natural Resources Board since 1984. April—as other coodinators and commissions also do—has profoundly influenced the nature of the development and land use patterns in her district. She holds a master's of science degree from the University of Vermont in natural resource planning and is a graduate of the Snelling Center for Government's Vermont Leadership Institute.

Ernie Pomerleau is a native Vermonter, born and raised in Burlington. He is one of the state's most accomplished developers, with dozens of profitable, community-building projects to his credit. Among them are several historic renovations, including the Follett House, a lavish, nineteenth-century Greek revival mansion that overlooks Lake Champlain and is listed on the National Register of Historic Places. It was a defining project for Ernie, galvanizing his interest in historic preservation and the redevelopment of Vermont's downtowns and village centers. Ernie allows that he probably holds more Act 250 permits than any other Vermonter. In 2010, he started work on a 1 megawatt solar power generation project in Ferrisburg. This project stands as the largest facility of its kind in the state; he's already in the planning stages of the next one.

Ernie is on the board of the Bank of Boston, serves on several boards in Vermont, and has recently stepped down as the chair of the Lake Champlain Chamber of Commerce. He was the chair of the 2007 Governor's Climate Change Commission and speaks frequently on climate change and renewable energy solutions.

Leonard Wilson's first "adult" job in Vermont was as a reporter for the *Bennington Banner*, a position he undertook after settling in Bennington in 1954, newly married to his wife, Priscilla. He rose to become managing editor and also became increasingly involved in Democratic politics. He left the newspaper and later ran unsuccessfully for lieutenant governor in 1960. After a stint in the Kennedy administration, he returned to Vermont in 1968, serving as state planning director in the Hoff administration. Over the next twenty-seven years, he alternated as state planning director and chairman of the Environmental Board, was secretary of environmental conservation for two years, and also sat on the Public Service Board; his career spanned the administrations of governors Hoff, Salmon, Snelling, and Kunin. Leonard retired in 1995, joining the VNRC board and eventually serving as vice chair.

Above: (l. to r.) Leonard Wilson, April Hensel, Ernie Pomerleau, and Richard Cowart

Rich, April, Ernie, and Leonard agree that consolidating a public mandate into law and using the force of law to protect the environment are both necessary and desirable. And they agree that Vermont's small scale—the personal, face-to-face nature of business and regulation—has helped its regulatory systems work, letting the Green Mountain State avoid many of the land use mistakes made in other states, where sprawling development, loss of farm and forestlands, fragmented wildlife habitat, and destruction of wetlands and water resources have diminished their citizens' quality of life and environmental security.

Ernie spoke of the growth center planning concept, originally explored in Governor Kunin's Costle Commission Report in 1987. The idea is to use tax and regulatory incentives to encourage compact settlement, leaving untouched the surrounding landscape of farms and forest. Ernie approves: "If you give me a circle and give me sufficient incentives to build inside it, I'm going to build

there, and that's enough." April disagrees. "The incentives are never enough to discourage development outside the settlement. Without the regulation, you might at worst have very obvious sprawl and at best maybe something that looks okay, but compromises or fragments the ecosystem beyond its ability to function."

The group talked about the value of the Vermont traditions of neighborliness, stewardship, and fairness as they extend to the political and permitting processes. These are part of the social capital that help make the regulatory system work—a foundation that other states and nations often lack. Rich notes that he has worked in many states, provinces, and nations and rarely has come across places where environmental issues are dealt with as thoughtfully as they are in Vermont. This has contributed to the state's ongoing reputation in the world at large: "Often," Rich says, "we meet decision makers around the world who know of two places in the U.S. that are leaders on environmental issues: California and Vermont. Many, are surprised to learn how small Vermont is in comparison to the size of California; the state looms large in their knowledge and expectations."

as amendments to one of the criteria laid out in Act 250, signed into law in December 1972. That achievement marked it as "one of the more successful experiments in public-private cooperation," as State Planning Director Leonard Wilson put it. But the final element of rational development called for in Act 250, the state Land Use Plan, never came into being. That plan proved more difficult to produce than the legislature had envisioned, and in 1972, Governor Davis announced that it wouldn't be ready for another year. Those who opposed it had time to campaign against it, roundly criticizing the proposed plan as "statewide zoning." Zoning at the town level was a novel practice in Vermont. Long accustomed to the Vermont they knew, which seemed an expansive and infinitely absorptive landscape, many Vermonters were still inclined to reject the idea that a panel of their fellow citizens ought to be given the authority to tell them, under law, what they could or couldn't do on their land. To add to town zoning an additional, statewide authority shaping land use was, in the traditionalist's view, a complete derogation of a fundamental civil right. Introduced to a slightly changed legislature in 1974, the plan was soundly defeated and was defeated again in 1975.

Davis later said that this failure to adopt a state plan was the greatest disappointment of his time in office.

With 587 miles of shoreline, 313,600 acres of open water, and 300,000 acres of wetlands in its basin, Lake Champlain is also a major provider of ecosystem services.

"The plan had generated so much controversy and the task to write it was so gigantic that I was unable to submit a finished plan until the eve of my departure from office." With his retirement in 1973, Act 250 lost one of its greatest allies. Enthusiasm for the plan remained high among environmentally minded Vermonters, and Davis's successor, Tom Salmon, worked to enforce Act 250 as best he could in his absence. (One way he found: by executive order all state investments were to be coordinated with Act 250 goals and policies. The state, at least, could make its development and investment decisions in a coherent fashion.) But support for developing and implementing the State Land Use Plan dwindled. In 1984, the authorizing language for it was quietly deleted from the law. "Without the land use plan," says Elizabeth Humstone, the amendments to Criterion Nine of Act 250 "took on great importance." "These would greatly influence the outcomes of major developments such as Pyramid Mall, ski area expansions and Wal-Mart."

The absence of a statewide plan—and the lack of any official and effective process by which to track the cumulative effects of incremental development—allowed for the piecemeal loss of the values Act 250 sought to protect. An individual project might not rise to the standard of "undue adverse impact," but a combination of such projects could and often did impose that kind of harm on Vermont's natural and cultural resources.

LAKE CHAMPLAIN

Lake Champlain stretches 120 miles from White-hall, New York (birthplace of the U.S. Navy), into Quebec and its outlet in the Richlieu River. It drains 8,234 square miles of New York, Vermont and Quebec. With 56 percent of the lake's total basin, Vermont has the largest catchment, almost exactly half of the state's 9,216 square miles. Well over half of all Vermonters—388,000 of 626,000—live there. When they do anything that affects water, the water they affect is connected to the lake.

Lake Champlain has been a conduit of transit for humans as long as there have been humans living near it. With the opening of the Champlain Barge Canal in 1823, it became part of a flat-water route between New York City and Montreal. The completion of the Erie Canal two years later connected the lake to upstate New York and all the territory reached by the Great Lakes. Vermont's forests and the lake's status as an important shipping corridor helped to make Burlington one of the largest lumber ports in America for a time in the nineteenth century.

With 587 miles of shoreline, 313,600 acres of open water, and 300,000 acres of wetlands in its basin, the lake is also a major provider of ecosystem services. As elsewhere in Vermont, those services have often needed protection from human activity. In 1963, concerned citizens in Vermont and New York combined to form the Lake Champlain Committee in order to resist plans for canal widening and river dredging that would have made the lake a much-travelled seaway for ocean-going vessels.

Environmental damage to most ecosystems is often visible only in retrospect.

The committee found that the need for protecting the ecological, recreational, and scenic values of the lake didn't stop there; and they found that citizens in Quebec were concerned as well. Forty-nine years old in 2012, the Lake Champlain Committee is a remarkable citizens' collaboration across state and national boundaries, and is the only non-profit citizens' group dedicated solely to protecting the lake's environmental integrity and recreational value. It has a legacy of action and a solid track record of achievements that aim toward establishing a sustainable relationship between the lake and the human residents of its drainage basin. The methods and strategies it has used typify the tool kit of the environmental movement: education, information, legislation, lobbying, citizen involvement, hands-on conservation work, pressure from the public on decision makers, and pressure on the public in the form of pointed, hard-to-avoid messaging.

Power, Law, and Land Trusts

While Act 250 was the dominant force shaping environmental politics in the decade, it was not the only ground on which the quality of the relationship between humans and nature was contested in Vermont. In 1970, the Public Service Board held hearings on the proposed licensure of the Vermont Yankee nuclear power plant in Vernon, which draws its cooling water from the Connecticut River. For Vermonters, the plant became and would remain a focal point for different visions of how humans and their economy would relate to nature and its ecosystems. (Vermont Yankee was and remains the only nuclear power plant in the state, thanks in large measure to the work of the Lake Champlain Committee,

which had, in 1968, helped quash an ill-considered plan to put a nuclear power plant on the shore of Lake Champlain in Charlotte.)

Construction on the Vernon plant began late in 1967, before the passage of the National Environmental Policy Act, and it took a while for the Atomic Energy Commission (AEC) to accept that projects underway would have to comply with the law as they moved forward. This meant that though the plant had been started without an assessment of its environmental impact, such studies would have to be done before its license to operate could be granted. The VNRC board voted to seek party status in the hearings, where they intended to raise questions about radiation as an environmental impact—an impact that would be felt by Vermonters far from the plant's site. As VNRC chair

Peg Garland explained in a September press release, "The evidence presented by the Conservation Society of Southern Vermont clearly demonstrated that the release of radioactive material permissible under the Atomic Energy Commission standard is far too high," and the presence of that radiation in Vermont was of interest to all Vermonters.

The resulting lawsuit escalated into a U.S. Supreme Court challenge to the constitutionality of the Atomic Energy Act. Several environmental groups, the VNRC among them, charged that the AEC was required to both promote and regulate nuclear power—an inherent conflict of interest. The case was in litigation but was rendered moot when Congress voted to split the AEC's functions between two new entities, the Nuclear Regulatory Commission and the Energy Research and Development Administration.

Other laws passed in the early 1970s helped shape the Vermont landscape for the better. In 1970, the legislature passed Act 252, the Water Pollution Control Act, establishing a classification system for the state's bodies of water and regulating for the first time discharges into public water that had any appreciable and detrimental effect on aquatic biota. Other laws—subdivision rules for water and sewer lines, a ban on phosphates in laundry detergent—also protected water quality in the state. In 1970, the state Agency of Environmental Conservation

Above: The state's only nuclear power plant, Vermont Yankee, was a continuing focus of effort and attention by the environmental movement.

was created, and in 1972, the state became the second in the nation to pass a bottle deposit bill, which had a quick and obvious effect on roadside litter while halting the ecologically oblivious practice of treating glass and metal as single-use items, as if the planet could give them to us in infinite supply. In 1973, the legislature passed a tax on profits from speculative land purchases, with the rate set on a sliding scale determined by the length of time the land was held and the profit made by resale. The operation of the law, though invisible to most Vermonters, worked to cool the speculative frenzy that had sent land values—and with them, property taxes—skyrocketing near ski areas and other centers of development. The 1973 amendments to Criterion Nine of Act 250 set legislative policies that were to guide all planning in the state, adding some considerations that weren't covered by the act's original ten criteria: the effect of development on agricultural, forest, and mineral lands, on open space, and on wildlife habitat; and the effect that development-led population growth would have on a town's ability to deliver services.

The enactment of forward-looking law to protect and conserve Vermont's common natural assets had become such a common feature of Vermont political life that by 1974 Governor Salmon could bemoan the fact that "we failed for the first time in years to enact any significant environmental legislation." Ominously, he also noted that "attempts were made to dismantle what we now have." To some Vermonters,

"environmentalist" had begun to be a pejorative term. Who were these people who presumed to tell Vermonters what they could and couldn't do on their land? The very idea, as Governor Davis had noted, went against long-standing practice. It violated the widely accepted if implicit terms of the social contract that defined what it meant to be a Vermonter—and the blame was put on environmentalism, not on the flurry of development that had made such legislation a wise response. "Environmental" had become such a charged term that one member of the Vermont Environmental Board seriously proposed

Among its goals, Act 250 sought to ensure that development would not have "undue adverse impact" on water resources, aesthetics, and scenic beauty.

that its name be changed to the "Land Use Control Board," to "get that word out of there." Evidently he thought that outright control of land use was an easier sell than anything that smacked of environmental concern.

Those anti-environmental sentiments were evident in an episode from the middle of the decade. Having been approached by the board of selectmen of the town of Hartland, VNRC staffer Darby Bradley and Chairman Jonathan Brownell produced, under a 1975 grant from the Conservation Law Foundation, a proposal for an open space protection program for the town. (They actually offered four alternatives, various combinations of tax incentives and conservation easements.) Brought to the town for a vote in May 1976, the proposal was

THE LIMITS TO GROWTH

In 1972, an international group of businesspeople, scientists, and state officials—the Club of Rome—published the results of a study they had commissioned. Titled *The Limits to Growth*, the study looked at exponential increases in human population, in resource use, and in emission of pollutants and projected those rates into the future. A research team consisting of Donella Meadows, Dennis Meadows, Jørgen Randers, and William Behrens III used what were then sophisticated computer modeling techniques developed at MIT by management professor Jay M. Forrester. The modeling explored five different possible scenarios of the human future. In the "business as usual" scenario, resources would become increasingly expensive, minerals and ores would become scarce, food would become scarce, and the environment would become increasingly degraded. As the researchers put it in the book's concluding section: "If the present growth trends in world population, industrialization, pollution, food production, and resource depletion continue unchanged, the limits to growth on this planet will be reached sometime within the next one hundred years. The most probable result will be a rather sudden and uncontrollable decline in both population and industrial capacity."

The book sold 30 million copies in thirty languages, and it shaped the environmental understanding of many Americans of that era, including many Vermonters in the environmental movement. Whether the particular numbers used were accurate or not, and whether or not one or another particular mineral or resource was depleted, the overall argument (many readers saw) was irrefutable: you can't have exponential growth of any physical thing within a physically finite system forever. A sustainable civilization would be a steady-state civilization.

The book was widely attacked. The Catholic Church objected to the implication that human population planning—contraception—was necessary to preserve the planet's capacity to support us. Business interests objected to being told that resources are finite, because the implications of that subvert much standard economic practice and would (they thought) deprive them of opportunities to expand, grow, and make money. Some in underdeveloped countries objected that the argument was made simply to lend support to continuing the world's unequal distribution of wealth. As one review of the book's history noted, "Continued growth is for many not an issue for debate; it is an indispensable condition of economic life."

'Economists and other critics charged that the book did not give enough credit to the human capacity for ingenuity and invention. The species had always invented its way out of ecosystem constraints before, and (these critics said) there was no reason to suppose it wouldn't do so for a long time into the future. Hadn't we just put a man on the moon? The power of technology to transform and improve our lives seemed limitless, and any talk of limits to growth was gloom-and-doom fear-mongering.

The argument that humans have always been able to invent their way around environmental limits is simply wrong, as the work of Vermonter George Perkins Marsh had long ago shown. And there are other reasons to suppose that the human capacity to invent its way around physical limits is itself limit ed, and in a very fundamental and crucial way. Humans will never invent their way around the laws of thermodynamics, the laws that forbid perpetual motion. Energy cannot be created out of nothing (the first law) and it cannot be recycled (the second). There will never be a pill that turns water into gasoline, or an engine that, when run backward, will take in heat, motion, and exhaust gases and then spew out valuable gasoline. This means we have to live within the energy budget that's available to us on the planet.

In our economy, everything we value is the product of three factors of production: human intelligence operating on matter

using energy. The matter and energy available to us are finite, and human ingenuity is limited by physical law. If we could create energy out of nothing, or recycle it over and over, we would never face any constraint on our economy; we'd be able to have infinite economic growth. With infinite energy, we could recycle every bit of matter that we use in the economy—even the molecules of iron that are lost to rust. Available energy is a limiting factor for the human economy, as it is for ecosystems. (The human economy is also limited by the finitude of "sink" services, the ability of the planet

The argument that humans have always been able to invent their way around environmental limits is simply wrong, as the work of Vermonter George Perkins Marsh had long ago shown.

to absorb our effluents. Natural systems do not generally produce effluents that natural systems can't absorb.)

These thermodynamic truths about economic activity are not appreciated by the vast majority of economists. Their professional optimism about the prospects for infinite economic growth—infinite expansion of the human ecological footprint—helped turn the tide of educated opinion against the book. But its argument that the biosphere has a limited ability to absorb human population growth, pollution, and economic growth in general is as valid today as it was forty years ago. In 2008, Graham Turner, a researcher in Australia, published "A Comparison of 'The Limits to Growth' with Thirty Years of Reality." It examined historical experience and the book's projections made in 1972 and found that changes in industrial produc tion, food production, and pollution are all in line with what Meadows, Meadows, Randers, and Behrens had predicted. An updated version, titled *The Limits to Growth: The 30 Year Update,* was published in 2004 by Chelsea Green Publishing.

rejected by a two-to-one margin. Marion MacDonald reported in the *Vermont Environmental Report* (the VNRC's quarterly magazine) that "interviews with local residents revealed concern that their taxes would rise, that they would lose their right to dispose of their land as they saw fit, [that they had] a general suspicion of government interference, and a sense that the whole scheme amounted to 'a lot of outsiders trying to cram something down our throats.'"

While Bradley termed the Hartland project a "major defeat," he credits it with having laid the foundation for development of two other methods of conserving open space—land trusts and the current use tax program.

With taxes on the fair market value of property providing the revenues for town services (including the largest budget item, the cost of local schools), some towns welcomed development as an opportunity to relieve budget

pressures. But development added to the other side of the ledger, as well, by increasing the cost of the town's provision of services. And when development increased land values, it priced some uses—farming—out of the market; some towns found that "a little development" was as hard to get as "a little bit

Vermont's streams offer scenic beauty—and a host of ecosystem services on which human civilization ultimately depends.

U.S. Senator Robert Stafford

1971–1989: REPUBLICAN

Senator Robert T. Stafford was a staunch environmentalist and champion of education whose name is familiar to countless college students through a loan program named for him. Stafford served two years as governor, eleven years in the House and seventeen in the Senate before retiring in 1989. As the ranking Republican on the Senate's environment committee, he repeatedly defended the Superfund program to clean up contaminated sites. Acid rain and automobile pollution were also among his legislative concerns. In 1988, Congress saluted his dedication to education measures, renaming he Federal Guaranteed Student Loan program after him.

Michael Dworkin

THE NUMBERS 'SCARE MY SOCKS OFF'

Michael Dworkin is a modern-day renaissance man, having achieved a high level of competence in a number of fields—from behavioral psychology to languages, from social justice to energy policy. His path has been a bit roundabout. Born into a family deeply committed to advocacy for social justice (his parents were foster care workers), he learned early on from his father that if you wanted to win someone over on a politically controversial issue, "you had to start with a conversation about cars." The secret was to begin on common ground and build trust, or you'd "never get to first base with them." Michael has fostered that trust in his hometown, where he has been elected moderator of the East Montpelier Town Meeting since 2005.

Michael started his college years at Middlebury. His interest in behavioral sciences led him to explore the lives of a dozen men who were patients "with serious behavioral problems" at the Brandon Training School (a state-run facility, now closed). Michael worked with these men for a year before returning to Middlebury to study the history of psychological sciences. After graduation, he earned his law degree at Harvard Law School. From 1979 to 1984, he worked for the Environmental Protection Agency defending standards that forbid the discharge of most of the toxic heavy metals into the waters of the United States. In 1984, he joined the legal staff of the Public Service Board (PSB), where he worked until the mid-1990s.

He considers his most important work was the introduction of least-cost planning and energy efficiency to the Vermont utility world. Michael also drafted the order that disallowed imprudent costs for the sale of both the Seabrook and the Vermont Yankee nuclear plants. After a stint in private practice he returned to the PSB in 1999 as its chair and presided until 2005, when he left to head the Vermont Law School's Institute for Energy and the Environment.

"If you care about the environment," he says, "energy use is the most important issue; and if you care about energy, envi-ronmental realities are the most important constraints." Those realities tell us we need to be efficient in our use of energy and that our energy has to be renewably sourced. If you care about social justice, you want that energy to be affordable and available to all. The problem, as Michael sees it, is twofold: over-population and populations who are underserved. "One-quarter of the world has no electricity," he says, "and yet worldwide [our energy use is] producing five times the sustainable level of CO_2. In the U.S., it's eight times." Here at home, "we could cut our energy use in half within twenty years" with no major new technologies needed, no major sacrifice in our standard of living. Why aren't we on that path? "We have the tools, but we don't have the will." Michael has a word of advice for managing what he sees as a necessary transition to a renewable energy, post-petroleum economy: "Don't back people into the corner. Give them reasonable options for reducing their energy demands."

As for the future, "I'm kind of a Pollyanna—optimistic at my emotional core. But the numbers scare my socks off."

pregnant." Market valuation has an optimistic ratchet: "fair market value" means the land is worth what someone will pay for it, and what they'll pay is determined by their own more or less realistic assessment of the profit they might make from it. To some extent, Act 250 slowed the ratchet, because profit could no longer be so certainly made by imposing costs and damage on Vermonters. But even so, valuable farmland and working forests were being converted to housing and other development at a steady pace, diminishing the healthy ecosystems that Vermonters

Wood is a renewable energy source, one that's produced locally in Vermont; purchase of it keeps energy dollars in the state. For reasons like these, Burlington voters approved the McNeil Generating Station (right), which turns wood chip fuel into steam and thence into electricity.

rely on for their well-being, threatening the agricultural foundation of the Vermont way of life, and threatening the tourist trade by nicking away at the visual appeal of the Vermont landscape.

The Hartland vote prompted Bradley and Brownell to take the lead in organizing a Fair Tax and Equal Education Coalition, precursor to the Current Use Tax Coalition. This organization brought together an unusual set of groups: the Vermont Hotel/Motel Association, the Vermont Farm Bureau, and the Vermont Timberland Owners Association, along with the Vermont Federation of Women's Clubs and groups representing snowmobilers (the Vermont Association of Snow Travelers) and anglers and hunters (through the Vermont Federation of Sportsmen's Clubs). In 1978, the coali-

tion succeeded in getting legislative approval for a current use tax program, which allows forest- and farmland to be taxed on the basis of how they're being used rather than on the speculative value of what the market says they might be worth for development.

In 1977, the Ottauquechee Regional Land Trust and the Lake Champlain Islands Trust were launched. The principle behind a land trust is simple: the organization negotiates with individual landowners for the donation or purchase of land or conservation easements as opportunities present themselves. Whether easements are purchased or donated, they restrict development —reducing the land's market valuation for tax purposes and retaining its ability to provide ecosystem services (including flows of food, fuel, and other needed products) that benefit the public.

Some towns have legitimate concerns about the piecemeal loss of their tax base through these conservation measures, and for some Vermonters, this is a roundhouse criticism of land trusts; they think the practice ought to be limited and controlled by public authority. Others take it to be yet another indication that wise land use planning is the preferred way to balance development and conservation, tax revenues a nd ecosystem services, public authority and private prerogative. Absent such planning, development decisions are made on a case-by-case basis, driven by private choices. Under such a system, it seems entirely reasonable, and only fair, that decisions *not* to develop would be made the same way.

Oil, Wood, and Highways

In 1971, the Organization of the Petroleum Exporting Countries (OPEC) exercised a newfound market power, a power given them by declining domestic production in the United States: they began restricting the amount of oil their member nations pumped from the ground and shipped. The resulting price shock profoundly affected Americans who waited in long lines to buy limited quantities of the fuel their lives had been built upon.

In Vermont, the high price of heating oil meant that wood once again became the heating fuel of choice. Many new Vermonters learned for the first time the truth of the old adage that "wood heats you twice"—once when you cut and split it, again when you burn it. Some forward-looking Vermonters began calculating just how much fuel (and other wood products) could be extracted sustainably from the state's forests. The Governor's Task Force on Wood Energy, convened in 1974, reported that development of a sound, scientifically managed wood

industry in the state could provide up to 25 percent of the state's power and home-heating fuel requirements.

That vision wasn't fully implemented. OPEC halted its embargo and raised production; the price of petroleum stabilized at its new, higher level, and Americans adapted to it. Indeed, in real terms, by the end of the 1980s Americans were paying less per gallon than they had at any time since the 1950s. This doesn't mean oil was less scarce than it had been in an absolute sense; it means it was pumped out of the ground faster—fast enough to make its price decline, even as demand steadily rose. One effect of the lower price was to discourage big users, the United States especially, from converting to renewable energy. But despite these national and international trends, the shape of the energy future was becoming clearer. Wood is a renewable energy source, one that's produced locally in Vermont; purchase of it keeps energy dollars in the state instead of sending them out to benefit other states and nations. For reasons like these, Burlington voters approved a 1978 bond issue to build the McNeil Generating Station, which turns wood chip fuel into steam and thence into electricity. At peak capacity, it provides nearly enough electricity—50 megawatts—to meet the needs of the city of Burlington. (A decade later, the plant was adapted to be able to use natural gas as well, though wood remains its primary fuel.)

As the price of oil stabilized and then declined in real (inflation-adjusted) terms, Americans saw little reason

to give up their reliance on personal automobiles as their primary means of transportation. Cars need roads, and in Vermont as elsewhere in the United States, a variety of highway improvements and expansions were on the drawing board, awaiting federal funding and federal, state, and local approval.

For Burlington, plans had long been laid for a partial ring road of the sort that surrounds other significant cities. (Burlington fronts on Lake Champlain, and while there had once been plans to create the sort of waterfront parkway that many another American city has—a highway barrier between people and a scenic and recreational resource—those plans came to naught and weren't part of the proposed Interstate addition.) Renewed interest in completing the planned highway surfaced in the late 1970s, but the proposal didn't meet with the kind of bright optimism that greeted the arrival of the Interstate in Guilford twenty-three years earlier. The oil shock of the early 1970s was gone but not forgotten—at least not by the citizens who mobilized to resist the Circumferential Highway, as it was called. The fight lasted thirty years and would spur the environmental movement in Vermont to forge new organizations, new alliances, and new ways of thinking.

As the decade came to a close, interest in forward looking environmental legislation remained high among a significant percentage of Vermonters, even as on the national scene environmental causes were soon to take a thorough drubbing.

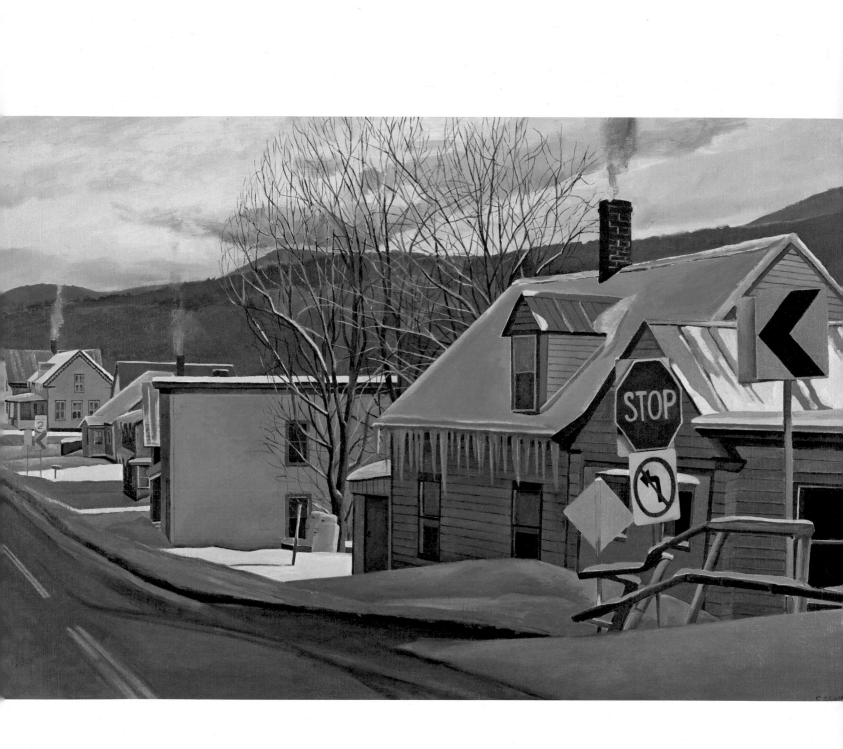

CHAPTER 3

The 1980s

Litigation

With new legislation in place, the environmental movement turns to the courts, challenging poorly planned development and seeking enforcement of the law.

O n a drizzly, misty evening in April 1982, partway into the second year of Ronald Reagan's presidency, a handful of reporters left the main lodge at Killington Ski Resort in Sherburne, Vermont. A few of them paused to count the cars in the parking lot: just thirty-five. The number was remarkable and was widely reported the next day. What made it remarkable was that inside the lodge, after the reception and press conference the reporters had attended, a statewide Republican fund-raising dinner was beginning. Just sixty-one tickets had been bought. The reporters, usually given a free pass to such dinners so they could bear witness to the strength and vigor of the party, had been ushered out of the building after the press conference.

By staying away from Killington that night, Republican contributors were following the example set by their party leaders. Congressman James Jeffords had sent regrets, saying he'd be unavoidably detained in Florida. U.S. senator Robert Stafford couldn't make it because he was planning a European tour. Governor Richard Snelling had another meeting he had to attend. Secretary of State (and future governor) James Douglas was unapologetically blunt, saying that an evening at home with his family appealed to him more. It was an election year, but not one single Republican holding a statewide office was in attendance.

What reduced the turnout that night wasn't the weather—unseasonably warm for April, with the drizzle releasing thick banks of fog from the still winter-deep snow—nor any quality of the food or setting. What kept people away was the company: the Reagan administration in Washington had sent, as its representative and draw, Secretary of the Interior James Watt.

VERMONT BY THE NUMBERS:

1980

- Population: 511,456
- Percent born in state: 64.2
- Cows: 186,000
- Farms: 5,890
- Total farm acreage: 1,537,751
- Registered motor vehicles: 347,323
- Seasonal homes: 34,279

On the national scene, Watt was second only to Reagan himself as a fund-raiser for the party. The sparse turn-out that night was a reminder that Vermont hadn't followed the rest of the country so completely in its embrace of Reagan. The former actor, General Electric pitchman, and governor of California had carried the state by a comfortable margin, but only because a third-party challenge from John Anderson got 14 percent of the vote. As did Reagan, Watt stood for environmental policies that fell far outside the Vermont consensus. Reaganism was a departure from a Republican tradition of support for conservation, beginning with Teddy Roosevelt and extending through the important environmental legislation passed under Richard Nixon; Reagan called not for conservation but for greater and greater development for

James Watt, Secretary of the Interior during the Reagan Administration, was not a popular figure in Vermont.

"unlocking" the resources that environmental legislation had put out of reach. In his time in office, Watt had decreased funding for environmental programs; restructured his department to hamstring it and decrease its regulatory power; halted expansion of national wildlife refuges; eased environmental regulations on oil and mining companies; directed the National Park Service to draft legislation decommissioning a number of national parks; and flat-out rejected donations of private land to the federal government when they were earmarked for conservation purposes. Under his direction the Department of the Interior set a record for fewest species listed under the Endangered Species Act.

The Reagan and Watt approach to resource management—not conservation but faster, less fettered use—found

strong support in the western United States, where the land seemed expansive and the federal presence large and intrusive. Resentments coalesced into what some media touted as "a Sagebrush Rebellion," which sought to reduce and set new, lowered limits to federal regulation. Particularly offensive to western farming interests were limits on grazing on public lands, limits on private appropriation of public waters, and legal constraints on use of private land, including protection for endangered species of no apparent economic value. Then, too, there was the sheer acreage that was owned and therefore controlled by the federal government in Washington (not, as could equally be said, by "We, the People of the United States"). The Bureau of Land Management, which Watt oversaw, was responsible for managing 340 million acres of public land, the vast majority of it west of the Mississippi. To Watt and Reagan, that was too much: they wanted to see that land put to use generating economic wealth. Sierra Club president Joe Fontaine offered a pointed summary of "Watt-ism": it "views our public lands, forests and other resources not as a legacy for the future, but as a bank balance to be drawn down as quickly as possible in the name of immediate development and a fast buck."

The national media speculated that Watt, a born-again Christian, was implementing environmental policies consistent with a belief that a Second Coming was imminent. If civilization was going to end soon, there was no need to preserve resources for the future.

The year before the Vermont fund-raiser, Reagan had ignored a million-signature petition gathered by the Sierra Club calling for Watt's ouster. His spokesman characterized the petition as emanating from socialist radicals bent on destroying America.

That view was not widely shared in Vermont, as Secretary Watt's visit made clear. About thirty-five miles downhill from that parking lot in Killington, in a dining hall at Castleton State College, a different fund-raising dinner was held the same evening. Billed as the "Watt Luck Supper," it was sponsored by the VNRC, the Lake Champlain Committee, the National Wildlife Federation, the Vermont Chapter of the Sierra Club, and the Vermont Audubon Council. It drew 600 people, many from as far away as St. Johnsbury and Brattleboro. The *Burlington Free Press* reported that the evening was "an enthusiastic protest against the policies of the Reagan Administration" and that it "looked like a cross between a family reunion and a pep rally." The program included speeches, comedy, singing, and audience participation: "elderly women in neatly tailored suits and long-haired mothers with small babies joined to sing 'This Land is Your Land,' a kind of anthem of the environmental movement." A year after the event, VNRC board chair Carl Reidel recalled that Watt's presence in Vermont became the catalyst for something else: "As the dinner went on, I felt that people turned away from simply attacking Watt, and instead were celebrating what we had, and what had happened over the last ten to fifteen years in Vermont."

It was a symbolic moment and a great celebration. But as important as symbols and celebrations are, there was also work to be done. With the advent of Reaganism and Watt-ism in Washington, Vermont's environmental commitment—and its young environmental laws—were tested again and again. Nor were those laws completely sufficient to protect the ecological and social foundations of Vermont life from being degraded by human acts and works; that goal—the achievement of a sustainable state—was still far from having been reached.

The 1980s, then, saw environmental developments on two fronts: a rearguard action (not always successful) against the return of infinite-planet, infinite-growth thinking of the sort that had come to reign in Washington and an extension, where possible, of existing efforts to secure from further harm the ecological and civil foundations of Vermonters' lives and livelihoods. In that latter effort, the decade brought some innovations that were sturdy and forward looking and that formed the basis for later successes. It also brought a major failure.

U.S. Senator Patrick Leahy

1974–PRESENT: DEMOCRAT

When Patrick Leahy of Middlesex was elected to the U.S. Senate in 1974, he was the first, and remains the only, Democrat elected to this office from Vermont. At thirty-four, he was the youngest U.S. senator ever to be elected from the Green Mountain State. In 2012, he ranked second in seniority in the Senate, served as chairman of the Senate Judiciary Committee, and is a senior member of the Agriculture and Appropriations Committees.

Always selected one of the top environmental legislators by the nation's foremost conservation organizations, Leahy successfully opposed attempts to allow oil and gas exploration in wildlife refuges, helped secure more than $70 million in federal funds to clean up Lake Champlain, and spearheaded congressional efforts to tackle the dangers of mercury pollution. He helped add more than 125,000 acres to the Green Mountain National Forest, an accomplishment matched by few lawmakers of any era.

Leahy has led bipartisan efforts to streamline the Department of Agriculture, and the 1994 Leahy-Lugar bill reorganized the U.S. Department of Agriculture by closing 1,100 offices and saving more than $2 billion. Leahy's Farms for the Future program—now the Farmland Protection Program, which was created in the 1990 Farm Bill—has helped preserve more than 350 Vermont farms. He played a crucial role in establishing the Milk Income Loss Compensation program, and is the father of the national organic standards and labeling program, which took effect in October 2002.

MAJOR MOMENTS IN LAND USE PLANNING IN VERMONT

1984

The legislature votes to remove the planning mandate from Act 250.

1984

The ten-acre loophole in Act 250 is closed.

1987

Governor Madeleine Kunin appoints a Governor's Commission on Vermont's Future. Also known as the Costle Commission, its report outlines thirty-two planning goals, calls for technical and financial assistance to towns developing plans compatible with those goals, and calls for empowering towns to charge developers impact fees to offset town costs related to their development.

1988

Act 200, the Growth Management Act, enacts the planning envisioned in the Costle Commission report. To protect working landscape and open land, it also provides assistance to farmers through the Dairy Income Stabilization program and the Working Farm Tax Abatement program.

1988

The Vermont Planners Association is formed to promote effective land use planning.

1989

Citizens for Property Rights is formed to resist and lobby against planning.

Litigation

Long ago, Alexis de Tocqueville noted that scarcely does a political issue arise in the United States before it becomes, in short order, a legal issue. Confrontation through litigation may not be an ideal means of resolving differences, but it's far from being the worst mechanism. (It has the virtue of being compatible with a democracy ruled by law.) The evolution of the Vermont environmental movement in the 1980s can be read in the succession of legal challenges to the state's environmental legislation and in the passage of new laws that clarified and extended the principles underlying the earlier achievements. During that decade, said Don Hooper, longtime VNRC staff member and subsequently the northeast regional director of the National Wildlife Federation, "the citizen activists of the '70s gave way to environmental lawyers and lobbyists." This was a natural evolution, as broad principles were brought down to manifold cases in their near-infinite particulars and as attempts to undercut the new policies were resisted. Litigation and lobbying are how both of these are done.

In 1984, Marion MacDonald of the VNRC reported that "the legislature has been less receptive to environmental initiatives in the years since the Reagan administration came to power," and "much of VNRC's [recent] legislative activity has been devoted to holding on to the gains of the 1960s and 1970s, rather than advocating new programs." Predictably, one arena

The Pyramid Corporation introduced into evidence photos of its existing malls, one of which tries to create the feeling of a public square indoors.

in which environmental gains needed protection was Act 250.

A decade's worth of experience had begun to show how the law could be, would be, should be used. Filling just nine pages in the Vermont Statutes Annotated when it was first enacted, it grew to sixty-four pages within a decade and a half. In his review of the law's history in a legal journal, attorney Paul Gillies notes that "it wasn't statewide zoning" because "zoning is practical"; it tells you what you can and can't do. Act 250 was "more relative" and "aspirational." Instead of carving the world of

potential land uses into "forbidden" and "allowed," it asked land owners to demonstrate that what they proposed to do wouldn't harm the interests of others, as those interests were defined under its criteria. As permits were reviewed (and mostly granted, usually with modification), and as permit seekers challenged in court the rare denials and the much more common imposition of modifications, the law gave increasingly detailed specifications of what did and didn't constitute a failure to meet its criteria. In those early years, every case set a precedent. Many drew little attention; a few, however, emerged as focal points for distinctly different visions of what Vermont was and would be.

Finite-Planet Retail: The Pyramid Mall Decision

One such case, decided early in the decade, began in 1977 over the future use of a cornfield at the corner of Routes 2 and 2A, in the rural town of Williston, about six miles east of Burlington. On that site, the Pyramid Companies of Dewitt, New York, proposed to build an eighty-two-store shopping mall with easy access to the nearby interstate. Never before had a project of such size and potential impact been introduced to the Act 250 process. Clearly the town of Williston would be affected; in exchange for a major increase in its tax base, it would become vulnerable to strip develop-

ment and suburban sprawl of the sort that Act 250 had in part been designed to discourage. But the mall would be large enough to affect the businesses in other retail centers in the area—South Burlington, Winooski, Essex, and downtown Burlington as well. Would it place "an unreasonable burden" on the citizens of these areas, and if so, could Act 250 provide relief?

A group of concerned citizens organized to fight the mall, getting help and legal advice from the VNRC, which had sought but was denied standing in the case. The proceedings dragged on for four years. One important element being contested in the case fell under Act 250's Criterion 7, which looks at the effects of development on the ability of local governments to deliver services. "Local" might be taken to mean the town in which the development is located, but the Pyramid proposal was for a mall that would draw customers from a larger region. As part of that region, the city of Burlington presented evidence on the status of its fire, police, and street departments, arguing that each was already operating at a minimal level and that further reduction in its tax base, as could be expected if Pyramid built the mall, would lead to unacceptable deterioration in their ability to perform, thus placing an undue burden on Burlington residents. The city was assisted by an unprecedented alliance—the state, under Republican Governor Richard Snelling, joined with the Chittenden County Regional Planning Commission (CCRPC) to present evidence and argument against

Left: two views of the same land in Taft Corners, before and after big-box development. Above: Burlington's Church Street Marketplace in winter.

the proposal. "Through [their] combined resources," writes Elizabeth Humstone (who coordinated the state's work on the case), "new data and analyses that projected the impact of a regional mall on both the host and surrounding communities were completed. This had never been done before in Vermont." Snelling directed all the relevant state agencies to devote staff to reviewing and evaluating the proposed mall under Act 250 criteria—a "huge effort," Humstone says, that was "a bit experimental," since it drew unprecedented connections and traced the effects of the proposed development into such areas as the impact on gasoline tax revenues and on state income

tax revenues from the development's effect on employment. "The analyses that were used in that case became the basis for many analyses of malls, strip centers, big boxes and others subject to Act 250."

In its 1978 judgment, the District 4 Commission agreed with Burlington, the CCRPC, and the state. That decision was appealed, with a final upholding of the District Commission coming in 1981.

To say that this decision was controversial is an understatement. To some, it represented clear affirmation of the principles the law sought to protect: the Vermont landscape and its vital town centers should not be degraded by sprawl and strip development, which would not only compromise ecosystems and their delivery of ecosystem services, but would reduce the quality of govern-

ment services and impose a wasteful, land- and energy-intensive building pattern on the landscape of Vermont. To others, the decision meant that one group of merchants had succeeded in using an environmental law to stymie competition from another set of merchants. If businesses downtown stood to lose customers to larger, more efficient retailers in the suburbs, too bad; the market should reward merchants who can sell at lower prices.

It's worth noting that big-box stores achieve some of their efficiency by transferring some of their costs to shoppers, including the cost of commuting—fuel and vehicular expenses and the loss of leisure time. There's also a subtler, less easily quantified cost in lost civic vitality and social capital. The see-and-be-seen exchanges of shoppers in the public spaces on Main Street—part of the human enactment of neighborliness—are displaced by more focused, single-purposed forays into distinctly private space at the mall. On Main Street, you meet other shoppers as fellow citizens. In the mall, you meet them as fellow consumers. The difference, when you reflect on it, isn't so subtle after all.

That social cost formed no part of the District Commission's decision. Years later, Darby Bradley, VNRC's staff attorney for the case, described its reasoning. The impact of the mall on Burlington was seen as an impact on its merchants, and that was relevant "only in so far as a drop in sales affected the assessed value of land (and therefore the property taxes yielded from) com-

**Nancy Bell, Darby Bradley,
Jon Groveman, and Darlene Palola**

THE VICTORIES ARE TEMPORARY

Nancy, Darby, Jon, and Darlene all have experiences litigating environmental cases, and all who won were dismayed by the temporary nature of their legal victories. Their stories begin like this:

Nancy Bell's busy parents routinely "turned (her) loose" to tramp outdoors with the family dog. Later in life, the daily chores of dairy farming in Lamoille County and running a large sugar bush also shaped her relationship with the earth. By 1982, she was living in Shrewsbury, where she became involved with an effort to protect what the locals called the Heartland—the mountains on the Shrewsbury-Mendon border. Nancy helped create the Raven Rock Land Trust, later renamed the Shrewsbury Land Trust. In 1989, working with Eric Palola, other staff, and the board at VNRC, she took on the protection of black bear habitat in Parker's Gore. The work led to a precedent-setting case that established criteria for determining when habitat is critical to the survival of a species. Reflecting on the high-stakes struggle that became adversarial and very contentious, Nancy allows that "during the Parker's Gore hearings, humans were my least favorite species." She much prefers her experiences working with The Conservation Fund, where she engages communities about conservation, having "conversations of the heart" that can lead to "finding common ground and better solutions to conflicts than litigation."

Darby Bradley is a native of the Upper Valley of the Connecticut River Basin and a graduate of Dartmouth College. But he cut his professional teeth far from home, on a longstanding, hotly contested issue involving a flood-control dam on the Snoqualmie River near Seattle, Washington. This experience as a volunteer with the Sierra Club while in law school helped him to see the limitations of contested case proceedings and the advantages of collaboration in resolving land use disputes. In 1974, he returned East and became the assistant director and counsel for the VNRC, a position in which he led the organization's four-year fight to stop the Pyramid Mall at Tafts Corner. He remembers thinking during this time, "Vermont is small enough that we each have a chance to make a difference." Wanting to make that

difference and frustrated by the "temporary nature of winning cases," Darby joined the staff of the Vermont Land Trust as general counsel in 1981. He became its president in 1990. In between, he served as chair of the Vermont Environmental Board of the Agency of Natural Resources, which oversaw the administration of Act 250, and was a member of Governor Kunin's Commission on the Future of Vermont. Since 2007, he has been special assistant for donor and government relations at the Vermont Land Trust, and he also serves on the board of the High Meadows Fund. Darby came to believe that in many cases litigation provides only a temporary resolution to land use disputes.

Jon Groveman came of age amidst the sprawl of Long Island. When he turned ten, he began to spend his summers at a camp in the Catskill Mountains and there developed a deep appreciation for the value of nature—and a growing intolerance for its destruction. As a young attorney, Jon worked for the City of New York to protect headwater areas in the Catskills and Adirondacks for the city's water supply. He later moved to Vermont and held positions with the Vermont League of Cities and Towns, the Water Resources Board, VNRC, and the Agency of Natural Resources, where he now works as their general counsel. When Jon was with the VNRC, he wrote much of the language for the Groundwater Protection Act of 2008 and fought attempts to weaken it in the ensuing years. He also led VNRC's recent challenge to the resurrected St. Alban's Walmart proposal, which, defeated in 1997, was proposed anew in 2003, for the very same cornfield two miles north of St. Albans. (Unfortunately, VNRC lost the seventeen-year-long case in the Vermont Supreme Court in 2011.)

Darlene Palola grew up in Seattle, just above Lake Washington, well within sight of Mount Rainier. With a bachelor of science degree from the University of Washington and a master's in public health from the University of Massachusetts, her career has been in health care policy and management. Darlene's environmental activism began in the early 1980s, with a local group, led by Malvine Cole, to stop uranium mining in the hills of Jamaica, Vermont.

Soon, Darlene became the leader of a group called the Stratton Area Concerned Citizens (SACC), which was organized to stop degradation of the North Branch and its tributaries by ski area development on Stratton Mountain. Their most important proactive work was to reclassify Kidder Brook from B to A1, thereby giving it the highest possible protection. Perhaps their most significant case

Above: (l. to r.) Jon Groveman, Nancy Bell, Darlene Palola, and Darby Bradley

was over the Stratton Ski Area's master plan, because it was in these proceedings that SACC fought for "14b Party Status," also known as party-by-permission status. They won their argument, establishing that those who are affected by development and who want a say in permit hearings should be granted standing in the proceedings.

Since then, Darlene says, the SACC "has been granted party status to all projects for which we have applied. We have appealed and worked out conditions with the help of VNRC" in many cases, "most recently the Stratton Water Quality Remediation Plan and a project in the Kidder Brook watershed." Stratton Ski Area may have a plan in place, but it still leaves plenty of work for SACC; as she says, "Stratton continues to develop and we continue to fight!"

Nancy, Darby, Jon, and Darlene all agreed that the 1980s were the testing ground for Act 250, with cases that set precedents for the battles that were to come in the decades ahead. But they also saw that the law was not completely effective, as individual decisions were made to approve projects that didn't meet its standard of "undue adverse impacts" but which in sum combined to degrade the state's landscapes and communities. This group of individuals still grapples with a truth noted by David Brower, founder of the Sierra Club: "The victories in conservation work are always temporary, while the defeats are permanent."

The sentiment captures Darby's experience of the Pyramid Mall case, which saved some farmland in Williston for fifteen years, until different proposals for big-box development succeeded. And as Darlene's ongoing vigilance at Stratton attests, a master plan is no guarantee that development in accordance with it will meet environmental criteria. Jon's "David versus Goliath" frustrations with the return of Walmart to St. Albans, and Nancy and friends' hard-won victory in Parker's Gore, suggest that "working it out, out of court" is often a better path. The resurrection of a poor land use proposal can snatch a victory away permanently; frequently that kind of defeat can be forestalled by mutual agreements collaboratively made.

Through a variety of strategies and laws, the Vermont environmental movement sought to preserve the state's compact village centers.

mercial buildings in Burlington." That, in turn, mattered only if the drop in tax yield interfered with the ability of Burlington to provide needed services. "Had Pyramid been able to establish that the decline of business activity in Burlington would have little impact on the City's total tax receipts, or that Burlington's budget had 'fat' which

could be trimmed without serious consequence, it would have received approval on this aspect of Act 250."

In effect, Act 250 had been used as a poor substitute for regional planning. This was evidence either that the law itself was being stretched beyond its original purpose, or that a permitting process designed to protect social and environmental values can't operate effectively without adequate regional land use planning that decision makers actually follow. As Bradley put it in

an update on the case he wrote for the *Vermont Environmental Report* in 1978, "Even if the mall is turned down, the same market forces which attracted Pyramid still exist. Unless we learn from the case, it seems inevitable that we will face the same threat again. Had there been an adequate plan stating where development of the magnitude of Pyramid should or should not be located, this proceeding would have been greatly simplified, and hours of time would have been saved. Unless the regional planning process is strengthened, the education afforded by the Pyramid Mall case will be largely lost."

There's another principle evident in the decision, one not explicitly stated in Act 250: a notion of limit. In its way, the controversy pitted partisans of infinite-planet thinking against those who worked toward a sustainable state. If the land is infinite, an economy can grow forever, and as it grows, it is perfectly capable of supporting both suburban malls and town centers. If the planet is infinite, then so too are potential customers and potential retail traffic, and any panel or group who presumes to apportion retail capacity between competing claimants is doing a disservice to the freedoms we enjoy as Americans. The decision said, in effect, that the population of any region has a finite capacity to support retail commerce. Once this limit is acknowledged, the difficult questions become: How shall that support for retail commerce be distributed? Where will the finite need for retail space be met? By whom?

The traditional answer to such questions has been "let the market decide." But an unfettered market system, like the one that drove development in the southern towns of Vermont with the advent of the Interstate, often gives bad answers—answers that impose real costs, harm, and loss on citizens who have done nothing to deserve them. A statewide land use plan might have provided guidance on these questions. Absent such a plan, the Act 250 process became, by default, the structure for

RATIONING RETAIL: WHO DECIDES?

On a finite planet, choices about retail capacity will eventually be made one way or another. To many, the options seem to be just two: choices could be made by individuals showing initiative and ambition in a free market, or they could be made by some sort of centralized administration that assigns scarce capacities, putting limits on individual prerogative for the common good. But there's a third way: it's possible to retain market incentives that reward initiative and ambition while structuring and in some cases fettering those markets so that their result is more effective at serving the public interest. "Structuring" means offering incentives or financial penalties to promote or discourage certain kinds of behavior—and it's important to remember that we wouldn't have the landscape we have now if huge incentives hadn't been given to Americans to use cheap gas and automobiles as their primary form of transportation. "Fettering" means declaring some market solutions simply off-limits—as we do when we prohibit child labor, or unsafe working conditions, or the siting of nuclear power plants on fault lines. There is no such thing as a completely free market; every market has been structured and fettered by public incentives, penalties, and prohibitions. Land use planning and enforcement would be one way to both structure and fetter a market to produce results that preserve values that most Vermonters want to see preserved. A real-estate market that doesn't have the right mix of incentives and prohibitions is fully capable of destroying a town center while encouraging land- and energy-hungry building on agricultural soils that have not been given to us in infinite supply.

THE UNSEEN SUCCESSES OF ACT 250

Many appreciative reviewers of Act 250's effects note that as important as its application to existing proposals has been, even more important are the proposals that are modified into compliance before submission—or that don't even enter the permitting process because they are so obviously ill-considered. Among the projects that were dramatically scaled down or abandoned completely in the face of Act 250 were a 700-unit campground in the unorganized mountainside town of Somerset (pop. 5); a 2,000-acre vacation home complex, including a 700-acre lake, near Randolph; and a plan to dam the Mad River to create a 21-acre lake solely so a developer could offer waterfront vacation homes for sale in Waitsfield, near the Mad River Glen and Sugarbush ski resorts.

deciding those questions in that place and time.

As much of the country has learned in the downturns that have been a regular feature of our economic experience, when entrepreneurial ambition is given relatively free rein in relatively unstructured markets, housing and retail capacity are overbuilt: land use goes to the highest bidder, a ratchet that escalates land use projects into the realm of the unrealistic and the financially unsustainable. The abandoned structures and cracked parking lots that get left behind are testament to the fickleness of fortune in a system driven by optimistic hopes that can't always be fulfilled. Act 250 has been credited with moderating speculative commercial investment in the state, thereby insulating its economy from the worst effects of recession. In particular, Act 250 has discouraged speculative housing construction and, in so doing, kept Vermont from feeling the worst effects of the recessions, housing bubbles, and collapses that have come over the decades. (That was the conclusion of a 1992 study done by Stephen M. Meyer of MIT, discussed in a sidebar in the next chapter.)

Today, a big-box suburban shopping "campus" stands in Williston, close by the Interstate, with a Walmart, a Home Depot, a Toys 'R' Us, and a dozen other retailers, as Darby Bradley (and many others) had predicted. Some stores are isolated behind their acres of parking while others are grouped into a bad imitation of a commercial city street. Bikes and pedestrians are clearly unwelcome. A car is a practical necessity to navigate the area—even to get from any of the stores to the stand-alone chain restaurants that fringe the complex.

This came to pass for many reasons, including in part because in the fifteen years after the Pyramid Mall decision, the population of Chittenden County grew, and the region further consolidated its status as a university hub, a center of commerce, and a tourist destination. While studies submitted in the Act 250 review of the new proposals showed that such development would still adversely affect the city of Burlington, the case was no longer so clear. Much of the growth in downtown Burlington came because, even as the Pyramid case was being contested, the city was in the process of transforming its primary commercial street into a pedestrian mall. Completed in September 1981, the Church Street Marketplace is an example of what a walkable downtown looks like at its best. Holding sixty-three specialty stores, thirteen national retailers, and twenty-six eating and drinking establishments, Church Street offers residential and office space above its street-level retail establishments. The stores have a 97 percent occupancy rate, and the street attracts three million visitors a year—many of them tourists. In the summer, the marketplace is host to twenty different food-cart vendors and a variety of street performers. With views of Lake Champlain and the Adirondacks from its cross streets, it wins unsolicited testimonials on tourist-oriented websites—"a great place to eat, walk around, shop"—and in 2008 was selected as one of the American

Planning Association's "Great Public Spaces in America." The denial of the Pyramid Mall permit in early 1981 gave the city time to finish the Church Street Marketplace, which, ironically enough, became such a powerful tourist and population draw that it helped to create the commercial opportunity, the economic niche, that big-box developers were eventually able to exploit.

In Williston, the original either-or decision between exurban and urban development was decided on several grounds, only one of which was the development's impact on the economic health of a nearby city; other grounds included Pyramid's failure to conform to the regional plan, impacts on agricultural soils, and impacts on transportation. (In fact, every single criterion of Act 250 came into play in the hearings.) The process chose a vital downtown center over the creation of suburban sprawl—but that original decision didn't stick. Should this be counted a failure of the Act 250 process, a result of not linking it to coherent land use planning? The answer is not clear-cut. But the processes and planning structures that existed could have been used to different effect. "The eventual fate of Tafts Corners," writes Humstone, "was more a product of political issues [that resulted in] ... changes in the leadership of the Environmental Board—not to mention the missteps by the town of Williston in ignoring its own Act 200 approved plan."

With the Pyramid case on record, bashing Act 250 as a constraint on growth became a familiar trope from

Many Vermont cities and towns are examples of multi-use walkable communities that provide alternatives to new development in countryside locations.

the business community. In 1981, the year of the Pyramid decision, Harry Behney, secretary of the Agency of Development and Community Affairs, began saying aloud, in public, what many developers had long been saying to whomever would listen: the law was driving away potential business and thereby harming Vermonters.

Behney's criticism of Act 250 gained enough attention and support that Republican Governor Richard Snelling felt he had to respond. He called for a thorough review of the law and the permitting process, choosing investigation rather than precipitate action.

The report of the Permit Process Review Committee concluded that, no, Act 250 had not caused economic damage. It did find that the state could do a better job of coordinating various permit processes and of making the sum total of them more accessible, transparent, efficient, and user-friendly.

While sniping at Act 250 would continue—"every year," attorney Gillies noted, "there are demands to make the process easier, faster, and more predictable"—no governor "has [ever] dared to criticize Act 250's values." The idea that individual pursuit of self-interest in the development of private property has social and environmental consequences, and that society therefore has a legitimate interest in shaping how private property is developed, is firmly entrenched as part of the social consensus that Vermonters hold.

Tailpipe Plugging and Bashed Noses

The governor's office passed from Republican Richard Snelling to Democrat Madeleine Kunin in 1984. Kunin's platform included a strong environmental plank, which she and a cooperative legislature soon implemented. Protection of the state's water resources was a priority, and in short order the legislature passed, and Kunin signed, several key pieces of legislation. In 1985, a groundwater classification law called for water quality assessment and mapping—if you don't know what you have, you can't know if it has been degraded. (Unfortunately, the law was

A landscape that is large and expansive seems infinitely capable of absorbing human acts and works, making environmental regulation seem unnecessary.

underfunded and largely ignored.) In 1986, the Water Quality Act extended regulatory coverage to indirect discharges of pollutants—the sort of water contamination that begins with a discharge on or under the ground. It also gave additional protection to upper-elevation waters and other wetlands that are especially fragile. The 1987 State Rivers Policy required the Water Resources Board to classify streams and rivers, set criteria for naming some of them "Outstanding Resource Waters," and also set limits to riparian gravel extraction—a practice by which farmers and

other riverside landowners had long supplemented their incomes but which degrades stream quality for wildlife and for human uses. The 1987 Solid Waste Act was remarkably forward-looking in placing emphasis on waste stream reduction and recycling, and it also mandated the closure of all unlined landfills—Vermont held about two hundred of them—by 1992.

Pesticide use by farmers had become a major threat to water quality, and 1985 brought passage of a pesticide monitoring law, along with a community-right-to-know law, so that both the state and

its citizens would know what pesticides were being used where and when. An underground storage tank law, passed in the same year, further protected groundwater by mandating new safety and construction standards and set up a state version of a "superfund" to help defray the costs to individuals and small businesses of bringing their storage tanks into compliance.

Mostly, this kind of environmental legislation amounts to "tailpipe plugging"—it forbids the discharge of toxic effluents rather than forbidding the production or use of the toxins themselves. (As noted, in some cases the new laws were even less effective, simply calling for the effluents to be catalogued.)

This approach is consistent with the criterion of freedom articulated by an old temperance slogan (and often misattributed to Supreme Court Justice Oliver Wendell Holmes): "Your freedom to swing your arm stops just short of my nose." Naturally enough, the focus is on the impact, the harm; but tailpipe plugging and lawsuits over bashed noses don't always succeed in protecting common assets. We control the speed of an automobile by regulating the flow of inputs to the engine, rather than trying to choke down the exhaust pipe; it's more efficient and effective. And arrests are sometimes made for "disorderly conduct" long before uncontrolled arm swinging has hurt somebody. Clearly, the law recognizes that some damage is best avoided altogether rather than being adjudicated after the fact as a tort. (This is something that public officials of every political persuasion know full well. Try approaching one with a shaving cream pie in hand and see how close you can get.)

One significant exception to the pattern had occurred a few years before: in 1978 the Lake Champlain Committee (a bi-state citizens' group dedicated to protecting and conserving the lake) succeeded in getting legislation in place to ban the use of phosphate-containing laundry detergent in Vermont. The phosphorous leads to algae blooms that degrade water quality and poison aquatic life, and the ban attacked this troublesome pollutant at its most common source. Other phosphorous reducing measures would follow.

An Unprecedented Coalition and a Lasting Achievement

As the national economy rose out of its slump in the mid-1980s, the increasing pace and pattern of development in Vermont brought substantial benefits, including jobs and a state budget surplus, but development also continued to threaten the state's ecosystems, its rural character, and the viability of its town and village centers. Much of that destructive dynamism had its origin outside the state: reduced enforcement from the Federal Environmental Protection Agency, documentable harm caused by acid rain that traced to the smokestacks of power plants in the Midwest, a resurgence of the kind of land speculation that had pushed its way into Vermont as the Interstate made its steady advance. Even with a tax on land sales—the antispeculative tax that grew progressively higher the faster the land was sold—profit could still be had by buying large parcels, subdividing, and selling them for housing development. The get-rich-quick opportunities available in Vermont drew the attention of the national financial press. Both *Fortune* and *Forbes* profiled one ambitious flatlander speculator, Harry S. Patten, who set up offices in Vermont and specialized in turning farmland into upscale subdivision. He offered wealthy, city-tired urbanites the opportunity to buy a ten-acre foothold on the Vermont way of life, a parcel large enough to escape Act 250 review. When his self-named corpora-

Put Blodgett and John Meyer

'JEALOUS OF NEW JERSEY'

Put Blodgett, co-chair of the Current Use Tax Coalition (CUTC), grew up on a dairy farm. The day after his graduation from Dartmouth College, he started work as a full-time dairy farmer and kept at it for over fifteen years. More recently, he turned his attention to the forested acres of his farm. He was "jealous of New Jersey" in 1978, because that state—known to many for the industrial development and suburban sprawl that's readily visible from its major highways—has a current use program. These programs allow farm- and forestland to be appraised at their use value instead of their potential value if developed. To participate, landowners have to sign on to a management policy, a relatively small burden in exchange for a considerable reward—a farm that has a chance at being economically viable. As an owner of forested property close to the Interstate and Dartmouth College, where property taxes are high, in 1978 Put realized he'd have to sell some building lots or cut his best lumber in order to generate some money from the land to make the payment. The choice pained him. In 1980, when the current use program became available in Vermont, he quickly signed up and has been enrolled ever since. Put sees that others have faced the same hard choice; the tax burden encourages unwise use, including parcelization of land into lots that are too small for either timber harvesting or to serve as habitat for a wide range of animals. Current use begins to fix a weakness in Act 250, Put says. The law "doesn't prevent parcelization," because the smaller projects that don't trigger Act 250 add up over time.

John Meyer, the other co-chair of CUTC, also heads up the Bardill Land and Lumber Company, where he oversees the management of more than fifteen thousand acres of timberland in and around the Worcester Mountain Range. He notes that the pre-Interstate, hand-shake culture of Vermont had its own informal way of dealing with the problem of high property taxes. "In the early 1950s, Vermont had a form of use value appraisal at the local level ... appraisers would simply assign timberland low values." But by the 1960s, things

started to change with the reapportionment of the legislature from one town, one vote to a population-based model mandated by federal law: "one man, one vote" was the slogan. In Vermont, one result was the sudden and dramatic loss of legislative over-representation for rural areas. As Vermont's population grew in the Interstate era, property taxes rose steadily while fewer and fewer Vermonters were connected to agriculture. Urbanites and recent immigrants to the state had little appreciation for the value of the informal systems of land use appraisal that had been in place, and they called for "fairness" in property appraisal. One hundred percent fair market value became the standard, and fair market value meant real estate value, not ecological value. That, says John, is "why current use became critical to save the working landscape." It formalized and restored the informal system that had been in place decades earlier.

John cites the 1978 film put out by the VNRC, *So Goes Vermont*, which shows that during the 1970s the rural, agricultural foundation of the state was disappearing rapidly. This, he says, was "a time when the annual per acre property tax exceeded [the dollar value of] the annual per acre [lumber] growth," which meant "at that point forestry was inherently not sustainable." Throughout the decade, more timber had to be cut to pay taxes than could be grown.

"Timber liquidation was the result—it was the only way to hang on. Landowners were going down in a spiral, rapidly accelerating." But what happens when all the timber is cut? Parceling out the land for housing is the only other option. "Current use, in one fell swoop, changed the dynamic." It created "a margin where land can be managed productively. It's true," John goes on, "that land lives and dies on current use. Working lands would vanish in a flash without current use. People would subdivide, sell out, get out."

The first to sign up for current use were forestland owners, not farmers, John notes. "Farmers didn't trust the state and felt the penalties were too high." And while much timberland is owned by people who live elsewhere, farmers usually reside on the land they work, and they had another concern: tax reduction on their land would hand a large problem over to the town—their neighbors—unless reimbursement came from the state. The current use program included that reimbursement—but "would the legislature actually do it?" Money for the program had to be appropriated every year. The CUTC, a group that played a critical role in getting the measure

Above: (l. to r.) John Meyer and Put Blodgett

passed, remained active "to ensure that the program would be fully funded annually, and people would stay in the program." It brought together a diverse coalition—agriculture, forestry, environmental, recreational, and landowner groups, as well as many people who simply cared about the agricultural heritage of Vermont and the retention of its working landscapes. The coalition was effectively the watchdog of the current use program. Many of its original members are still active in it today.

After a decade-long hiatus, the coalition returned, because by 2010, the legislature, feeling budget pressures, went looking for money from the current use program again. A compromise was hammered out, one that divided the forestry and agricultural communities: Was it too little? Was it the best that could be gotten? John sighs, "Compromise is an important learning process. It is an artful proposition to get everyone to say yes."

Put, commenting on the public perception of the program, says "I don't like to refer to the program as a tax abatement program." It's not about giving a "special interest" a tax break; it's about preserving the foundation of the state's economy. "Vermont will lose its rural landscape if it doesn't recognize the value of its use as a working landscape."

John agrees. "Conceptually, use value appraisal on undeveloped land is really no different from market value appraisal on developed land. Both systems are based on actual use. Current use taxes land on the same rational basis as other appraisal values on developed land. It's simply a matter of equity. Frankly, the most successful working lands legislation is current use." He went on to say that he's hopeful about "keeping the working lands of Vermont working." "People are finally beginning to talk about working lands, agriculture, and forest together. Agriculture has always been a sacred cow. I think the [legislature's] agriculture committees should be agriculture and forestry committees because that's what they deal with: working lands."

Together, Put and John have developed an interesting idea that John expresses as "a filter or lens—a working landscape filter—that all legislation has to pass through regarding its impact on Vermont's working lands. Will any given bill help or hurt the working lands—does it help both economies to survive? Somebody has to ask that question …Will a proposed bill make Vermont a more enduring place, or spur the spiral of decay?"

tion went public its stock price tripled in a year on a profit increase of 175 percent. Vermont was the engine of his personal fortune. "Forget Florida," advised the subhead to the *Forbes* article; "Today's undeveloped land hype centers on Good Old New England."

During the Reagan era, some Vermont environmental organizations enlarged their scope of operations to take on regional and national issues, lobbying for control of the emissions that were producing acid rain and for better enforcement of existing regulations at the federal level. Other

organizations began making a new and productive linkage between housing, land conservation, and preservation of both farms and compact village centers. Speculative pressure and distant money were sending housing prices beyond the reach of average Vermonters and raising land values so high that on many agricultural soils farming was no longer an economically viable option. If lack of affordable housing and loss of farms and ecosystems had a common cause, then a successful strategy for dealing with either might be fashioned from tackling both.

In the fall of 1986, a group of like-minded individuals met near Montpelier to work up a new idea: the creation of a semi-public agency devoted to pursuit of three interlocking goals—preserving the working landscape of Vermont, promoting development and redevelopment within historic town centers, and increasing the stock of affordable housing available in the state. The group included Monty Fisher and Eric Palola from the VNRC; Robert Klein from The Nature Conservancy; Rick Carbin and Darby Bradley from the Vermont Land Trust; Paul Bruhn from the Preservation Trust of Vermont; Steve Kimball; Jim Libby; and Gus Seelig, then head of the Central Vermont Community Action Council. The plan they formulated was a novel one, and it drew inspiration from Carbin's experience with the Vermont Land Trust (which had begun as the Ottauquechee Regional Land Trust about a decade earlier). There, Carbin and his board had realized that they could sometimes achieve their goals without spending a whole lot of money. What they needed was a grubstake and a bit of backing in case the numbers didn't work as planned. As Jim Libby and Darby Bradley reported the story: "When an important property in South Woodstock came under contract for sale in 1980, the Vermont Land Trust, with $5,000 in the bank, exercised its right to match the developer's offer of $1 million." They then sought underwriting from "charitable creditors" and with that financial backing "bought the property, created a limited development plan that

preserved the essential open space, and resold the property subject to conservation easements. The Vermont Land Trust managed to recoup its entire investment, planning, and holding costs, so it never had to call on the charitable creditors to make up a loss." What they had done was a public-interest version of the low-down-payment real estate flip, similar in form to the deals that brought profits to developers like Patten, but executed instead to conserve farmland and ecosystems.

Carbin and the others thought that elements of this model could be used to preserve other important land and property in the state and to provide affordable housing to low-income Vermonters. Without drawing on "charitable creditors," but using instead grant money and public funds to match or augment expenditures by towns, non-profits, and even the state itself, such an organization could help tip the balance and make a greater number of conservation, downtown development, and low-income housing projects economically feasible. The Vermont Land Trust and The Nature Conservancy had already been lobbying for a state trust fund to conserve farmland and open space. The group decided to invite affordable housing advocates to join the effort, creating the Vermont Housing and Conservation Coalition.

In politics, as in comedy and cooking, timing counts for a great deal.

Top right: Landscape conserved by the Vermont Housing and Conservation Board. Bottom: affordable housing in Montpelier.

Previous efforts to conserve farmland with state support, as recommended by an agricultural policy task force in 1984, had come to naught, mostly thanks to the state's $35 million budget deficit. But, by 1987, budget discipline and the economic boom (including, ironically enough, the boom in land speculation) had fattened the state treasury, and at the start of her second term, Kunin was looking for a bold initiative to energize and define her governorship. "And," Libby and Bradley wrote, "Vermonters were ready." The coalition had enormous appeal. As state senator Scudder Parker, chair of the Finance Committee, said, "this is the first time low income advocates, the green sneaker crowd and the farm bureau all want us to do the same thing."

In 1987, a statute authorized the creation of the Vermont Housing and Conservation Board (VHCB), gave it a mission (to "encourage and assist in creating affordable housing and in preserving the states' agricultural land, historic properties, important natural areas and recreational lands"), and appropriated $3 million for it to begin its work. The next year, the legislature received the findings of the Governor's Commission on the Future of Vermont, also known as the Growth Commission or the Costle Commission. It was chaired by Vermonter Douglas Costle, who had served as the head of the Environmental Protection Agency in the Carter administration and returned to serve as dean of the Vermont Law School. Responding to the report's

Between 1986 and 1988, Vermont lost more than three hundred dairy farms, 10 percent of the total.

call to strengthen the VHCB, the legislature appropriated an additional $20 million and gave the VHCB an income stream by dedicating a portion of property transfer tax receipts to the fund. The money would be leveraged by being lent or granted to non-profit developers (for development costs, not operating expenses), to towns and municipalities, to regional and local housing authorities, and to the state. Conservation easements and guarantees concerning rents would have to be written into deeds, even though real estate law at the time was not fond of deed restrictions in perpetuity. Work-arounds were developed, including ninety-nine-year, renewable ground leases with resale restrictions. (Housing subsidy covenant restrictions were codified into law by the legislature in 1989.)

Dedicated to pursuing multiple goals that were newly seen as complementary rather than antagonistic, the VHCB came to serve as a model for other states. Rhode Island copied the enabling statute word-for-word in creating its version in 1989, and by 2005, Connecticut, Massachusetts, and Hawaii had similar programs. In 1999, the Sierra Club cited Vermont as the number-one smart-growth state in the nation, specifically crediting the VHCB as the key instrument of this achievement.

By 2012, the VHCB had leveraged more than $950 million from private and public sources, helped build more than 10,000 units of affordable housing, and conserved 390,740 acres of the Vermont landscape.

Planning, Again: All Carrot, No Stick

The Costle Commission report that recommended increased funding for the VHCB made other recommendations for preserving the social and natural capital of Vermont. Subtitled "Guidelines for Growth" and issued in final form in January 1988, it seconded and extended the findings that had been adopted as the Vermont Land Capability Plan in 1973, and it echoed the findings of the final report of the Vermont Planning Council from 1968. Many of the guidelines for growth that the report offered were unexceptional and would have had nearly unanimous support in any sampling of Vermont opinion: "The quality of air, water, wildlife and land resources should be maintained and improved." "Natural and historic features of the Vermont landscape should be protected and preserved." "Citizen participation should occur at all levels of the planning process, and decisions should be made at the most local level possible consistent with their impact." "Sound forest management practices should be encouraged." "Decent and affordable housing should be available to all Vermonters."

Statements of practical purpose that could put those goals into effect had strong majority support from Vermonters: "Strip development along highways and scattered residential development not related to community centers should be discouraged." "Economic growth should be encouraged in designated growth areas."

In sum, the pragmatic imperatives of its guidelines led the commission to its major recommendation: "A coordinated, comprehensive planning process and policy framework must be established to guide decisions by local governments, regional planning commissions, and state agencies." The report showed in detail how that could be done while generally steering clear of top-down mandates and prohibitions. The result is a model of clarity and coherent presentation. Rooted in a wide-ranging series of public hearings that surveyed Vermonters' values and concerns, as well as in the hard and difficult facts of the changing Vermont landscape ("Since 1986, the rate of farm decline has accelerated….Vermont has lost more than 300 dairy farms—10 percent of the total—in just the last two years"), it offered a clear diagnosis of the problem before laying out a set of institutional structures and policy guidelines to address it.

What the report offered was an impressive synthesis: a bold and (on paper) successful resolution of the tensions between local control and non-negotiable, big-picture constraint; between individual human prerogative and our shared physical reality; between economic growth and ecological limits. The limits, constraints, and reality that defined one side of the balance wouldn't be articulated by a central authority and imposed on the citizenry but would instead be coded into policy by town and regional planning commissions (with the help, to be sure, of a cadre of professional planners whose

Madeleine May Kunin

OPTIMISTIC AND ENGAGED

Among Vermont governors, Madeleine May Kunin is a standout on two counts: the only woman ever to hold the office, she is also the only governor to support integrated land use planning from the grassroots to the grass tops and to see those efforts become law. Her 1989 creation of a Governor's Commission on Vermont's Future, also known as the Growth Commission, led to the passage of Act 200, a forward-looking planning law. It also secured a funding stream for the Housing and Conservation Board.

Some political observers think Act 200 also cost the former governor her job. With public sentiment aroused against any form of planning, in 1991 she chose not to run for a fourth term.

During her three terms as governor, 1985 to 1991, Madeleine marshaled significant environmental legislation through a receptive statehouse, including laws that established statewide water quality standards and closed the ten-acre loophole in Act 250.

On today's energy issues, she has a clear and strong opinion. "The time has come to shut down [Vermont] Yankee and use every other clean, renewable energy source available. And that must start with, especially, conservation and efficiency." She worries that economic pressures will erode environmental gains. "When people are frightened, they see black-and-white, and what has happened in economic hard times is that regulations tend to, in people's minds, equal loss of jobs." She well understands that lack of good jobs is a problem for Vermont and the country at large. "Some of the major issues of our day are related to high levels of poverty. This country has as much as 20 percent of children in poverty and a minimum wage earner will spend a half to a third of her income on childcare. And, of course, there is a growing discrepancy between the rich and the poor." This all spells trouble for the environment, she warns.

In 1989, then governor Kunin served on a commission that monitored the first democratic elections in Bulgaria. There, in the former Soviet bloc country freed by the fall of the Berlin Wall in

1989, she saw a clear connection between poverty and environmental degradation. The winning candidates ran on environmental platforms, and "their first policy initiatives were for a clean environment. This was a country where their environmental movement gave birth to democracy." The success of the democratic elections was clear evidence of "this little country's potential for change," and by the time she and her policy advisor, George Hamilton, returned to Vermont, they had decided to do what they could to help Bulgaria and other nations in Eastern Europe address environmental, economic, and social challenges. After consultations with Douglas Costle, Jonathan Lash, and others, then governor Kunin conceived a new non-profit organization: the Institute for Sustainable Communities (ISC).

The idea received a seed grant from the Rockefeller Brothers Fund in 1990, and in 1991 the ISC was officially incorporated. It began work in Eastern Europe—Bulgaria, Romania, Albania, Kosovo—but now reaches into Russia, China, and Japan as well. Domestically ISC runs a national Climate Leadership Academy with workshops on Low-Carbon Transportation and Green Economic Development. The academy has drawn more than five hundred practitioners from sixty-one cities and regions throughout the United States.

At seventy-nine, Madeleine shows no signs of resting, let alone resting on her laurels. On a tour with her latest book, *The New Feminist Agenda: Defining the Next Revolution for Women, Work, and Family*, she tackles the social, environmental, and economic issues that stem from the fact that women have entered the workforce in record numbers without public policy to support them or their families.

In addition to having written two previous books, *Living a Political Life* and *Pearls, Politics, and Power*, she holds the position of Marsh Professor at University of Vermont and she is a frequent commentator on Vermont Public Radio.

As to the future: "We need to do a better job, to make a greater effort to sit down at the table with a variety of interests, with new allies, because we have some serious social and economic issues, not to mention climate change, which will only make these troubling situations worse." Her personal credo is clear. "You must be optimistic and engaged. You cannot give up, you cannot cede the ground to the opposition." Perseverance is her plain recipe for success.

advice could be presumed to be based in knowledge of ecological and social reality).

The report formed the basis of Vermont Act 200, the most ambitious and far-reaching planning legislation of the decade. That law offered towns and regions incentives and financial help for the kind of community planning that Act 250 needed, a bottom-up process that would slow the dynamic by which the Vermont landscape and its communities were being compromised and degraded through piecemeal, one-by-one decision making.

The law had some notable successes —its substantial funding for the VHCB, for instance—and it remains on the books, but it failed to achieve its larger object. If the report the law was based on was so clear and far-reaching, and its ends had such widespread support, why did the legislation not produce a sturdy system of land use planning that integrated local, regional, and state efforts to secure the ends that Vermonters valued?

The simplest answer: the law wasn't effectively enforced. Despite the clarity of the logic behind it, despite the input from thousands of Vermonters who attended hearings or sent written comments to the commission, and despite what was, to many, a clear and obvious need for its remedy, in 1998 enforcement of systematic land use planning was still politically unacceptable in Vermont. Some towns still had no zoning laws, and many of the ones that did were finding them extremely unpopular. In towns that lay some distance from the development pressure released by the arrival of the Interstate, Vermonters had yet to accept the idea that they had to get a town permit in order to do things their parents and their parents' parents had freely done on their own property. While Vermonters were nearly unanimous in wanting to see their working landscapes and ecosystem services preserved, and a strong majority supported the concept of growth centers and wanted to see suburban sprawl stopped, fewer Vermonters were ready to accept land use planning as the vehicle for achieving this. The same feature of the Vermont experience that allowed it to leapfrog fifty years of other states' experience to create a model land use permitting law in Act 250—its isolation from the pressures and damage of incoherent development—now worked against the adoption of anything that looked like additional government constraint on the free disposition and development of property. The social capital of Vermont—the mutual trust, publicly held knowledge, and shared understandings that underlie its political and social life—hadn't developed in a direction that would have made the virtues of planning as obvious to all Vermonters as they had become to the Costle Commission.

Act 200 was resisted because it was considered statewide zoning, but that's not what it was; it didn't seek to impose definitions of "forbidden" and "allowed" on various types of land use in Vermont. Like Act 250, it sought to implement a process by which Vermonters themselves would make

these decisions. That process had to be coordinated among adjacent towns and within and among the state's regions to reflect the reality that, just as some effects of development reached beyond the boundaries of individual properties, others reached beyond the boundaries of individual towns and individual groups of towns.

There are also more particular reasons that crucial elements of the planning process outlined in Act 200 withered and fell into disuse.

One was a backlash from a property rights movement that tended to equate planning with zoning, zoning with unnecessary control, and unnecessary control with oppression. In 1990, Citizens for Property Rights succeeded in placing an item on town meeting ballots in 121 of Vermont's 251 towns, instructing town officials "not to adopt an Act 200 plan." Much disinformation was broadcast about what Act 200 would do; VNRC volunteers going door-to-door to solicit support for it found people who had been told it forbade hanging out laundry, forbade gun ownership, and included other similarly offensive controls on the use of property. At town meeting in Duxbury, Governor Kunin had to wait out a floor vote on whether or not she'd even be allowed to speak on the issue (a second vote by paper ballot reversed a voice vote in which the "noes" were loudest). Ninety-nine towns approved the resolution. Some outspoken proponents of planning suffered vandalism of their private property. With the election or appointment of property-rights parti

A backlash against Act 200, and its perceived oppression, was the property rights movement that tended to equate planning with zoning and zoning with unnecessary control.

sans to some town planning commissions and selectboards, many meetings weren't productive efforts to secure a common and desirable future but became occasions for rancorous argument and belligerent debate.

Other factors contributed to the ineffectiveness of Act 200. While the Costle Commission had foreseen that implementation of an effective, locally controlled planning process would cost money—between $2 million and $5 million, they estimated—the process was underfunded. It gave no additional money to state agencies to perform their part in the process—the review and approval of local and regional plans to ensure consistency and compatibility with state goals. This meant that the work suffered from being shoehorned into existing job descriptions. At the local level, the process relied heavily on the citizens who served as town officers—volunteers, essentially, whose ability to donate time to public purposes was already severely taxed and whose willingness to do so was further reduced by the behavior of the opposition. Town planning commissioners were assisted and advised by circuit-riding professional planners, a money-saving approach that had the disadvantage of guaranteeing that no matter how respectful, facilitative, and consensus building these professionals proved to be, planning could easily be portrayed as the work of outsiders coming into town to tell the locals what they must and mustn't do. Many of the Vermonters who rejected planning remembered the handshake culture they had enjoyed before the wave of "flatlander" immigration of the 1960s and 70s. Planning, often supported by recent arrivals to the state, seemed the complete abandonment of the values they most wanted to see preserved.

Enforcement was hampered by a lack of authority—an absence of the kind of "mutual coercion mutually agreed upon" that was crucial to the success of the billboard law decades earlier. While the report had recommended that "a series of meaningful sanctions must be implemented" to ensure that towns prepared plans and that these plans would be reviewed and coordinated at the regional and state levels, the law as written offered incentives—limited financial assistance—but held no penalties for towns that didn't comply. Some towns embraced planning, used the funds wisely, and created plans through exemplary processes of public participation. But some towns returned the planning money on principle; others found that the money was more trouble than it was worth; still others found ways to spend it on things like a new dump truck for the road commissioner.

Finally, these obstacles might have been met and diminished if the Act 200 process had had strong support in Montpelier. Among voters, opponents of planning were more vociferous and motivated than proponents, a fact that tended to diminish the legislature's enthusiasm for seeing the law succeed. Strong leadership from the governor's office might have influenced both public and legislative opinion, but in 1990 Governor Kunin chose not to run for office again, and neither of her two immediate successors (Republican Richard Snelling and then Democrat Howard Dean) chose to associate themselves with the cause. In the first year, the review of plans was a cumbersome learning experience; a second round the next year showed improvement; but in its third year, the process sputtered out from lack of execution by towns, regional commissions, and state agencies. Certainly for state agencies, and perhaps for towns and regional commissions as well, a strong commitment from the governor's office would have produced greater effort and attention.

Although Act 200 did expand the scope and quality of local planning efforts and was the foundation of some notable successes, Madeleine Kunin's stirring call in her 1988 State of the State address for "a new planning era" that would have Vermonters "taking more direct responsibility for decision-making in order to assure greater control over our destiny" was not fully realized. As we shall see, other key elements of the Costle Commission report would eventually influence environmental policy in the state.

CHAPTER 4

The 1990s

Confrontation

Vermont's environmental and planning laws are widely debated and attacked, as big-box development makes inroads in the state. Efforts at planning and conservation meet with resistance.

Early in the morning of August 14, 1991, James Bressor, Republican Governor Richard Snelling's press secretary, was awakened by a phone call from the state trooper assigned to drive the governor from his home in Shelburne, over the Green Mountains, and to his office in Montpelier. He'd found the governor dead at the edge of his backyard swimming pool. Snelling's wife Barbara was away in New York, on a business trip.

Bressor called the governor's cabinet and their deputies to summon them to an emergency meeting in the fifth floor conference room of the Pavilion building, where the governor's office is located. They'd meet with the new governor, Democrat Howard Dean. By 8:45, the group of twenty-some appointees had assembled, somber in their grief, anxious in the expectation that they were about to lose their jobs. Dean, a doctor whose duties as lieutenant governor hadn't kept him completely away from the practice he shared with his wife, Judith Steinberg, had had to pause to cancel patient appointments. When he arrived, the meeting was brief. Dean's message: This is a time to grieve our loss. There will be no sudden changes to the cabinet, now or into the foreseeable future. He would meet with each of them, one-on-one, in the weeks to come.

Snelling's death from a heart attack came just eight months into his return to office. He'd had four previous two-year terms as governor, from 1977 to 1984, before Madeleine Kunin took the office for three terms, 1985 to 1991. As an experienced but also newly elected governor, he had been painfully aware of the stresses on Vermonters brought by the lingering economic recession and had been lobbied by the Chamber of Commerce and other business interests to "streamline" Act 250 and make it "more efficient" in order to get the economy going again.

VERMONT BY THE NUMBERS:
1990

- Population: 562,758
- Percent born in state: 59
- Cows: 163,000
- Farms: 5,496
- Total farm acreage: 1,315,000
- Registered motor vehicles: 461,796
- Seasonal homes: 45,443

On the death of Richard Snelling, l., in 1991, Lieutenant Governor Howard Dean, r., became governor.

This call from a segment of the business community is typically repeated during downturns; from the point of view of some businesspeople, the world is full of entrepreneurial possibilities that are foreclosed by environmental limits embodied in law—and they tend to see the law, not the environmental limit, as the constraining factor.

The values coded into Act 250's criteria have widespread support among Vermonters, making them hard to attack directly. What some in the business community proposed were reforms to the process. Redundancies in it slowed things down, they said. It would be better all around to have one unified hearing, with an "irrebutable presumption" that permits from towns and state agencies demonstrate compliance with Act 250 requirements.

What wasn't said, but what was in some quarters quite clearly understood, was that local governments could be outspent and state agencies could be influenced by political pressure.

A Showdown: Finite-Planet Airshed

This was the inheritance of the new governor, Dr. Howard Dean. Despite his decision to keep the Snelling cabinet intact, business interests in the state were uneasy about the transition from a Republican to a Democrat, and Dean knew that their confidence was necessary if Vermont was to weather the recession and return to prosperity. Pressure from the champions of commerce and "efficiency" mounted. In 1991, both houses of the legislature

were as evenly divided as a legislature could be. In the House, Republicans had a nominal two-seat edge, but the two representatives from the Progressive Party often voted with the Democrats. The Senate was even-steven, fifteen to fifteen. In November 1992, when Dean was elected to the office he'd gained through Snelling's death and Barbara Snelling, Richard Snelling's widow, was elected lieutenant governor, Republicans picked up one seat in the Senate, shifting the balance sixteen to fourteen.

That slim majority gave the newly elected governor his first Act 250 challenge. Consistent with his desire to maintain continuity with the previous administration, Dean had submitted the names of Snelling's Environmental Board chair and four other members for reappointment. The Senate would need to confirm those appointments, and Dean expected them to do so when the legislature convened early in 1993. But, in an unusual move, the Senate Committee on Natural Resources and Energy decided to postpone the confirmation decision until the following January, 1994—and to hold a series of hearings on the performance of the appointees in the interim. It would be a way of keeping the work of the Environmental Board, and the question of whether and how environmental regulation stymies business, in the public eye while Dean found his way in his first full term as governor.

One of the cases before the Environmental Board was a proposal from a wholesale grocery operation in

DOES RESOURCE PROTECTION HURT THE ECONOMY?

The short answer is no.

In 1992, Stephen M. Meyer, a professor of political science at Massachusetts Institute of Technology, investigated this question and concluded, in a peer-reviewed paper titled "Environmentalism and Prosperity: Testing the Environmental Impact Hypothesis": "The benefits of environmental protection are obvious and demonstrable. It is clear from the data and analyses presented in this report that the states can pursue environmental quality without fear of impeding economic prosperity." Six months later, he had completed a study focused specifically on New England and reported, with academic caution, that "there is reason to speculate that the more extensive planning required by Act 250 actually may have contributed to lessening the overall impact of the recession on Vermont's construction, real estate, and banking industry." Act 250 moderates speculative, overly optimistic commercial initiatives, and so when bubbles eventually burst, the effects of the ensuing downturn are less severe.

A longer answer takes into account that for a state like Vermont, in which tourism accounts for nearly a third of the economic base, preservation of the working landscape, compact village centers, and the state's natural resource base are crucial to economic vitality. Clearly, environmental regulations prevent some businesses from expanding and adding jobs; but those same regulations protect and add jobs elsewhere in the economy, and the net effect is positive.

A complete answer to the question "Does resource protection hurt the economy?" needs to look beyond economic benefits as meawsured

Drying laundry in the breeze is one mundane example of an ecosystem service.

by market transactions—Gross State Product— to include the real, economically valuable but unpriced services that Vermonters get from healthy ecosystems. If we include these services in our understanding of "economy," the answer is clear: environmental protection is absolutely crucial to our economic well-being.

And there is yet one further frame of reference that ought to be taken into account: economic well-being is not the sum total of human well-being. Beyond specifically economic considerations, environmental quality is a key aspect of quality of life. Economic activity is a means to an ultimate end, and it doesn't make sense to degrade that end—a higher quality of life—in order to give freer rein to just one of the instruments for achieving it.

Brattleboro, a case that became "the mother of all Act 250 battles," in the words of one commentator later. C&S Wholesale Grocers was the largest privately held company in Vermont; its 600,000-square-foot warehouse was the largest building in Vermont, and from it the company shipped groceries as far as Georgia and Maine. Its work consisted of buying grocery items in bulk and repacking shipments for delivery to individual stores, most of them owned by large chains up and down the length of the eastern United States. C&S sought a permit to add capacity by building an additional 200,000-square-foot warehouse in a business park in Brattleboro. The company let it be widely understood that it would leave the state and relocate

in Greenfield, Massachusetts, twenty miles to the south, if it didn't get what it wanted.

Brattleboro, on the Connecticut River, is surrounded by mountains and hills. The setting is scenic but has air quality issues, as the basin tends to trap pollutants. The area has frequently been at risk of violating U.S. Environmental Protection Agency air quality standards. The additional warehouse would have been served by tractor-trailers—refrigerated trucks that need to idle to keep the compressors pumping—and would have increased truck traffic in the airshed by as many as a thousand trips per day. The additional diesel exhaust was a major concern in the review process.

The District Commission approved the project, but with conditions that limited the gross volume of trucks to six hundred trips per day and limited the amount of idling they could do. Depending on where you stood, this was either an example of the sort of ridiculous micromanagement that the Act 250 process regularly perpetrated on the business community, or a good-faith effort to squeeze additional economic activity into an area that couldn't readily absorb it without ill effect. As in the Pyramid Mall case, here again the Act 250 process was being called on to apportion a finite capacity—in this case, an ecological capacity: the ability of an airshed to absorb diesel exhaust and still meet air quality guidelines.

The permit was appealed, and C&S Wholesale Grocers cross-appealed the decision. The Environmental Board upheld the conditions of the District

Commission. But the company rejected the conditions, saying it couldn't live with the hourly and total limits on truck traffic. It didn't take the matter further—didn't appeal the decision in court—but was loud and prominent in both its criticism of the Environmental Board and its promise to leave the state.

In a historically unprecedented move, Dean, as governor, also publically criticized the Environmental Board's decision, calling it a "non-permit" and saying it threatened the economy of Brattleboro and the region. Prior to this case, Environmental Board decisions had been treated as being beyond politics: the questions that Act 250 permits deal with (including air quality, as in this case) are technical, not political, questions. Dean's public opining about the work of the Environmental Board gave support to those who wanted to see a regime change in Act 250's administration and a reform of the permitting process.

Dean's criticism of the C&S decision drew a great deal of criticism in return: the Conservation Law Foundation, the Vermont Public Interest Research Group, the Vermont Natural Resources Council, and the two largest-circulation daily papers in the state, the *Rutland Herald* and the *Burlington Free Press*, were prominent among the voices that took him to task for encouraging the perception that the work of the Environmental Board was political rather than legal and technical. As the *Burlington Free Press* noted, "a high fence built of custom and good sense has protected Act 250 from political meddling"—

C&S Wholesale Grocers balked at accepting limits on total truck traffic and the amount of idling refrigerated trucks could do.

and the governor had just helped dismantle that fence.

Dean's response was to allow that he should have been a bit more careful in discussing a quasi-judicial procedure, but he went on to defend the reasonableness of his criticism: "It's not like they [C&S Wholesale Grocers] were locating on a farm or cutting down a virgin forest." Whether this was a spontaneously ill-considered remark or part of a strategy to send a sympathetic signal to those with pro-commerce, anti-Act 250 sentiments, it had the predictable effect of further outraging environmentalists and further strengthening criticism of the Environmental Board and the whole Act 250 process.

Dean's press secretary tried to smooth things over by noting that the governor supported but had no role in Act 250 hearings. But, by then, the governor's response had firmly established that he shared C&S's interpretation of the Environmental Board's decision. C&S Vice President Joel Cherington had said, of the conditioned permit, "It's almost impossible to do business in this state with its sort of misuse of the environmental legislation which is going on now." The process, he said, "doesn't need a facelift; it needs a heart transplant."

Left out of the C&S version of the narrative are a few relevant details. In the year and a half that the C&S permit application was under review, the company's business volume doubled, which meant they had outgrown the proposed additional warehouse before the permit was even approved—a development that its officers, including Cherington,

The Brattleoro airshed had a finite capacity to absorb diesel exhaust without ill effect.

certainly must have appreciated. Instead of building the 200,000-square-foot warehouse it had proposed (and had been given a permit for), it soon bought a 335,000-square-foot space in South Hatfield, Massachusetts, and also went on to build a new 465,000-square-foot facility in North Hatfield. The company couldn't have expanded to that degree in Brattleboro without hitting other limits besides air quality—including a sheer lack of open space flat enough to hold buildings of that size. Most likely, corporate plans for the additional capacity had been laid before Cherington took to criticizing Act 250, which invites us to view his remarks with some skepticism about his purpose.

Another relevant detail: during the hearing process, C&S offered estimates that had been worked up by company-paid consultants about the volume of truck trips from the existing and the proposed facility. The numbers sounded fishy to a *Rutland Herald* reporter covering the story and to some local citizens. Those citizens went out and counted the existing truck traffic, providing the local commission with actual data instead of estimates—and also discovering that C&S was in violation of its existing permit, a violation serious enough that it eventually warranted a $100,000 fine.

The largest neglected consideration —it can hardly be called a "detail"—

is the fact that the planet is finite and has ecological limits. Nothing that the Environmental Board could decide, nothing that Governor Dean could say or do, and no amount of complaint and criticism from C&S Wholesale Grocers could change the fact that the capacity of the Brattleboro airshed to absorb diesel exhaust is fixed and finite. This or that business's desire to expand operations can't always and forever be satisfied in a finite world. Transportation planning by the state and by the regional planning commission might have found a way to accommodate business growth within fixed and finite limits; it might, for instance, encourage the development of transportation infrastructure that allows for commerce to be accomplished with a smaller ecological footprint. Railroads offer 400 ton-miles of transportation per gallon of fuel burned; trucks hover around 130. Had the C&S operation been moving its freight into and out of Brattleboro by rail instead of truck, the burden on the finite capacity of the air shed would have been significantly reduced. But construction of rail lines is beyond the piecemeal, this-case–that-case purview of Act 250.

A final detail: with more than two dozen warehouse facilities, mostly in New England and the Mid-Atlantic states, C&S Wholesale Grocers continues to operate its facility in Brattleboro; it never left the state.

A Lone Vote Decides

The 1993–1994 legislative session convened for its second half in January 1994. One order of business was to review legislation that aimed to streamline Act 250 by curtailing citizen participation, and C&S Vice President Cherington and President Rick Cohen both testified in favor of the bill. It didn't pass. But Act 250 did suffer a setback as the Senate Natural Resources and Energy Committee, under the chairmanship of Senator Tom McCauley, took up the matter of the confirmation of the governor's appointments to the Environmental Board. A vote of the Senate on January 19, 1994, confirmed only two: Sam Lloyd and Steven Wright. The others—Ferdinand Bongartz, Terry Ehrich, and Chair Elizabeth Courtney—were rejected. The C&S case—and Cherington's complaint about it—featured prominently in that decision, as did a pending appeal by Wal-Mart Stores, Inc., on their application to build a store on farmland at Tafts Corner in Williston.

This result aroused the environmental community. "This is a volunteer board," the VNRC said in a letter to all state senators, Governor Dean, and Lieutenant Governor Barbara Snelling. "Subjecting these individuals to a tortuous confirmation process hurts the Vermont tradition of volunteer service

Newspapers editorialized about the political football the Environmental Board had become, with some speculating that the controversy wasn't about environmental protection at all.

to the state." Op-eds and letters to the editor characterized the Senate's actions as "environmental McCarthyism" and as a "witch hunt," in which public servants who had done no wrong were sacrificed so that some senators could appease pro-growth, anti-environmentalist sentiment. In more measured tones, newspapers editorialized about the political football the Environmental Board had become, with some speculating that the controversy wasn't about environmental protection at all. "Don't think most Republicans care deeply about eliminating Act 250," said the *Rutland Herald*, noting that environmental protection had too much support in Vermont for Act 250

to be taken down. "It has just been a handy target to gain attention while [Republicans are busy] contemplating further political moves." One of those moves, the paper suggested, was that Republicans wanted Governor Dean to seem weak in order to improve the electoral chances of his likeliest challenger, Lieutenant Governor Snelling. By presiding over a senate that rejected Dean's appointees, she could appear to be decisively pro-business and stronger than the governor in this battle.

Either because he felt the heat of all that public censure, or because he recognized that Republican electoral strategy required a strong response, or because he simply thought it was the right thing

to do, Dean returned fire in what one paper described as "his best moment." Speaking at a packed press conference, he set aside his notes and planted his feet. "There is not one shred of evidence," he said, "unveiled at any of these hearings that would indicate that there is any reason whatsoever that all three of these nominees shouldn't be confirmed. I can tell you," he added, "that I will not cave in to those senators who want me to lower environmental standards." He renewed the reappointments of Courtney, Bongartz, and Ehrich to the Environmental Board, initiating round two of the confrontation.

The reappointments came to a roll-call vote on the floor of the Senate on February 22, 1994. When one Republican senator from Orleans County, Michael Metcalf, broke ranks and voted to confirm, an audible gasp arose from the gallery: the vote was headed for a tie. VNRC Deputy Director for Policy Steve Holmes was in the chamber as the vote was taken. "You could have heard a pin drop," Holmes reported, "as Lieutenant Governor Snelling paused for what seemed like several moments before casting the vote on Elizabeth Courtney." Snelling voted no; Courtney, Bongartz, and Ehrich were again rejected.

In Holmes's judgment, "This vote set the tone for what would be a long and partisan session, which didn't adjourn until June 12," more than four weeks after the part-time legislators usually return to their citizen lives.

The Fallout

The effects of the confrontation and vote are difficult to measure. Act 250 remained in force, administered by other hands. But the Senate's actions had sent a clear message: members of the Environmental Board had better be more accommodating to business interests in their permit conditioning or face a similar fate. In his autobiography, Ralph Wright, who was then speaker of the house, said of the final vote: "I don't think I was ever more disappointed than I was at that moment. It bothers me to this day." Reflecting on the Senate's actions years later, one veteran *Burlington Free Press* journalist, Candace Page, remarked, "The refusal to confirm the appointments of three proven moderate candidates to the Environmental Board was arguably an abuse of power. And Act 250's effectiveness suffered from this abuse." Before the 1994 session, Act 250 had been hampered by the lack of a coherent land use plan to guide decisions. In the wake of the reappointment confrontation, the process was further damaged; the Environmental Board and District Commissions were hesitant to dismiss any permit on any grounds whatsoever.

Ultimately, legislative oversight of administrative processes is part of an effective and democratic system of government. But some governmental administration is rooted in physical reality, and that reality can't be changed by majority vote—not by legislators, not by citizens. In the effort to accommodate patterns of human land use

to the fixed capacities of ecosystems, there's room for practical and political disagreement, but the physical limits themselves can't be changed by human choice. In effect, in this episode the Senate shot the messenger so it wouldn't have to hear the message; and this response—outright denial of environmental limits—continues to be a difficulty faced by efforts to move in the direction of a sustainable state.

There is no easy solution. "When Reason is against a Man," the political philosopher Thomas Hobbes wrote centuries ago, "a Man will be against Reason." The same applies to evidence. Powerful interests often challenge and controvert factual evidence when acceptance of it would threaten their purposes. Challenging the well-established factual basis of policy on a subject, any subject, degrades the stock

To some, the world is full of entrepreneurial possibilities that are frustrated by environmental regulation.

of publicly held knowledge, a crucial element of social capital that allows a society to function. As with built capital, our social capital sometimes needs upgrading, improvement, replacement; change in what we collectively know and think and believe is not always bad. But when basic factual matters are contested and made the subject of political processes, when reality itself (and not just appropriate ends and means of policy) becomes the subject of polarized division, then effective, reality-based governance is made more difficult—and governance, democratic or otherwise, becomes less certain of being sustainably successful in promoting the general welfare and securing the blessings of liberty to ourselves and our progeny.

The District Commissions and the Environmental Board had been generous in granting permits. Between 1990 and 1994, 2,444 permit applications entered the process and only thirty-eight were denied. But the conditions that had been imposed on the permits that were approved were seen by business interests as unwarranted constraints that harmed their profit margins. This, of course, was precisely the point of Act 250: the process was intended to ensure that market-driven development didn't degrade the non-market values that Vermonters cherish. The market is a good allocator of resources and an effective vehicle of the public interest only when prices tell the truth about costs, and that's what the additional costs imposed by Act 250 permitting conditions began to address: they brought the otherwise uncounted social

and ecological costs of development into the price of the project.

If a development can't be profitable under Act 250, chances are it brings no net benefit to Vermonters.

That's not a logic that everyone accepted. If you think infinite economic growth is possible, if you think the planet's resources are effectively infinite, you see much environmental regulation as mostly cost, little gain. As one prominent state Republican said, defending his colleagues in their rejection of the appointments, "The Senate Natural Resources Committee believes that the main problem is that the [Environmental] Board has allowed itself to develop a culture that allows them to place extreme conditions on an applicant's permit." One person's "extreme

GETTING PRICES TO TELL THE TRUTH

Economists have long talked about "externalities"—costs and benefits that aren't reflected in the prices of goods--and they acknowledge that markets are not good allocators of resources when these externalities are significant. But most economists seem to believe the earth is infinite—they believe that it's possible to have infinite economic growth—so they don't see environmental externalities as being very large. Ecological economists and others concerned about the size of our human footprint on the planet have called for "true cost pricing," arguing that environmental costs are large enough that any system that fails to take them into account is misguided and will lead to irrational, "uneconomic," even catastrophic outcomes. The matter was outlined succinctly in a statement attributed to Oystein Dahle, a former vice president of Exxon Norway who went on to head the World Watch Institute (an unusual career track). In a conversation at the State of the World Conference in Aspen, Colorado, in 2001, he offered this perfectly balanced, pithy observation: "Socialism collapsed because it did not let prices tell the economic truth. Capitalism will collapse if it does not let prices tell the ecological truth." Much environmental policy, including Vermont's Act 250, can be seen as being directed toward this end, trying to ensure that prices tell the ecological truth.

Paul Bruhn, Howard Dean, John Ewing, and Michael Metcalf

VERMONT, AN ENDANGERED PLACE?

The conversation among these four individuals begins with a fact: in 1993 and then again in 2003, the National Trust for Historic Preservation, recognizing the threat of mall-and-sprawl development in the state, designated all of Vermont one of the nation's eleven most endangered places.

Paul Bruhn is a native of Burlington. His family owned an office equipment and stationery store on Church Street, where Paul's office is now located on the third floor. Since the Bruhns lived a mile from downtown, "I could ride a bike to wherever I was going." The city was a smart-growth community before anyone had heard the term—"a great community to grow up in," Paul says. He was a founding board member of Smart Growth Vermont and instrumental in the start-up of the Vermont Housing and Conservation Board. He is the longtime director of the Preservation Trust of Vermont.

Howard Dean lived his youth in East Hampton and New York City and graduated from Yale University and the Albert Einstein School of Medicine. On moving to Vermont, he and his wife, Judith Steinberg, shared a medical practice in Shelburne until, as lieutenant governor, he became governor in 1991 with the death of Richard Snelling. One of Howard's most notable accomplishments during his five-term tenure as governor was the Champion Lands deal of 1997. In 2003, Dean left the governor's office to run a campaign for the U.S. presidency, in which his social–liberal, fiscal–conservative position, and his innovative use of social media, brought him great success. Eventually, he lost the Democratic primary battle to John Kerry, despite an endorsement from former vice president Al Gore.

John Ewing "spent a great deal of time outdoors" as a youth in rural Pennsylvania northeast of Philadelphia. Graduating from law school in 1957, unlike most of his classmates he steered clear of urban centers and moved to Vermont. He loved Burlington, where he chose to live, with its compact community center surrounded by working landscape. It was there that John got involved in conservation work with organizations like the Audubon Society and The Nature Conservancy. He was the longest serving member of the Vermont Housing and Conservation Board, with a tenure of thirteen years, from 1998 to 2011. He helped form the Winooski Valley Park District and, later, the Forum on Sprawl, which evolved into Smart Growth Vermont and then merged with VNRC in 2011. John was the president of Bank of Vermont in Burlington and served as an economic and environmental advisor to Governor Dean, who also appointed him to chair of the Environmental Board from 1995 to 1998.

Michael Metcalf has been happily immersed in local politics, attending town meetings from the age of eleven and not missing more than two or three in the fifty years since. During the last four years, he and his wife have walked the Long Trail. Being able to commune with nature this way, he says, is fundamental to his well-being. He served as a Vermont state senator from Orleans County from 1989 to 1994. He has taught government and history at Hazen Union School in Hardwick since 1974 and at Johnson State College as an adjunct since 1987. During his tenure in the Senate, he exercised courage and leadership by voting his conscience rather than the party line. In one dramatic episode, his was the sole Republican vote in favor of Governor Dean's reappointment of Snelling's chair of the Environmental Board, Elizabeth Courtney. Michael's break with party ranks meant that Lieutenant Governor Barbara Snelling, Governor Snelling's widow, had the tie-breaking vote, which she used to reject her husband's own pick for the position.

The former governor starts the discussion: "Vermont has all of the incentives to encourage sprawl, which is why I took conservation so seriously and why easements are so important." The state has identified growth centers and has policies in place to give incentives for developing there, but, Howard says, "so long as you can build outside of growth centers, people will do that." He continues: "Act 250 has saved Vermont from much worse," but as important as regulation is, it's "not the answer" because "ultimately it erodes through economic pressures, such as we saw in 1994," when the Environmental Board was caught in a highly partisan political storm and the quasi-judicial process of Act 250 was compromised.

Paul agrees. "Review boards rarely say no to development, no matter how inappropriate a proposal is." And John adds, "The environmental board had a preference for attaching conditions, rather than [issuing] outright denials."

Howard adds, "Now here is a legitimate jobs-versus-growth issue. You can circumscribe where growth is expected, but those borders

Above: (l. to r.) Howard Dean, John Ewing, Michael Metcalf, and Paul Bruhn

can always be expanded. An important insurance policy against that sprawl-creep is land conservation. It's the most effective thing we've got. In the end … there must be some line beyond which you cannot go."

As Michael sees it: "Towns that trusted local government more than they mistrusted state government are those that continued to plan, and this reflects a belief in the efficacy of some kind of governance." Howard responds that "it helps to have land use planning. The more money there is, however, the more confrontation there will be. It's inevitable and it's about money, that's a plain fact. Economic recessions especially put pressure on planning to be ignored."

Paul, in agreement, extends the thinking: "Strip development and sprawl undermine the brand of Vermont. Our brand is the best economic advantage that Vermont has, and if we become 'anywhere USA,' we risk undermining our economic future." Land use planning, then, is crucial to the long-term economic health of the state. Paul elaborates: "We are not talking about pickling Vermont, and this isn't about making the state a museum, but instead, we need to plan for what is appropriate for the state. Walmart in downtown Rutland is a perfect example—located in an existing building in the town center, rather than in a sprawl-inducing location. We get that people need

these services, but let's do it in a way that fits with the identity of the state." John wraps up the conversation with a reference to town planning becoming more effective. "In many towns today, planning is the third leg of the land use stool, along with regulation and conservation."

For Michael, the environmental movement's high point in the 1990s was the Champion Lands deal and the low point was the political polarization that came to a head with the rejection of then governor Dean's appointees to the Environmental Board. "It was terribly ugly. I regret that I wasn't able to do more to stop it."

John adds that behind that same process "was a lot of misunderstanding about the Act 250 program."

Howard also thinks the Champion Lands deal was the environmental high point of the 1990s. The worst? "The stuff on the ground, the sprawl of Williston."

John's "worst" is the failure of Act 250 to control sprawl. His "best" is the downtown growth center bill, which he notes is improving our chances of guiding growth to the right places.

Paul rates the creation of the Vermont Housing and Conservation Board and the downtown location of the Rutland Walmart as the best moments, with the sprawl of Williston as the worst, because it gobbled up working land and undermined downtowns and village centers.

Coming Soon to a Town Near You

DANZIGER
IN AISLE 256 NO ONE CAN HEAR YOU SCREAM

condition" is another person's justifiable protection of a commonly held public asset that is finite in supply. Our system has processes, like depoliticized judicial and quasi-judicial proceedings, to sort out such basic differences of factual interpretation. But, through the appointment controversy, district environmental commissioners and members of the Environmental Board were put on notice that their decisions would not be seen as factual, technical exercises in administering values widely shared by Vermonters; their interpretations would be subject to political review and judgment.

Brawling, Malling, and Sprawling

In the mid-1990s, Vermont was the only state that did not have a Walmart store within its borders. That fact seemed to trouble corporate officers, who persisted in their efforts to establish a presence in Vermont. Aware of the pressures that were being brought on the state, and also of the value of its landscape and compact population centers, in 1993 the National Trust for Historic Preservation had taken its own unprecedented step: they designated

the entire Green Mountain State as one of the Ten Most Endangered Historic Places in the country. Their listing made headlines, raising public awareness about sprawl and what unchecked development could cost in social and cultural terms. It also helped generate in some Vermonters a modest pride in being citizens of the only state in the nation that was Walmart-free. But corporate pressures were unrelenting, and quite a few Vermonters accepted the logic behind big-box development: a Walmart would mean lower prices, and who could be against that?

The objection, of course, is that those lower prices can impose costs on others, and sometimes the others who pay those costs are fellow Vermonters: city and village residents who see their local economy decline and who soon don't have a choice but to drive to the suburbs for their shopping; farmers whose land values increase, threatening the economic viability of their livelihood; fellow citizens who lose time and money to congestion, traffic, and travel; Vermonters who see their consumer dollars shipped out of state to stimulate economies somewhere else.

But what if such development could be constrained to existing buildings that are in or near downtowns? Many of the objections would be met—and the retail traffic would enliven the downtown, strengthening instead of diminishing its tax base.

And so it was that the Preservation Trust of Vermont, the VNRC, and several local citizens' groups gave notice: they would not resist, and would even actively support, the arrival of Wal-Mart Stores, Inc. in Vermont if the company would scale back its proposals to a size that could be accommodated in existing empty buildings, in locations that didn't drain vitality from urban centers. The groups supported Wal-Mart Stores, Inc. in Act 250 hearings on their proposal for a store in Rutland, since the store would be in the downtown, would make use of an existing building,

An "infill" alternative for the St. Albans Walmart, with parking below the new structure.

Mollie Beattie, 1948–1996

"Vermont will always remain the keeper of an alternative American dream; where bigger is not always better; where community is more important than personal riches and partisan politics; where the distinction between village and countryside remains; where people can live close to the land; where they can see stars at night, clean snow and a hawk on the wing; and where none of these things are subject to the myopia of short-term economics."

In 1997, Patrick Parentau, director of the Environmental Law Center at the Vermont School of Law, published an appreciation of the life and work of Vermont forester and conservationist Mollie Beatty. "Deep within the labyrinth of the Department of Interior," it begins, "down one of the side canyons that radiate off the main hallway, is the Office of the Director of the United States Fish and Wildlife Service. Thirteen people have occupied this Office; their portraits hang in the entryway. Twelve are men in suits with serious expressions. The thirteenth is a woman wearing waders, standing in an icy Alaskan river, holding a pair of binoculars…. She is smiling broadly, and her expression seems to say, 'Is this a great job or what?'"

And that begins to capture who Mollie was and her approach to her work. Despite a career that took her into the halls of power, she never lost her love of engagement with the outdoors. One of the first female professional foresters in Vermont, she became the first woman commissioner of the state's Department of Forests, Parks and Recreation, appointed by Madeleine Kunin. In 1993, she joined the Clinton administration, becoming the first woman director of the national Fish and Wildlife Service, another male-dominated bastion where (Parentau says) she broke the mold of its "'hook and bullet' culture."

As a forester, she had developed management plans for forests around the state, including those at Shelburne Farms and on the properties of the Windham Foundation in Grafton. As commissioner of State Forests, Parks and Recreation, she helped revitalize and extend Vermont's state parks system, achieving a major expansion of Kingsland Bay state park, acquisition of Knight Island, and protection of Victory Bog. She worked within the administration and with advocacy groups to keep ski areas from decimating bear habitat and other critical ecosystems as they expanded to attract (and keep) increased skier traffic. A strong advocate for the creation of the Vermont Housing and Conservation Board, she became one of its founding board members, representing the Agency of Natural Resources. She fully grasped the board's dual mission and was an effective advocate for affordable housing.

Mollie died in 1996 at the age of forty-nine of brain cancer, back in her home state of Vermont. In recognition of her extraordinary contribution to conservation in the United States, Congress named the second largest designated wilderness in the United States—the Mollie Beattie Wilderness in the Arctic National Wildlife Refuge—in her honor. Mollie Beattie State Forest in her home town of Grafton is named after her as well.

and wouldn't contribute to sprawl. Bennington and Berlin also permitted Walmarts that made use of existing buildings: a disused five-and-dime store near downtown Bennington and an empty anchor store in a semi-rural mall in Berlin. Both developments contributed to the salvage of existing built infrastructure, helping to conserve resources and reducing the possibility of blight: there's nothing quite so wasteful or ugly as an abandoned downtown building or a dying shopping mall falling gradually into disrepair.

The proposal for Williston, though, didn't fit this pattern. It was to be a new store, built in the area that the Pyramid Corporation had eyed a decade earlier. First proposed in 1990, the store's permit was eventually approved by the Environmental Board in the wake of the Senate confrontation, and the store opened for business in 1997.

The Williston store wasn't the only proposal from the company: in 1993 it applied for a permit to put one of its standard stores next to an Interstate exchange in a cornfield near St. Albans, population about eight thousand, just twelve miles from the Canadian border. Clearly the proposed 100,000-square-foot store would have an effect on the city's commercial center, drawing out its life, its property values, its ability to sustain municipal services. The District Commission and, on appeal, the Environmental Board decided the St. Albans case on the grounds established in the Pyramid Mall case in Williston years earlier, and the permit was denied in 1994.

MAJOR MOMENTS IN LAND USE PLANNING IN VERMONT

1990
Legislative confrontation over land use planning leads to a consolidation of Act 200's thirty-two goals into a shorter list of twelve.

1993-1995
The legislature finances a Growth Center Pilot Project.

1994
Act 200 and Act 250 are widely debated and attacked.

1995–1997
Funding for municipal planning under Act 200 is cut to zero in the state budget.

1998
State funding for municipal planning efforts is restored. The Downtown Development Act, encouraging development in concentrated centers, is passed and signed by Governor Howard Dean. It establishes requirements and incentives for designating downtowns as growth centers. The incentives include tax credits, rebates, and planning grants.

1998
In one year, the Vermont Land Trust conserves (through easement or outright purchase) 52,000 acres, or more than 1 percent, of Vermont's privately owned undeveloped land.

Wal-Mart Stores, Inc. appealed the decision and pursued that appeal as far as it could be taken. "Wal-Mart Permit Denied: [State] Supreme Court Upholds E-Board Decision" announced a headline in the VNRC's *Vermont*

Environmental Report three years later. The case had symbolic significance—through its Act 250 process, Vermont had said, to one of the largest, best-known retailers in the world, that the benefit that commercial activity brings has to be weighed against the social and economic costs it imposes, particularly on the viability of downtown centers. But the symbolic value had already been undercut by the granting of the permit to the store in Williston. Vermont had been the only state without a Walmart; then it was the only state without a Walmart store built for that purpose; then it became the only state that had one such Walmart store.

Still, the St. Albans Walmart case was significant legally, for it established that the Environmental Board was within its legitimate authority to require Wal-Mart Stores, Inc. to provide data on secondary growth that its proposal would spawn, and that these considerations were relevant to the case. Having been denied standing before the District Commission, the Environmental Board, and the courts, the VNRC nevertheless filed a "friend of the court" brief, arguing that "spin-off" development (fast-food restaurants, gas stations, convenience stores) would be induced by the presence of a Walmart, and that this development would impose additional costs on the community: loss of employment, need for additional public investment in downtown revitalization, costs of traffic regulation, road maintenance, construc-tion of infrastructure for water supply, sewage, and storm-water disposal. Those costs had to be explored and become part of the deliberations; and the VNRC, in collaboration with the Preservation Trust of Vermont, had done just such a study, which was submitted in evidence. Wal-Mart Stores, Inc. had done such a study also and had come to very different conclusions. The Environmental Board found the joint VNRC-PTV study to be based on sounder, sturdier assumptions. The Vermont Supreme Court agreed. In the absence of a land use plan, the environmental movement was again successful in using the Act 250 process to accomplish some of what such a plan would have done.

As in Rutland and Bennington, Wal-Mart Inc. had been offered an alternative in St. Albans: site the store in the downtown. But despite years of negotiation, various incentives, and a great deal of free design work, Walmart renewed its application for a larger version of the project on the same green-field site out of town. In 2011, the Vermont Supreme Court approved the permit, demonstrating once again that in many land use cases the victories are only temporary. The pressures for unwise land use—for sprawl—don't simply go away. For some consumers, the lure of cheap products made overseas is compelling. And for some developers, the opportunity to cash out the state's natural and social capital for private gain will continue to be more attractive—more profitable—than adapting plans to existing structures and civic infrastructure.

U.S. Senator Jim Jeffords
1989–2007: REPUBLICAN/INDEPENDENT

Jim Jeffords entered politics in 1966, winning a seat in the Vermont State Senate. He followed that success in 1968 with a victory in the race for Vermont attorney general. In 1974, he won Vermont's sole seat in the U.S. House of Representatives, where he served for fourteen years and was the ranking Republican member of the House Education and Labor Committee. In 1988, Jeffords was elected to the U.S. Senate and was reelected in 1994 and 2000.

Jeffords's work in Congress focused on legislation involving education, job training, and individuals with disabilities. In his later years in the Senate, his emphasis shifted, as he pushed several important pieces of environmental legislation through Congress and was a leader on other fronts as well. Together with Paul Simon, he actively lobbied the U.S. administration into mounting a humanitarian mission to Rwanda during the Rwandan Genocide.

Jeffords was one of the founders of the Congressional Solar Coalition and the Congressional Arts Caucus. Recognized frequently for his performance as a legislator, in 1999 he received *Parenting* magazine's "Legislator of the Year" award and the Sierra Club's highest commendation in 2002. Reelected to a third term in November 2000, on June 5, 2001, he officially dropped his Republican party affiliation and became an independent who caucused with the Democratic Party, a move that broke the 50-50 balance in the body and denied the vice president his regular tie-breaking vote.

Fighting Sprawl: New Methods, New Organizations, New Laws

In 1997, outgoing Environmental Board chair and retired bank president John Ewing had seen enough: clearly, existing application of environmental law, especially as administered through the Act 250 process, wasn't enough to stop the degradation of Vermont towns and landscapes. The battles over Walmart had helped others, too, come to the same conclusion. In 1997, Ewing joined with Elizabeth Humstone to found the Vermont Forum on Sprawl, an organization dedicated to getting interested people talking to each other and to raising public awareness of the processes by which Vermont's landscape and values were being degraded by unwise land use policies. Humstone, with a graduate degree in city planning from Harvard University and decades of experience in the field, became the organization's first executive director. Among the Vermonters on the organization's Steering Committee was Paul Bruhn, former staffer to U.S. Senator Patrick Leahy and founding executive director of the Preservation Trust of Vermont, established in 1980.

The intention of the Vermont Forum on Sprawl was first to understand the causes and effects of sprawl on the state and public attitudes toward development—information that would

A stretch of roadway uninterrupted by strip or sprawl development leaves a buffer at the river's edge.

David Deen

STRICTLY TROUT

As a youngster, David Deen summered at his grandparents' farm in Bucks County, Pennsylvania, where he developed a passion for an old-fashioned form of fishing, "cane pole and bobbers." It was his full-time summer preoccupation—"until I discovered girls," he admits. And then, "after I was married with two kids, I took it up again." His avocation became a vocation, as he went on to create a trout fishing guide service, *Strictly Trout*.

But trout fishing is not David's sole passion. From his college days, he found himself gravitating toward the "community action world." Coming of age in the 1960s gave him plenty of opportunity to participate in social change movements. While a student at University of Connecticut (UConn), he joined the SDS, Students for a Democratic Society, where he steadily grew to understand that he was a natural-born organizer.

At UConn he met Jeanette White (now the senator from Windham County, Vermont) and her husband, Bill, and together the friends decided to move to Vermont. In 1972, after an Americorps Vista stint in Connecticut and a road trip to Chicago to sit at the feet of community organizer Saul Alinsky, David moved to a piece of land that Bill and Jeanette had purchased in Westminster West. He and the Whites lived in tents for the first several months. With a twinkle in his eye, David reports that "since then, I've never lived more than two miles from that tent site."

After a string of building projects, David organized a state-wide housing coalition and began picketing to protest the lack of affordable housing in Vermont. In 1973, his engagement with social justice took a different form as he went to work for Southeastern Vermont Community Action (SEVCA). By 1974, he was its executive director. He left SEVCA in 1983, in frustration over Reagan era budget cuts and that administration's policies toward low-income populations.

The decade he spent with SEVCA was the foundation of David's political career. In the anti-war movement's successful effort to end the war in Vietnam by denying it funding, David saw how grass-roots organizing and education could bring about change. "From that moment I wanted to be involved in public policy." In 1986, he became the first-ever Democratic senator from Windham County. A policy disagreement with the National Rifle Association cost him his seat, but by 1990 he was back in the statehouse as a state representative from Dummerston, Putney, and Westminster.

During his prior term as the senator from Windham County, David made significant contributions. He championed the passage of the gravel extraction law, which prohibits the commercial extraction of gravel from Vermont waterways, a bill that was to play a prominent role in the recovery from the 2011 Tropical Storm Irene. He was also the cosponsor of the bill that created the Vermont Housing and Conservation Board.

Serving in the Vermont Legislature is a part-time venture, so a "day job was necessary." David joined the staff of the Connecticut River Watershed Council in 1998 as their river steward. Naturally, the river steward would have an interest in the operation of Vermont Yankee on the river's western shore. But Yankee's presence there "really wasn't an issue until 2005, when Entergy requested an amendment to its discharge permit to increase its thermal discharge." The Agency of Natural Resources issued that permit amendment, allowing the plant to increase the temperature of the Connecticut River by one degree—which may not seem like much but which would have known and unknown deleterious effects on the river's ecosystem. David organized opposition, helping to instigate a case that went eventually to the Vermont Supreme Court, where the permit was affirmed. Since then he's been active in efforts to shut down Yankee in 2012 when its permit to operate expires.

David's experience of success at the grassroots level shapes his perceptions about best strategies for conserving ecosystem health: "We should be having all the fights at the local planning level. The missing ingredient in Vermont over the past fifty years has been state-level leadership and financial support for local planning."

identify what key steps needed to be taken to change wasteful (and ultimately unsustainable) land use patterns. The organization brought together diverse, and sometimes opposing, interests to discuss how Vermont could have strong downtowns and village centers while preserving the qualities of landscape and community life that have been important in defining Vermont and what it means to be a Vermonter. As with many another environmental organization, discussion soon led to action. The forum's mission grew beyond facilitating public conversation and came to include preparing and offering legislative solutions to promote downtown development and alternative, town-specific development models that could do a better job of accommodating economic activity to the landscapes and traditional settlement patterns of Vermont. The group also offered practical tools and professional assistance. The goal was not to halt growth, but to see it managed intelligently. As Bruhn put it, "We're not in favor of pickling Vermont. On the other hand, we've got to find ways to grow that reinforce what's important about our place. It's essential that we are good stewards of our place."

Within the environmental movement, the forum (which became Smart Growth Vermont in 2007) filled a distinctive niche: it operated at the junction between development and conservation, between economic change and the preservation of ecological and community vitality. As its website put it, it served as "the state's only organization that looks at the future of Vermont from both a conservation and development perspective." In 1999, it surveyed Vermonter's attitudes toward sprawl and found that a clear majority—61 percent—wanted sprawl stopped, and an even larger majority—72 percent—understood that "sprawl" and "economic development" were not synonymous. It established and published widely a list of ten principles of smart growth, which included concentrating development into walkable neighborhoods, leaving more of the landscape untouched; building pedestrian-friendly commercial and residential areas that have a diversity of businesses and housing types; and encouraging town centers that provide access to civic service and amenities, including formal and informal public space.

In 1994, three years before the Vermont Forum on Sprawl was organized, the legislature (with the help of those who organized the forum) had begun to realize that action was needed if Vermont was to retain its downtown centers and working landscapes and not see both degraded by sprawl. The Vermont Downtown Program of that year was created "to provide training and technical assistance to support community revitalization efforts"—exactly the sort of thing that the forum aimed to do. By supplementing state efforts, by publicizing the problem of sprawl, and by fostering conversations among stakeholders, the forum helped build the social capital—the popular understanding and political support—that the program would need to be effective. Under the law, participation by towns was voluntary. If a town or

Smart Growth

According to the Principles of Intelligent Growth produced by the Vermont Forum on Sprawl, for development to be "smart" it must:

1. Maintain the historic settlement pattern of compact village and urban centers separated by rural countryside.

2. Promote the health and vitality of communities through economic and residential growth that is targeted to compact, mixed use centers, including resort centers, at a scale convenient and accessible for pedestrians and appropriate for the community.

3. Offer choices in the mode of transportation available and ensure that transportation options are integrated and consistent with land use objectives.

4. Protect and preserve environmental quality and important natural and historic features of Vermont, including natural areas, water resources, air quality, scenic resources, and historic sites and districts.

5. Provide public access to formal and informal open spaces, including parks, playgrounds, public greens, water bodies, forests, and mountains.

6. Encourage and strengthen agricultural and forest enterprises and minimize conflicts of development with these businesses.

7. Provide housing that meets the needs of a diversity of social and income groups in each Vermont community, but especially in communities that are most rapidly growing.

8. Support a diversity of viable business enterprises in downtowns and villages, including locally owned businesses, and a diversity of agricultural and forestry enterprises in the countryside.

9. Balance growth with the availability of economic and efficient public utilities and services, and ensure the investment of scarce public funds consistent with these principles.

10. Accomplish the goals and strategies for smart growth through coalitions with stakeholders and broad engagement of the public.

More information on each of these principles, including concrete guides to their implementation, can be found on the website for Smart Growth Vermont (www.smartgrowthvermont.org).

Right: The Champion Lands Deal serves as a model by balancing competing land use interests.

city saw the benefits that would come from controlling sprawl and building more livable and walkable commercial centers, it could get state (and sometimes forum) help to accomplish that; if it didn't, well, it wouldn't come looking for training and technical assistance.

It soon became clear that providing towns with information and advice alone was insufficient to the task of halting sprawl. In 1998, the legislature passed the Downtown Development Act, which went beyond advice and technical support to authorize the creation of downtown development areas that would be eligible for tax credits and grants from state agencies and for the financing of transportation projects through the State Infrastructure Bank. The language of the bill was clear, and its intention would have been familiar to any reader of the 1969 planning council report or the 1989 Costle Commission report. It aimed "to preserve and encourage the development of downtown areas of municipalities of the state; … to reflect Vermont's traditional settlement patterns, and to minimize or avoid strip development or other unplanned development throughout the countryside on quality farmland or important natural and cultural landscapes." The incentives it offered made this law stronger than its predecessor, but it still included no penalties, no outright prohibitions; it made the carrot larger and more obvious but did not wield the stick of state enforcement.

The law certainly created a broader awareness of the need to concentrate development in downtowns and existing growth areas, and by offering incentives, it certainly slowed the process by which businesses across the state were migrating out of downtowns and toward arterial and feeder roads, adding to sprawl on the landscape. But advocates of smart growth are split on whether positive incentives alone—no penalties, no prohibitions—are sufficient to halt the kind of development that unnecessarily degrades ecosystems and imposes additional losses, burdens, and costs on Vermonters.

Vermont's Largest-ever Conservation Deal

As the environmental movement struggled to rein in the economic forces that were producing sprawl in Vermont's built-up areas (and saw some notable successes and setbacks in that effort), on another front the 1990s brought a major success. The Champion Lands Deal, as it was called, balanced conservation, preservation, ecology, and development in a way that served as a model for other efforts.

The work began with the announcement, in October 1997, by Champion International, a multibillion dollar

Above and right: Victory Bog, part of the land protected in the Champion Lands deal.

international paper and forest products company, that it would receive bids on lands it owned in New York, Vermont, and New Hampshire. All told, it was looking to sell 325,000 acres in what a company spokesperson said was an effort to increase profitability by focusing on its softwood products like plywood. The office-paper and newsprint markets had been proving volatile of late. (A downturn in 1996 had knocked Champion's annual sales down from $7 billion to $5.9 billion

and its profits from $742 million to $141 million.) The paperless office was on the horizon, and plywood sales were booming; the company was looking to make a strategic shift. Most of the land that Champion put up for sale had been recently harvested and was in regrowth, anyway; profitable reharvesting was years away. The company was ready to focus on its very profitable South American operations. Just the year before, it had bought nearly half a million acres in Brazil, including 128,000 acres of pine plantation, a chipping plant, and port facilities on the Amazon.

The call for bids sent a charge through Vermont's environmental community and the Dean administration. The Vermont Champion lands were the largest privately held forest parcel in the state, consisting of 132,000 contiguous acres in fourteen towns in three counties, more than 2 percent of the entire land area of the state. Larger than Vermont's smallest county (Grand Isle, at 194 square miles), the land had long been recognized as being of immense ecological and economic value. On the ecological side: despite the recent harvesting, the parcel contained some of the richest and most diverse ecosystems in the state (testimony to the value of regulations that had balanced that extraction with ecological constraints). It held twenty-six natural heritage sites; 90 percent of the Nulhegan watershed; thirty miles of the Nulhegan River and its major tributaries; eleven miles of Paul Stream; three miles of Moose River; the complete shorelines of fifteen lakes and ponds; sixteen rare or exemplary natural ecosystems, including black spruce swamps, dwarf shrub bogs, and lowland spruce-fir forest; breeding grounds for migratory songbirds; the only Vermont population of the threatened spruce grouse; habitat for several small and endangered mammals, including the rock vole and the southern bog lemming; 10,000 acres of the state's largest deer-wintering yard; the largest, most concentrated population of moose in the state; and habitat for bear, bobcat, and other northern native species. The Champion parcel abutted other conserved and protected land—the 31,500-acre John Hancock Timberlands, The Conservation Fund's 5,000-acre McConnell tract, and the 2,000-acre Wenlock Deer Management Area.

On the economic side, the lands were crucial to the forestry and outdoor recreation economy of the Northeast Kingdom, the hardscrabble, less developed counties of the state's northeast. While the forest-products industry had thrived with harvest and declined as that extraction tapered off, the land continued to support hunting, fishing, hiking, snowmobiling, snowshoeing, cross-country skiing, canoeing, kayaking, and boating. Its

attractions were mentioned in every major guidebook and brochure that touted the Northeast Kingdom as a recreational destination. In addition to the increased life satisfaction these pursuits offered to Vermonters and visitors, there were other benefits as well: the local economy of the region depended heavily on them. Snowmobiling alone brought a $3-billion-a-year boost to the Vermont economy, and with its ready access to miles and miles of trails on the Champion lands, the Northeast Kingdom town of Island Pond had become the acknowledged capital of the pastime in the state.

Preservation of the land and continued public access to it for these pursuits would secure another, more traditional foundation of the local economy. For many Vermonters, the hunting, trapping, and fishing that the land offered weren't "sport" but a chance to supplement the household food budget. Securing the land through conservation would let those Vermonters continue to participate in an economy that offers the satisfactions of intergenerational historical grounding (one of the social values that is strained by sprawl), while letting them maintain a traditional, direct and immediate relation to the natural sources of human sustenance.

According to a 1993 study done for the Northern Forest Lands Council, each one thousand acres of forestland in Vermont supports 1.1 manufacturing jobs and 4.2 travel and tourism jobs; at that rate, conserving the Champion lands—preventing them from being parceled out for vacation homes, for

instance—would support 700 jobs in an area that sorely needed them. As The Conservation Fund, the Vermont Agency of Natural Resources, and the Vermont Land Trust would put it in the application for funding they submitted to the Vermont Housing and Conservation Board, "Essex County is the most economically impoverished county in the state. Its heritage is a

wealth of landscape that has been sold out from under it, load by load. Absent a conservation strategy, these forests will continue to be exploited, the lands will ultimately be parcelized and developed, the shorelines and special places degraded, and public access denied, all at the expense of the rural communities whose livelihood and heritage is integral with this land. This," the application said in boldface, "is not only the first chance the public has had to protect the rich natural and cultural resources of these lands, it is almost certainly our last."

Securing the land for public use became a top priority for environmental organizations and, under the leadership of Governor Howard Dean, the state. Effective action would have to be timely, and there was no time to lose. Other states were seeing large timber holdings being broken up for development, for parceling out as housing lots and private game preserves, and that prospect brought added urgency.

Champion released a prospectus for the sale in mid-June, and the first bids in a two-round process were due in July. None were accepted, but some bidders were invited to participate in the second round. The announcement came in October: the winning bid for lands in all three states was offered by The Conservation Fund, a national non-profit that specializes in working with land trusts and state and local governments to leverage its funds in pursuit of conservation. The Conservation Fund then faced the daunting task of coming up with the money it needed to purchase the lands—$26.5 million for just the Vermont parcel. Serving as the central clearinghouse, it helped organize a public-private funding partnership that included The Vermont Land Trust, the state Agency of Natural Resources, the Freeman Foundation, the U.S. Fish and Wildlife Service, and The Nature Conservancy. The bulk of the state funding came through an application to the Vermont Housing and Conservation Board (whose state-funded mission was to encourage, assess, and, where appropriate, help fund exactly this kind of effort).

Immediately after Champion's announcement of its intentions, Connie

One of the many streams protected by the Champion Lands Deal.

Motyka, commissioner of the state's Department of Forests, Parks and Recreation, had convened a panel of thirty-one scientists, land managers, and foresters to study the Champion lands and make recommendations. Their report formed the basis for the overall conservation and disposition plan for the lands. The entire parcel would be kept in public access, though in some places particular recreational activities would be limited, based on ecological impact. (For instance, snowmobile trails in and near deer wintering areas would be rerouted.)

Just over half of the $26.5 million cost—$13.5 million—was borne by

The Conservation Fund, which aimed to cover its commitment through fund-raising and borrowing against the eventual resale of some of the land to private holders after conservation and access easements had been added. The Freeman Foundation kicked in $4 million and a non-Vermont foundation pledged to match the state's proposed share of $4.5 million, which came through the VHCB application process and was supported by a single, dedicated appropriation. The deal closed in 1999. The federal government got a twenty-six-thousand-acre addition to the Silvio O. Conte National

Wildlife Refuge. Twenty-two thousand acres went to the state to create the West Mountain Wildlife Management Area, to be managed by the state Fish and Wildlife Department under conservation and public access easements held by the VHCB and The Nature Conservancy. Title to the largest portion of the parcel, eighty-four thousand acres, was sold to the Essex Timber Company under easements to ensure conservation, public access, and sustainable yield management practices.

The public-access easements served to formalize (and in some areas improve upon) the informal policies that Champion had long established for the land. The land could have been posted against trespass but wasn't—a corporate generosity that could have been revoked at any moment and that wasn't guaranteed to be maintained by subsequent owners. All told, for a cost of less than $33 an acre, the citizens of Vermont secured for themselves and their progeny the perpetual use and benefit of a broad swath of the continent's Northern Forest, with its glens and bogs, pristine rivers and undeveloped lakes, wildlife habitat, working forest and recreational opportunities. In doing so, they also secured into the future the financial and ecological foundation of the recreation- and timber-dependent communities of the Northeast Kingdom: the "cut and sell" approach of the private owners would be replaced by sustained yield and multiple-use management of the forests. And Vermonters could be certain that land that was by long custom available for public use wouldn't be fenced and posted or turned into private game preserves accessible only on payment of hunting fees, as was increasingly the case in other New England states.

There were, to be sure, vociferous complaints about resources being "locked away" and about which parcels, exactly, would be available for hunting and fishing and which would be protected as refuges. There was also vociferous complaint that the largest parcel had gone to a timber company and would continue as working forest instead of being set aside as a wildlife preserve. The fact that there was principled criticism from both sides of the issue suggests that the deal as structured was an effective, centrist accommodation. On the whole, since the result protected the most ecologically sensitive land and conserved the rest, the people of Vermont supported the move and were pleased with the investment.

Vermonters were lucky to have the opportunity to make that investment. The same macroeconomic forces acting on Champion International were acting on other large landholding companies in New England; all across the region, timber and paper companies were cashing out land inventory after harvest. In just two months in 1996, two-and-a-half million acres in Maine changed ownership, and in most cases, the public learned of the sale only after a contract had been signed. Unlike Vermont, Maine had little or no opportunity to pursue outright public ownership and the purchase of conservation easements as a way to protect the public's interest in maintaining a flow of natural capital services from these large, undeveloped properties.

And Vermonters were lucky in another sense as well. In the closing of the Champion Lands Deal, they benefited from the educational and organizational efforts of generations of environmental and conservation activists who had come before. To make this purchase and secure a public interest in these lands, a strong, hastily convened public-private partnership had to act boldly and with great dispatch to leverage funding from inside and outside the state. The conversations and compromises between participants were fast, pointed, and effective: the goal was clear and the time line unforgiving. The effort could not have succeeded, and perhaps couldn't even have been undertaken, if the social capital of Vermont hadn't included a strong shared understanding of the value of ecosystem preservation and the need to sustain the flow of benefits that humans derive from nature. That shared public understanding, embodied in law and in such innovative organizations as the Vermont Housing and Conservation Board, was a product of all the work that had come before it. In its way, every brochure and press release written by an environmental group, every public meeting or hearing about an environmental issue, every visit to an elementary school classroom by an Environmental Learning for the Future volunteer helped to secure this unprecedented achievement.

CHAPTER 5

The 2000s

Collaboration

The confrontations of the 1990s give way to a new era of cooperation across party lines. Climate change demands attention and effective collaboration.

The last tick of the clock before midnight on the evening of December 31, 1999, was met with great expectation and quite a bit of anxiety around the globe as that moment swept, east to west, through the twenty-four time zones of the planet.

It wasn't that the change marked the start of a new millennium—as pedants never tired of pointing out, the new millennium began with the start of 2001, not the end of 1999. And it wasn't just that round numbers have a visceral appeal that pedantry can't dislodge. What worried everyone is that we had managed to become totally dependent on computer systems that might fail because they would not recognize that "00" meant "2000" instead of "1900." Some predictions had it that the economic systems of humanity would collapse, as electrical generation, air travel, government services of all sorts, payroll generation, banking, commercial exchanges, credit card use, and the burgeoning Internet would all come to a crashing halt.

The rollover of 1999 to 2000 invited us to recognize how vulnerable our civilization had become. It seems likely that much of the anxiety over Y2K was sheer displacement, the product of a larger but amorphous sense that human society, with its high-tech, resource-hungry economy, had become exceedingly precarious in ways that were less easy to understand (or fix) than a bit of computer programming. The planet's stock of oil is fixed and finite, but we continued to use more and more of it every year. Science was telling us that climate change was no hoax or fluke but a real and established fact that we had better organize to do something about.

VERMONT BY THE NUMBERS:
2000
- Population: 608,827
- Percent born in state: 54.3
- Cows: 156,000
- Farms: 6,521
- Total farm acreage: 1,255,900
- Registered motor vehicles: 514,883
- Seasonal homes: 43,106
- Percent of homes with Internet access: 51.2

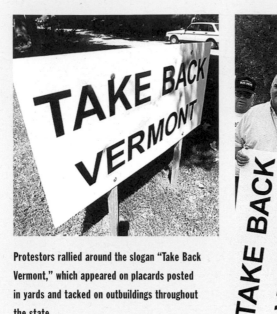

Protestors rallied around the slogan "Take Back Vermont," which appeared on placards posted in yards and tacked on outbuildings throughout the state.

Long thought to be too large to be affected by anything mere mortals could do, the planet was proving to have a delicate balance that humans had disturbed.

The remedy for both climate change and oil addiction was easy to imagine —a world in which humans live and thrive in an economy run on renewable solar energy—but the path to that solution was difficult to see. The un-remedied future was easy to imagine as well, and also deeply disturbing. Oceans would rise, drowning cities. Increasingly, fierce storms would batter our lands and works. Deserts would spread where productive lands had fed us before, propelling hordes of ecological refugees to move in search of food and water. Vermont, famously verdant and relatively unpopulated, might see

a renewed influx of migrants seeking escape—not just from the pressures and "disamenities" of urbanized and sub-urbanized life, as in previous decades, but from food insecurity and social upheaval. Climate change and a precipitous fall down the back slope of peak oil were likely to produce enormous dislocations exactly like those predicted for Y2K. On the whole, it was easier to worry about the damage that a bit of computer code might cause.

In the 1990s, the United States had seen an increasing polarization of political discourse, driven by new, rabidly partisan media outlets along with safe-seat redistricting that let congressmen play to an ideological base rather than encourage them to enter into policy-making in a spirit of cooperation. That change threatened to halt prog-

ress however you cared to define it. National politics became suffused with cynical posturing and the dysfunctional idea that party interest is, in all cases, the national interest—that opponents are essentially traitors. Bill Clinton survived a politically charged impeachment proceeding, a hotly contested presidential election came down to hanging chads in Florida, and a remarkably rapid Supreme Court decision halted a recount and gave the office to George W. Bush.

And then there was 9-11.

While the Bush administration moved into two controversial wars that would last more than a decade, Vermonters managed to hold the partisanship and rancor—and even the issues—of national politics mostly at arm's length. In a 2002 poll conducted by the University of Vermont, only 2.3 percent of Vermonters identified "terrorism and the war in Afghanistan" as the most serious issue facing the state in the coming decade. And on matters closer to home, the state's long tradition of civil discourse continued to serve it well.

There were divisive, us-versus-them moments, to be sure. In the spring of 2000, prompted by a controversial Vermont Supreme Court decision, the legislature took testimony from more than a hundred Vermonters on a proposed same-sex civil union bill. Many legislators reported that their minds were changed by hearing Vermonters—neighbors, friends, constituents—speak movingly and eloquently in support of it. But when

the bill was passed and signed into law by Governor Dean, reaction was loud and long. Protestors rallied around the slogan "Take Back Vermont," which appeared on placards posted in yards and tacked on outbuildings throughout the state. The clear supposition was that Vermont had been taken away—away from native Vermonters, who had seen their influence diminished and their ways of life changed by the influx of "flatlanders" who had altered the demographics of the state in the Interstate era. Many of the same Vermonters who had opposed state land use planning and other environmental legislation saw civil unions as yet another unwanted and intrusive government initiative imposed on them by recent arrivals. Ruth Dwyer, the Republican challenger to Governor Dean in the fall election, played to that sentiment, speaking of "a clash of outlooks" between many Vermonters and "new people who make the rules for others and don't listen."

Dwyer lost, and by the end of the decade civil unions had been displaced by legislation granting full marriage and legal rights to same-sex couples. While some aging "Take Back Vermont" signs were brought out at rallies decrying the law, it was considerably less controversial than the original civil unions law had been. The us-versus-them, native-versus-immigrant division that civil unions had reopened had in some measure been repaired. The social capital on which a sustainable political society depends had been strained by the change but not broken.

GOATS AND BISCUITS

"Real Vermonters Don't Milk Goats," published in 1983 by UVM political science professor Frank Bryan and Bill Mares, offered a humorous but pointed look at the differences between traditional Vermont culture and the outlook—and agricultural practices—of some of the recent arrivals. The back-to-the-land movement of the 1960s and 1970s had driven a good portion of that influx, and nearly every town had its resident commune, its resident organic farm housing young people who were mostly unfamiliar with rural and agricultural life. While many of the new arrivals had been drawn by Vermont's rural beauty, its tradition of face-to-face democracy, and its ethos of live-and-let-live self-reliance, their expectations and values often clashed with the outlook of Vermonters whose roots in the state reached back several generations.

Lisa Alther's 1976 novel *Kinflicks*, set in Vermont, treats the cultural chasm between the two groups as the occasion for both comedy and broader cultural insight. One aspect of flatlander culture that rubbed many "real" Vermonters the wrong way was a disregard for cultural context; as one (flatlander) political observer put it, "Town Meeting didn't cease to exist the first time a newcomer stood up and spoke their mind in front of it. But something was certainly lost when new arrivals felt free to stand up and begin their remarks without first saying 'I know I've only been here for a few years …'" To be a real Vermonter, your roots had to be several generations deep. Could the offspring of flatlanders be Vermonters? Not really. "A cat can have kittens in the oven," said a newly minted Vermont folk saying, "but that doesn't make them biscuits."

Vermont's Flagship Environmental Law under Assault

That doesn't mean that the Bush years (2000 to 2008) were all smooth sailing in environmental matters. In 2002, when Howard Dean's political trajectory took him onto the national stage and he chose not to run for governor again, Republican Jim Douglas won the office with 45 percent of the popular vote (a third party candidate drew 10 percent of the vote). Douglas held the office until he stepped down in 2011, sustaining a longtime pattern: since 1962, no incumbent governor has failed to be returned to office. Having served as Bush's Vermont campaign manager, Douglas emphasized themes familiar on the national scene: taxes

should be cut and government should be smaller. He spoke often and enthusiastically about Vermont's environmental heritage and the qualities of character that make Vermonters and their communities strong, but much of his agenda amounted to a reprise of the Watt-ism seen in the Reagan era, adapted for the constraints of context: a Vermont version of small-government, free-market, infinite-planet ideology.

In his first inaugural address in 2003, Douglas spoke of Vermont's "two great economic advantages—our natural environment and Vermonters themselves." The landscape, he said, "nourishes the soul," and he vowed to uphold the traditions that had made Vermont "a leader among states and nations in protecting the quality of our water and air." But Vermonters need jobs, and

the economy had to recover and grow to provide them. As he saw it, "sincere but misguided" people thought there was conflict between these two goals. He announced a "third way"—"The Vermont Way"—that would recognize "the codependence of our economy and our environment. My administration," he promised, "will work on behalf of each so that we may improve on both."

The words might have been spoken by the leader of any one of dozens of environmental groups in the state, who had long been arguing that environmental protection need not conflict with economic progress. Since the earliest days of the struggle against nuclear power, the environmental movement had been making the case that public investment in renewable energy could put Vermonters to work—faster and better than nuclear construction could, since much of the money spent on nuclear plants leaves the state, and much of the construction money spent in the state goes to transient workers brought in for the building. Investment in renewables would also preserve environmental values and ensure that the economy would be stronger in the future, since solar and renewable energy must eventually displace coal and oil. That basic argument had been expanded to include other aspects of the sustainable economy: investment in sustainable agriculture would grow jobs, revitalizing downtowns would grow jobs, investment in energy efficiency and retrofitting would grow jobs. Reducing energy demand—the harvesting of "negawatts"—was cheaper and

MAJOR MOMENTS IN LAND USE PLANNING **IN VERMONT**

2002

The second Downtown Development Act is passed, creating a new category of designation for Village Centers.

2006

The legislature passes and Governor Jim Douglas signs the Growth Center legislation, building on the two existing Downtown Development Acts from 1998 and 2002, offering permitting advantages and financial incentives to develop in state-approved designated Growth Centers.

Jon Groveman interrogates a witness in the St. Albans Walmart Environmental Court proceeding.

more forward-looking than any other approach to meeting the economy's energy needs and would reduce our ecological footprint while stimulating the economy by keeping more of our energy dollars within the state.

But pursuit of energy efficiency was not part of Douglas's third way. Efficiency Vermont, the state's widely admired, negawatt-generating state-regulated utility, had been in place since 2000, saving Vermonters money by saving them energy. Douglas came to office in 2003 proposing to slash its budget in half. He appointed David O'Brien, who previously had fought the establishment of the utility, as commissioner of the Department of Public Service charged with overseeing it. "As commissioner," says Vermont energy activist and commentator Carl Etnier, "O'Brien continued to support the governor's anti-efficiency and anti-renewables stances."

In practice, Douglas's third way fell much more in line with one of the "sincere but misguided" beliefs he criticized, the belief that effective environmental regulation is incompatible with economic progress—and his administration was clearly in favor of economic progress. While paying lip service to the benefits Vermonters enjoy by virtue of their shared landscape, as well as to the tradition of environmental activism that had done so much to preserve it, he also struck another consistent theme in his campaign and first inaugural address: Act 250 was cumbersome and its administration needed to be "streamlined" to make it more efficient.

Here, Act 250 served as whipping boy for redundancies and confusing overlaps in the permitting system as a whole, which had become a concern to thoughtful observers from both ends of the political spectrum. Many development proposals faced a confusing welter of a process   there were permits needed under local zoning bylaws, permits needed under various state regulations on water quality and other matters, and sometimes permits under federal regulations on wetlands and navigable waters. Projects that affected more than one town would need permits from each, for there was no mechanism of coordination between towns, nor was there any guarantee that the decisions would be similar. If the project triggered Act 250 review, there was yet another process to navigate. In the public mind, Act 250—the most visible and, thanks to some high-profile cases, the most controversial element in the system—came to represent the system as a whole. One former Environmental Board member from that era reports hearing complaints about difficulties with Act 250 from applicants whose proposals hadn't ever been under Act 250 review.

The changes Douglas proposed aimed to "simplify a complex process" and make the system more "efficient," a purpose worthy enough (and vague enough) to gain bipartisan support. But his efforts to change the administration of Act 250 seemed very much a solution in search of a problem, since the problem actually lay elsewhere.

Soon after taking office, the Douglas administration proposed, and the legislature eventually approved, a restructuring of the Act 250 process that turned its quasi-judicial appeals proceedings into formal court proceedings. The authority to review permit appeals was taken away from the citizens empanelled on the Environmental Board and handed to a judge on the newly repurposed Environmental Court. Instead of a board of nine citizens hearing other citizens speak about their concerns, one lone judge would hear arguments from lawyers and almost only lawyers; few

citizens were prepared to risk speaking on their own behalf in a lawyered-up, formal proceeding. In the system as redesigned, the deepest pocket would often win. The state would have standing to participate in the proceedings but public participation, constrained by the practical necessity of expensive legal counsel, would be sharply curtailed in another way as well. Only individuals who could demonstrate a "particularized interest" in the case would be granted party status. In a Windsor County case, the court had set

A court decision set a high bar for defining "particularized interest" in the agricultural soils of Vermont.

as precedent a very high bar for defining "particularized interest" in regard to agricultural soils. Caring about the future of agriculture in Vermont wasn't enough. Such general environmental values (the court had indicated) are adequately represented by the state and local governments as instruments of the popular will. (Citizens and environmental groups could have input into Environmental Court proceedings by filing *amicus curiae*—friend of the court—briefs, but friends of the court don't have the right of appeal as do parties with legal standing.)

The result: under the "permit reform," Act 250 increasingly became a means for defining the public interest as the interest of the applicants. It was no longer as effective as it had been as a means for ensuring that private, for-profit development doesn't impose harm and loss on the general public. In choosing "efficiency" over open and participatory governance, the Douglas administration also chose poorly examined development over protection of environmental values.

The reforms to Act 250 point to a tension that Vermont, and the nation, will eventually have to resolve. As human culture builds out to (and beyond) the limits of planetary ecosystems, it becomes increasingly obvious that land use decisions have consequences not just for landowners and those who live near them, but for all of us, and that those public and social consequences make them fit subjects for public influence through legislation and regulation. Two fundamental principles of democratic freedom are that citizens have the right to be left alone in all matters that don't harm or damage others, and they have the right to participate in decisions that may affect their lives and well-being. As the economy builds out its ecological footprint, more and more of our private decisions have consequences for others. Thus, with "non-smart" economic growth the very ground on which democratic free-

WHAT DOES 'EFFICIENT' MEAN?

Whether a system can be judged efficient or not depends a great deal on what we mean by the term. Common sense is a useful guide: a system is more efficient if it gives us more of what we want (outputs, benefits, or what have you) for a lesser amount of what we don't want to give up (money, time, or materials, for instance). It isn't "efficient" for most people to grow their own food; food can be bought more cheaply from bulk producers (farmers) than most households could produce it if they paid themselves the going wage rate for serving as their own gardener. But that kind of calculation ignores the satisfactions that some people derive from participating in the production of their own sustenance, the pleasure they get from nurturing growing things, the additional increments of well-being they derive from physical engagement with soil and from seeing their work embodied in something that has obvious value and worth.

> It's good to keep in mind what Winston Churchill once said: "Democracy is the worst form of government, except for all the others."

The same sort of problem arises when we apply the standard of efficiency to governance, and it's why we put the word in quotation marks here. One of the potential benefits that governance offers is the increase in citizen satisfaction and well-being that comes when people are effective participants in decisions that affect them. This is one of the basic justifications for democracy. Participation also increases the perceived legitimacy of governmental processes, which has other beneficial effects; among others, it increases voluntary compliance with laws as varied as traffic regulations and tax codes, reducing enforcement costs. "Efficiency" means quite a different thing if these benefits are taken into consideration. Democracy is inherently inefficient when judged by narrow cost-and-result standards. By those standards, the most efficient form of government is a dictatorship. It's good to keep in mind what Winston Churchill once said: "Democracy is the worst form of government, except for all the others."

Finite-Planet Water

The Clean Water Act of 1972 instituted a national cleanup of the nation's waterways, which had too long been treated as an open-access "sink"—a dump into which anyone could freely discharge wastes and pollutants. Under the CWA, wastewater treatment facilities were built or upgraded and "point source" discharges—those coming from a single facility—were regulated and controlled. Water bodies that were considered dead in 1972 have made remarkable recoveries. Regulatory "tailpipe plugging" (see text) accomplished a great deal.

Even so, by 2002 over 20,000 bodies of water in the United States were ranked as "impaired" by the EPA—more than 40 percent of all that had been assessed, and adding up to more than 300,000 miles of river and lake shoreline and 5 million acres of lakes. Clearly, if water quality was to be fully restored, more needed to be done.

The problem was and continues to be "non-point" discharges—the diffuse pollution that is carried into waterways by runoff from land. Anything that is put on land can and will find its way into our waterways. The most problematic pollutants vary from basin to basin, watershed to watershed.

Some of the most troublesome: the oil and gasoline and road salt that find their way into our soils and streets and parking lots as we use automobiles; untreated animal waste, including the burdens produced in some areas by farm animals and in others by pets; and fertilizers and pesticides, used by suburbanites to feed their lawns—and by farmers to increase their yields in order to feed us.

The CWA outlined the manner in which non-point pollution was to be judged and limited: states were to identify bodies of water that are "impaired"—too polluted to be used for their "designated beneficial uses"—and then set water quality standards for them. EPA rules written in 1985 and 1992 offered further guidance: states were to identify the pollutants that cause the impairment, and for each of those pollutants they were to identify the Total Maximum Daily Load (TMDL) that the body of water could absorb without being impaired. Their work would be reported to and reviewed by the EPA.

Behind the notion of TMDL is solid, sustainable, finite-planet thinking: the capacity of bodies of water to absorb pollutants isn't infinite, and the limits need to be discovered and respected.

Implementation and enforcement of the new rules wasn't immediate. States, faced with significant research and regulatory expense, declined to comply with the law. Some sued to have the EPA do the job. The scientific work was and has been slow going. Between 1996 and 2003, a total of 7,327 TMDLs were approved nationwide, representing just 17 percent of the 42,193 bodies of water listed as impaired.

In Vermont, the issue of TMDLs came to a head in 1999, with an application from Lowe's to build a store in South Burlington. The company received the necessary storm-water permits from the state in July of 2001, despite the fact that the store and its parking lot would force acres of runoff into Potash Brook, an impaired waterway. The Conservation Law

Foundation immediately appealed that decision. Under the CWA, the appeal said, additional pollutants could not be discharged into the brook unless a mitigation and cleanup strategy were in place—a strategy that would require determination of the appropriate TMDLs, which hadn't been prepared.

There were no TMDLs for Potash Brook because the state had not calculated any TMDLs for that type of impairment at all. Meanwhile, well over one thousand state-issued storm-water discharge permits had expired and were up for review. The Conservation Law Foundation (CLF) had brought to light a major problem in the way that Vermont was managing its water resources—and had revealed that the state was violating laws established under the Clean Water Act. "Vermont's Agency of Natural Resources," said Chris Kilian, then the CLF's Natural Resources Project Director, "can no longer turn a blind eye to our serious water pollution problems. Rubber-stamping permits that will add more pollution is not acceptable."

CLF appeals were pending when the two sides announced a settlement in May 2006. Lowe's agreed to implement higher cleanup standards than the state had required. Measures included storm-water retention ponds and filtration systems for runoff for not only Lowe's twelve-acre site but the entire Southland Commercial Plaza. Taken together these remedies were designed to eliminate all new impact on Potash Brook. As part of the agreement, Lowe's will monitor upstream and downstream conditions of the brook to gauge whether the "zero harm" standard is met.

The suit prompted the state to begin the process of identifying TMDLs for impaired bodies of water. TMDLs remain a controversial and difficult topic, as might be expected of a regulatory device that operates at the intersection of human activity and biophysical limit. For the fifty water bodies in Vermont that are officially classified as impaired because of acidification, the source of the pollutant—acid rain—is well beyond the power of the state to control. And much non-point-source water pollution in Vermont has its origin in agricultural practice, which legislators and regulators are loathe to tackle. As the strong base of the state's economy and as a prime preserver of open (undeveloped) land, farming provides all Vermonters with many benefits, and the environmental movement is unanimous in wanting to see a healthy agricultural economy. But farming practices are responsible for 38 percent of the phosphate pollution that leads to regular algae blooms in Lake Champlain (making it the second largest category, after urbanization at 46 percent). The blooms can be toxic to wildlife, humans, and domesticated pets, and they prevent recreational use of the parts of the lake that are affected. If Vermont is to achieve a sustainable balance between humans and the bodies of water in the state, it will have to enforce TMDLs for all waters that drain into its lakes, even if those limits require changes in agricultural practice. By 2012, Vermont had established TMDLs for roughly 60 percent of the waters that had been identified as needing them.

The concept of a TMDL for diesel exhaust would have clarified (and made more precise) the concerns about air quality that were raised in the C&S Wholesale Grocers case in 1993. The concept can be extended further: sustainable use of any of nature's sink services means limiting each and every one of our effluents to the total maximum daily load that ecosystems can absorb and reprocess without ill effect. Paired with a similar understanding of the limits of source services—like the maximum sustainable yield figures that can be calculated for forests and fisheries—TMDLs point the way to achieving a sustainable balance between human activity and planetary systems. The burden of research, regulation and restraint is regrettable, but it's made necessary by the growth of our economy out to, and beyond, the limits inherent in natural systems.

doms are exercised tends to disappear. If we are to continue to have a large ecological footprint on the planet, either the realm in which we have the right to pursue our own purposes without public regulation or influence must grow smaller, or our ability to influence the decisions that affect us must be curtailed. The Douglas reforms pursued the latter path.

The Environmental Movement Responds

The Act 250 reforms had three effects on the environmental movement. First and most obviously, they made litigation more formal and expensive and in many cases precluded concerned citizens or environmental groups from having standing. Even with standing, the increased costs reduced the sheer number of cases that such groups could address. This produced the second effect: the reforms reduced the bargaining power that the prospect of litigation gave to environmental groups.

The third effect was the adaptation the environmental movement made to this change. Shut out from many avenues of direct influence in the Douglas administration, and with Act 250 a much more costly arena in which to participate, the momentum of the environmental movement found new outlets. One was a reopening of the conversation about regional land use planning, in terms that Vermonters could readily hear: halting sprawl and supporting smart growth in compact village centers and downtowns. And

while the environmental movement continued to use litigation in an effort to get existing laws enforced, it also moved beyond struggles over policy to encourage direct action—not just marching in the streets or rallies on the statehouse lawn (although there was plenty of that), but the constructive work of using existing programs and new initiatives—often grassroots and volunteer-staffed—to push for necessary change.

Much of the work was motivated by an awareness that climate change and the transition to a post-petroleum society are the largest challenges facing our society. It came in the form of weatherization programs, solar and wind energy projects, "transition town" groups dedicated to preparing for peak oil, community gardening groups, agricultural revitalization programs, and a variety of informational programs and initiatives that furthered the goals of reducing energy use, making the switch to renewables, controlling sprawl and growth, and reducing culture's impact on the planet: everything from installation of solar panels to car-pool coordination to farmers' markets to "support local agriculture" sloganeering to handing out compact fluorescent lightbulbs.

Thus, the environmental movement found other ways to continue building the physical and social-capital infrastructure that a sustainable state needs and that public policy wasn't giving them. A case can be made that in the Douglas years, the environmental movement did a better job of implementing his "third way" than his administration did.

Tackling Energy, Town by Town

In a truly sustainable society, all the energy used by humans will come from sustainable sources. The recognition of this need for a post-petroleum economy gave greater clarity to the goals of the environmental movement and helped its participants find a language in which to express those goals. They could see, better and more fully than ever before, that cheap oil is the driver of both climate change and exurban, landscape-gobbling sprawl. They also began to see more fully that a post-petroleum, sustainable society could be imagined, communicated, and sold to the public,

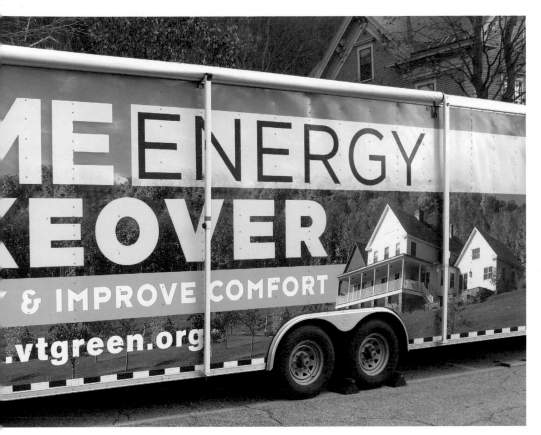

not as a mingy, stingy alternative to the anything-is-possible, infinite-planet vision of the post-war American dream, but as a world in which human life satisfactions and the values that Vermonters hold dear would be easier to have, preserve, protect, and extend: nothing less than a new American dream.

The desire to bring that vision into reality drove the efforts of the environmental movement in a variety of ways, and regularly brought energetic, visionary groups together in common cause.

One such partnership: in 2005, five Vermont organizations—the Ten Percent Challenge; the Sustainable Energy Resource Group (SERG); the New England Grassroots Environment

A variety of programs encourage Vermonters to make their homes more efficient.

Fund; the Vermont Energy Investment Corporation (VEIC), and the Vermont Natural Resources Council—began to meet regularly to instigate and support community-based efforts to reduce Vermont energy consumption. They formed a non-profit, the Vermont Energy and Climate Action Network (VECAN), to "inspire, support, connect and align community-based energy and climate action initiatives." The chosen vehicle would be town energy committees: small groups of citizens that would work to inform their neighbors about energy issues, assist them in find-

ing ways to reduce their energy use, and help them connect with the resources they'd need to do that. By the close of the decade there were more than one hundred of them in the state.

Development of wind-generated electricity moved by fits and starts in the decade and was a divisive issue in the environmental movement. Some existing laws and regulations promoting renewables encouraged it, but economic uncertainties and siting and permitting issues—as well as resistance to the ecological and aesthetic consequences of large-scale applications—held it back. Wind power development got little help from the Douglas administration, which went on record as opposing it. (This pleased some environmentalists and displeased others.)

Nor did the Douglas administration avail itself of a once-in-a-lifetime (and much less controversial) opportunity to purchase hydroelectric dams on the Connecticut and Deerfield rivers, which in total production would have supplied the state with as much as 40 percent of its electricity needs from an existing, reliable, renewable source. The dams were lost in competitive bidding. Vermont, with two corporate partners providing technical expertise, simply bid too low. The state's offer was based on assumptions—perhaps infinite-planet assumptions—about future energy prices that have been criticized for being unrealistic. Those familiar with peak oil, and with the need to put a price on carbon emissions in order to deal with global climate change, had long been making predictions about

Paul Costello, Beth Sachs,
Gus Seelig, Lisa Steele, and
Jennifer Wallace-Brodeur

FIVE PEOPLE, FIVE PARTNERSHIPS

Paul Costello's father, a district court judge for Chittenden County, was "an Augustinian—a deeply moral man, who knew right from wrong in a fallen world." Paul says he came of age in "the consumer society of the '70s, with a deep sense of alienation." As a student and young man, he questioned the naive idea of progress. After his undergraduate work he earned a PhD in history from McGill University. Reflecting on the challenges that environmentalism faces, Paul offers an analysis that draws on his knowledge of history: "A harmonized society was the Enlightenment's idea of progress, and slowly through history notions of progress originally based on faith became attached to materialism, which has led us in an unsustainable direction." In his job as the executive director of the non-profit Vermont Council on Rural Development, Paul encourages himself to be an extrovert and an optimist, but personally, he admits that he is actually more introverted and that he battles a deep pessimism about our environmental future.

The Working Landscape Partnership. "We are thinking very differently from the way we were even ten years ago," Paul says of the environmental movement. "We're in a different period of environmentalism, and everyone knows it. We are investing in the economy to create the solutions" that we need to build a sustainable society. This "economic seed work," he says, "is critical." And it needs both popular and institutional support. "We need to look at the interaction of values, investments, and regulation, and this requires cultural learning, otherwise the votes aren't there. We need those votes to promote real changes in budgets and fiscal priorities and policies."

To help facilitate this change in thinking, Paul helped instigate the Working Landscape Partnership, which he leads as head of the Vermont Council on Rural Development. The partnership has developed a campaign to support local agriculture and forestry and to attract and incubate farm and forest entrepreneurs. These, Paul says, are crucial to conserving Vermont's working landscape for the next generation. The plan aims to encourage strategic investment in farm and forest enterprises through a development fund premised on the reality that the working landscape benefits all Vermonters. According to Paul, this is the kind of investment that is needed if we're to maintain the economic viability of farm and forest enterprises and, through them, the landscape of Vermont. One crucial part of the work is educational outreach for broad-ranging collaboration and buy-in. "Successful collaborations require bold planning and sacrifice. But no one wants a prepackaged vision. We all want to create it and own it. And that process takes time." That attitude paid off with the passage of a "working lands" bill in the 2012 legislative session.

Beth Sachs early in life had a growing sense of outrage at the cultural discrimination she encountered for being Jewish. She was in her first year of college when the United States invaded Cambodia in 1970, a unilateral presidential action to expand a war that many wanted to see brought to an end. The event prompted her to join a Black Panther support group; she wanted to broaden her understanding of and help stop the social injustices of a system that generated ethnic discrimination, racism, and war. Later, inspired by the life and work of 1920s labor and community organizer Mother Jones, Beth developed a passion for worker empowerment. She started thinking about environmental issues in 1973 after meeting Blair Hamilton, who had an infectious enthusiasm for innovative architecture: lightweight structures designed to minimize the human footprint on the land. She began to think about the human impact—positive and negative—on the natural environment. After working in energy-related organizations and businesses in Montreal, California, and Montana, she and Blair moved to Vermont in 1979. In the 1980s, they conceived of the idea of an organization dedicated to helping people and communities reduce the economic and environmental costs of energy use—a combination of both their passions.

The Vermont Energy Investment Corporation. In the early-to mid-1980s, Beth recollects, "energy was not a huge issue." The gas rationing and gas lines of the 1970s were long gone, and most people "felt like the crisis was over" (that is, except for low-income people, for whom the energy crisis has never gone away). Blair and Beth had been researching energy efficiency for "quite a while," and they thought enough was known to inform good

Above: (l. to r.) Jennifer Wallace-Brodeur, Beth Sachs, Lisa Steele, Paul Costello, and Gus Seelig

action; the time was ripe for practice. But there were barriers—the lack of access to trustworthy information and capital, and the "hassle factor" of getting the work done well. Soon after Blair and Beth moved to Burlington, they recognized a path forward: several municipal agencies were coming to the rather obvious conclusion that wasting energy was costly. The Vermont Housing Finance Agency, the Burlington Electric Department, the Champlain Valley Office of Economic Opportunity, the City of Burlington's Community and Economic Development Office, and the Burlington Housing Authority were interested in efficiency improvements, but no single one of them was large enough to justify the hiring of a dedicated staff energy efficiency expert. The non-profit organization that Blair and Beth

envisioned, the Vermont Energy Investment Corporation (VEIC), could fill that need. By the mid-1980s, VEIC had helped reduce energy costs for buildings in Burlington and had paved the way for the city's 1990 energy efficiency bond. That bond was approved by voters, many of whom were opposed to meeting the city's growing need for electricity through purchase from Hydro Québec. VEIC had helped them see that efficiency was a better, more economical choice.

Beth believes that the fundamental environmental issue isn't about growth anymore: "It's about climate change—and maintaining the health of the planet to support life." Ecologically unsustainable development not only gobbles up landscape and the values that tra-

continued following page

Paul Costello, Beth Sachs, Gus Seelig, Lisa Steele, and Jennifer Wallace-Brodeur

continued from previous page

ditional environmentalism seeks to protect, it has real, demonstrable, and negative effects on human health. She's not optimistic about the future. "The only way to be successful will be to combine good public policy with mandatory regulation, appropriate incentives, and public education." Mandatory regulations are unpopular, she knows, but "I don't see how incentives and education alone will get us to where we want to be."

Gus Seelig, a native of New York City, came to Vermont to attend Goddard College in the 1970s. He was much influenced by his father, a union organizer active in the civil rights movement; Gus has memories of walking picket lines on the weekends with him. Gus doesn't think of himself as an environmental professional or activist—though it seems both are integral to his role as executive director of the Vermont Housing and Conservation Board. He struggles with how to pursue both social and environmental justice. Gus has a love of nature, rural communities, and living in places where people know and care for one another. He is the town moderator in Calais and was a long-time volunteer firefighter, two positions that have allowed him to know the community in an intimate way. That kind of knowledge has been important to his work. Gus was much influenced by his mentor at the Central Vermont Community Action Council, Ben Collins, who had been Governor Hoff's secretary of civil and military affairs; Collins' innovative thinking and commitment to social justice were inspirational. The challenge for Gus has been and continues to be how to advance both the idea of conservation and housing as related problems and the work of finding collaborative solutions to them, which means helping Vermonters find ways to make a decent living in sustainable relationship to their environment.

The Vermont Housing and Conservation Board. The Vermont Housing and Conservation Board (VHCB) was created in 1987 to pursue the goals of supporting both affordable housing and the working landscape of Vermont. "We have good tools," says Gus, but the work of the semi-public VHCB has been challenged by the same mood of public austerity that challenges other governmental agencies. "The myth is that we will figure out how to do things better, more efficiently and do more with less. But we need resources in order to make an investment in housing and conservation. How do we have that conversation with Vermonters? Without further financial investment, we won't make substantially more progress." As the work of the VHCB amply attests, "Public dollars will pull in private dollars." Gus's organizer DNA has helped make the VHCB a success.

Lisa Steele felt privileged to come of age in the 1960s, with its world-historic social issues energizing student movements across the country. She grew up in Florida when it was "pristine and undeveloped." After college, Lisa came back to find Florida a different place. With no planning or zoning to guide growth, chaotic and thoughtless development had taken over; native ecosystems had been transected almost to death by roads and housing developments, and the structures of a burgeoning population obscured the land she loved. This experience gave direction to her professional aspirations. As an adult living in Vermont, she saw opportunities. One was the chance to help fund efforts to protect the environment through her philanthropic giving. She particularly wanted to encourage collaboration among non-profits that were competing for funding and recognition, losing sight of the end result. She helped them to collaborate and cooperate to be more effective in achieving results such as reducing greenhouse gas emissions through energy efficiency and conservation.

Lisa's other significant opportunity came in the form of derelict property on the Burlington waterfront. With her business partner, Melinda Moulton, she took what were polluted, abandoned properties and redeveloped them into an attractive complex of buildings that serves community needs and reconnect Vermonters to a lakefront that had been lost to, and then abandoned by, industrial development. The area, like the lake, is a glittering jewel and is one reason Burlington is consistently on various lists of the nation's "most livable cities."

The Main Street Landing Company. In 1982 the Burlington Waterfront was a place that most people avoided. It had oil tanks, barbed wire fencing, a scrap metal yard, a working granary with a "handsome rat population," and empty brick buildings and was filled with accidental urban landscaping—overgrown with weeds and shrubs. The Union Station was owned by Green Mountain Power, and the Haigh Mill and McKenzie buildings were up for sale. The old coal-fired McNeil power plant was still in operation, but soon to be closed down.

Lisa bought some of the property, undertaking what she soon thought might be "an albatross of a restoration project." She turned to Moulton. Through their Main Street Landing Company, they transformed the waterfront; today it hosts a community sailing center, the ECHO Aquarium and Science Center and its Leahy Center for Lake Champlain, a skate park, day-care facilities, a performing arts center, a variety of restaurants, a lake-view tree-shaded park, and a boardwalk. The Burlington Bike Path connects the place to other parts of the city. The renovated buildings are alive with commerce and retail and arts venues, the tourist boating industry has its footprint there, and, in the summer, outdoor festivals bring tens of thousands of people to the shores of Lake Champlain.

Through effective collaboration and a willingness to serve the community, their work gave Burlington a healthy green environment for people to work, live, play, and enjoy the arts. The social justice component to their development is evident throughout their work. Their lakeside development has been acclaimed as the way for the future for smart development: locally based, socially responsible, financially viable, community oriented, publicly assessable, and environmentally healthy. "The key to this success," Lisa remarks, "is that Melinda and I are always trying to ensure we improve our environment, the experience of our tenants, clients, and visitors—and our financial sustainability."

Jennifer Wallace-Brodeur grew up in the eminently walkable downtown of Montpelier, where "the environmental ethic was implicit as a way of life." The city, she says, "hasn't changed much since then." Jennifer was in college during the Reagan administration and when Madeleine Kunin became governor. Kunin's environmental commitment turned land use planning back into "kitchen table" conversation in Jennifer's house and others, but too late for that cornfield in Taft Corners that was lost to development. That was a turning point for Jennifer; she "still grinds her teeth" when she passes that quintessential example of suburban mall-and-sprawl. She never considered herself a professional environmentalist until she began working with AARP on rural transportation issues. There she began to see how transportation systems affect community and individual health, social equity and equality of access to work and jobs, and also patterns of land use—and through these, the environmental values that leaders like Kunin championed.

AARP Vermont: Transporting the Public. Jennifer saw clearly that the state's transportation systems had been "developed for cars and not for people"—a major cart-and-horse inversion. She resolved to do something about it. As associate state director of State and

Community Development of the AARP Vermont, she knew that her constituency was particularly affected: when Vermonters lose the ability to carry a driver's license, they become trapped. She launched an ambitious collaborative that brought together other groups who represent those adversely affected by America's love affair with the automobile: public health organizations concerned about obesity and depression, as well as social justice groups concerned with low-income mobility, and others whose missions involved land use planning and economic development. She helped them see their common interest. "I want Vermonters to become more aware of what shapes new development today and how to dial [it] back and claim our communities for people." During its first year, the initiative succeeded in getting "complete streets" legislation passed. The bill requires that the state and municipalities plan for all users, of all ages, in all project phases when developing or reconstructing roads.

Jennifer continues to think about the design of communities that balance all modes of travel. The ambitious goal is to give every Vermonter expanded transportation options, to make car-less living practical. "There is a palpable aversion to talking about moving away from the single occupancy vehicle," she says. The auto-centric paradigm still prevails, and as budgets are squeezed by the end of the era of oil affluence, "the expectation is to do more with the same resources or even less. But, communities need a much more robust set of tools. Funding and an evidence-based strategy are what will make a difference."

EROI AND THE COST OF ENERGY

All the different forms of energy that humans use can be expressed in common units; the work-potential of a lump of coal, a kilowatt hour of electricity, a cord of wood, or a gallon of gas can all be expressed by measures of horsepower, British Thermal Units, or calories. When the cost per unit of energy sources vary widely, it can sometimes make economic sense to switch from one type of fuel (from heating oil to wood, for instance)—though there are costs of change-over that have to be taken into account. Prices send us signals about what energy source it makes sense to use; the energy source with the lowest dollar-per-BTU cost is the economical choice.

The prices we pay for energy are a result of the interaction of supply and demand, and both supply and demand are affected by policies and individual human decisions. The faster we pump oil, the more of it enters the economy and the lower its price will tend to be (and the faster we will run out of it). Dollars per BTU isn't always an accurate reflection of the physical realities of energy systems. A useful addition to the traditional dollars-in-energy-out analysis is to calculate the energy cost of an energy system. How much energy does it take, for instance, to get a barrel of petroleum out of the ground and into the economy? The answer, in 2012, is "about one twentieth of a barrel." The Energy Return on Energy Invested, or EROI, of oil averages 20:1 worldwide. In 1960, at the start of our story, energy was much cheaper in physical terms: the EROI of oil was about 40:1.

The declining EROI of oil is a physical fact that can't be altered (much) by human effort. (New, more efficient extraction techniques can have some small effect.) That decline has driven and will drive price increases in energy. While the average EROI for oil worldwide is 20:1, for new oil it is lower—just 5:1, by some estimates. (It takes a lot of energy to drill five miles under the seabed and pump the result ashore.) Wind energy has an EROI that falls in a range between 14:1 and 17:1, making it a much better energy investment than new oil.

energy prices that have since come true: the cost of energy is on an upward march. In its winning bid, TransCanada used more realistic assumptions about future energy prices, hence offered a higher bid for the chance to receive income from the dams. "Of course, hindsight is 20/20," said Representative Michael Obuchowski later. "But if people had had a little bit more courage and a little bit more foresight, we would be sitting on top of the world." Instead, Vermont can now watch as "the utilities that were successful are making money hand over fist."

Climate Change Dithering

Unlike the country at large, by 2005 Vermont's shared public knowledge included a strong consensus that climate change was real, challenging, and would not be effectively or efficiently met by individual acts of conscience and foresight. In December of that year, halfway through his second term as governor, Jim Douglas signed an executive order establishing the Governor's Commission on Climate Change (GCCC) and charged it with developing a comprehensive set of policy recommendations for reducing Vermont's greenhouse gas emissions to targets he proposed: 25 percent from 1990 levels by 2012; 50 percent by 2028; and, if practicable, 75 percent by 2050.

The Commission drew on expertise from the Center for Climate Strategies and on insight from a thirty-one-member plenary group, which represented a cross-section of Vermonters with relevant experience. The GCCC delivered thirty-eight policy options to the governor in October 2007. These it summarized under six broad strategies that would, the report said, "build ... on Vermont's energy efficiency leadership and renewable energy potential." The six strategies:

1. Expand energy efficiency policies by extending Vermont's very effective demand-side management programs (which had kept growth in electricity demand nearly level, even as the economy grew) to other energy uses besides electricity and natural gas, especially heating oil; and establish viable mechanisms to stimulate the development of renewable energy facilities, including wind turbines, in ways that meet the needs of local communities.

2. Keep farmland in farming and forested areas forested with two main strategies: promote innovative marketing (including a "virtual marketplace") for Vermont farm and forest products and develop additional policies and incentives to protect farmlands and forests from development pressure.

3. Reduce emissions from transportation (the second largest category, after heating) through several approaches. One called for consideration and careful evaluation of new policies, like offering a state-funded rebate for fuel-efficient vehicles (paid for by a tax on inefficient vehicles, perhaps) or taxing gasoline on a sliding scale—an increasing percentage at the pump as you pumped more,

A rally demanding action on climate change brought a crowd onto the streets of Montpelier in April 2007.

instead of the customary flat, per-gallon tax. Highway funds could be reassigned away from fuel-inefficient road construction that encourages sprawl. Intercity bus and rail service, both passenger and freight, could be expanded and improved, with provision made for "intermodal connectivity": the pairing of this kind of energy efficient transportation with bicycle use, shuttle services, and pedestrian-friendly compact town centers, which should be promoted by planning efforts.

4. Educate and engage Vermonters about climate change, through state programs within the Agency of Natural Resources and through the Vermont Department of Education, which should establish that all teachers licensed in Vermont "possess a fundamental level of environmental literacy and stewardship and have the capacity to teach with and about nature."

5. Have the state government lead by example by creating a climate change cabinet to coordinate climate change efforts across all agencies; by switching out the fleet of state vehicles to fuel efficient models; by developing a program for obtaining carbon offsets for government functions that can't be made carbon-free (like air travel); and by challenging other major institutions and enterprises in Vermont to follow the government lead.

6. Create a Vermont Climate Collaborative to bring together government, academic, and private sector partners to research climate change effects on Vermont, articulate possible green energy futures, analyze the benefits of a green economy, and seek federal and other funding for efforts at implementation.

The commission closed their report with this optimistic message: "Vermont can harness the challenge of climate change, turning [it] into an engine of economic innovation, to the ultimate benefit of our economy, our landscape, and the well being of our citizens." The sustainable, post-carbon economy is coming, the report can be read as saying, whether Vermont wants it or not; and were Vermont to lead the way, it would be well positioned to emerge as the strongest regional economy in the post-petroleum era, attracting sustainable jobs and securing the health and well-being of Vermonters in other ways.

The report met with a mixed response from the governor. He embraced several of its recommendations—the Vermont Climate Collaborative, the ecological literacy standard for schools, creation of a Center for Climate Change and Waste Reduction in the Agency of Natural Resources, and some elements of implementation of a green economy (increased timber harvesting for wood fuel and expanded sugarmaking in state forests). The rest of the report was relegated to the limbo of "further study" by the Vermont Climate Collaborative. The administration was disinclined to pursue any measure that either raised taxes (call them fees, revenue enhancements, or what you will), increased spending, or expanded the scope and authority of government, however difficult it would be to solve climate change under those constraints.

In the meantime, Peter Shumlin, then president pro tempore of the Senate, joined with House Speaker Gaye Symington to begin the 2007

Downtown Rutland, with train service to New York City, is a transportation hub for its region.

legislative session with three weeks of joint hearings on the legislature's own climate change bill, lining up testimony—"graduate seminar presentations" would also be accurate—by experts that included longtime energy analyst Amory Lovins, Middlebury College Scholar-in-Residence, writer, and climate change activist Bill McKibben, and Pittsford climate scientist Alan Betts. Never before had so many legislators—eight full committees' worth—spent so much time in a tutorial on a single topic. "Climate change is the single greatest challenge—the single greatest catastrophe—our children and grandchildren will face," Shumlin said in opening the sessions.

In his testimony, McKibben cited our dependency on automobiles for most of our transportation as the biggest "nut to crack." "Sprawl, the Circ highway—they are global warming machines," he told the legislators. They heard the message, as several developments showed.

Circumventing the Circumferential Highway

Back in 1982, Congress had put $50 million into that year's Surface Transportation Act for completion of Interstate 289, the circumferential highway around Burlington that had been planned as far back as 1965. Designed as a 15.8-mile highway that would relieve congestion in the town of Essex and let traffic loop around the city through open countryside, by the 1980s, the Circ (as it was called) began to look to many people like the best solution to traffic snarls brought by growth and congestion on Route 2A from Williston to the village of Essex Junction. Particularly troublesome was a five-cornered intersection in Essex Junction that twice a day became a notorious bottleneck for commuters—approximately eight thousand of whom were headed for the IBM plant nearby. The company was a strong supporter of the Circ, which had gotten its environmental impact statement and some other necessary paperwork in 1986. Land acquisition for the highway began soon after. But even so, an increasing number of Vermonters had become aware that highways do not always bring wealth, ease, and prosperity; they also and quite regularly bring sprawl, congestion, and inconvenience. The highway began to meet with organized opposition.

The road had undergone its Act 250 review in 1986. The permit issued by the District Commission required that the regional planning commission and the towns that hosted the right-of-way review the proposal to assess its direct and indirect effects on the farmland and water resources in its path; these would have to be minimal if the road was not to pose an "undue burden" on Vermonters and the environment. "This is a case where Act 250, through the conditions of a permit, ensured that resource planning happened at the local level," says Sandy Levine, a Conservation Law Foundation attorney. "This [planning] resulted in permanent easements on properties along the highway and zoning changes to reduce the likelihood of sprawl development in those resources." And, she says, "quite frankly, it worked."

The roadway had been designed in sections, lettered from A to J, and each was reviewed separately. A section of the highway that could begin to give relief to the congested five corners of Essex Junction was constructed in 1992. It was an isolated four-lane highway to nowhere, throttled on either end by connection to lesser roads.

By the time the rest of the Circ rose to the top of various funding and approval queues, the plan needed a fresh environmental impact statement. The state offered one in 2002, with

U.S. Senator Bernard Sanders
2007–PRESENT: INDEPENDENT

Bernie Sanders was elected to the U.S. Senate in 2006 after serving sixteen years in the House of Representatives. He is the longest serving independent member of Congress in American history. Born in 1941 in Brooklyn, he moved to Vermont after graduation from the University of Chicago in 1964. He was elected Mayor of Burlington by ten votes in 1981 and served four terms in that office.

Sanders is one of the strongest voices in the Senate in support of sound environmental policy. "Good environmental policy is good economic policy. We are not only helping to save the planet in terms of global warming, we are also moving to get this country out of the economic crisis that we are in right now. Are we making some progress? We really are. In the stimulus package, for example, we are spending more money on energy efficiency and sustainable energy then in the history of the United States of America. We certainly have moved far more aggressively in the last year then Bush did in eight years. Here is what I think we have got to do. I think the low-hanging fruit and a real job creator is energy efficiency. As we struggle with the most significant economic crisis since the Great Depression, it is imperative that we create millions of good-paying jobs and, as I said, the interesting thing here is that good environmental policy is good economic policy."

The Smart Growth alternative to the CIRC includes a series of rotaries such as this one at the Five Corners in Essex Junction.

findings that were contested and quickly litigated in federal court by the Conservation Law Foundation and Friends of the Earth. They found a ready ally in the newly formed Smart Growth Collaborative, coordinated by Beth Humstone, who was director of the Vermont Forum on Sprawl. The suit successfully argued that the state's environmental impact statement used old data and information in its studies, and the state was "sent back to square one," as Sandy Levine says.

It's one thing to say no to a proposed solution and quite another to show how the problem could be better solved. The permitting delay gave the Smart Growth Collaborative time to develop alternative plans to the Circ—plans that would, they said, do several things: solve the five-corner congestion problem without the sprawl-inducing side effects of the highway; accommodate a variety of transportation modes, including bike and pedestrian ways; improve commuter access to IBM; and, all told, cost significantly less than the Circ would cost.

The Circ became a rallying point for those who envisioned a different, less car-dependent, less energy-intensive future for Vermont. While the environmental impact statement had been held up over such technical issues as water quality, wetland integrity, and runoff, for many who opposed the Circ the quarry was much larger: Would we continue to spend tax dollars expanding old-fashioned petroleum-society infrastructure through sheer inertia and thoughtlessness, or would we begin to plan and build for a sustainable future?

The federal Environmental Protection Agency sided with the Conservation Law Foundation and the Smart Growth Collaborative—not on the larger issue but on the narrower grounds of environmental impact, the issue that had held up the repermitting of the road. In a strongly worded letter to the Douglas administration, the recently appointed EPA regional administrator for New England, Curt Spalding, said that the road as planned would cause "unacceptable damage" to nearby wetlands and streams and would not receive a federal permit. He had visited the site and agreed with

the engineering reports, saying later that he found "those impacts would be very, very substantial, [with] secondary impacts in the hundreds of acres." No doubt aware of the Smart Growth Collaborative's alternative, he added: "We think you could work with the existing Route 2a and do the things you need to do and not have such a substantial impact."

Governor Douglas was not pleased. His administration had already come under fire from the EPA for failing to implement the measures necessary to bring Lake Champlain water quality up to standards, earning a strong and well-publicized rebuke from Spalding's predecessor. And now a plum, federally funded, job-creating, and (as he saw it) people-pleasing investment was being denied to Vermont on his watch. "The recommendation is wrong," he pronounced. "Everybody agrees that this is the right thing to do, and yet special interest groups and now some federal bureaucrats are saying something different." Note the reprise of the Reagan-Watt themes: environmentalists, but not corporations, are special interests; the government (especially the federal government) is the problem, not part of the solution. And clearly, the "everybody" that matters doesn't include smart-growth advocates, environmentalists, or federal environmental administrators.

The Circ, long on the drawing boards, had finally died, though there were some who continued to hold out hope for an improbable resuscitation. The official pronounce-

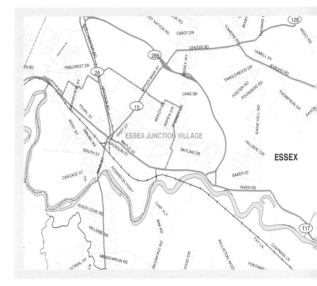

The Circumferential Highway would have let traffic loop around Burlington through open countryside and farmland.

ment of death came from Douglas's successor, Governor Peter Shumlin, in a 2011 press conference in Williston, not far from those five corners: "The Circ, as originally conceived thirty years ago, will not be built. Let's face that reality while also recognizing that significant transportation problems exist in this region that need to be addressed.

By bringing together stakeholders in the spirit of collaboration, I believe we will find more cost-effective and modern solutions to our current challenges."

The section that was completed is, of course, still there, an aberrant concrete fixture on an otherwise rural landscape of farms and wetlands. A single strip mall occupies a prominent place at the end of an off-ramp, looking lonely and out of place.

Chris Kilian and Paul Burns

TWO UNIQUE OPPORTUNITIES
FOR LEADERSHIP

Chris Kilian, vice president of the Conservation Law Foundation and director of the Vermont office, has had a long history in environmental advocacy in Vermont. He established his legal credentials in the 1990s, as general counsel and water program director at VNRC. During that time the Federal Energy Regulatory Commission (FERC) was in the process of reviewing the fifty-year-old licenses for hydroelectric dams on rivers in Vermont and across the nation. This gave Vermont an opportunity to address water quality impacts of these dams over their first fifty years. Chris was well positioned and ready to take full advantage of this once-in-a-lifetime occurrence. It was as if he had been preparing for this moment from the time he was a boy. His parents were "deeply conservation-minded" and involved the children in the management of their land in upstate New York. Fly-fishing with his father in the Mohawk River near Cohoes, New York, was both an ecological and aesthetic experience for this young avid angler. It was there he learned about the consequences of allowing corporations to flush pollutants like polychlorinated biphenyls (PCBs) into waterways and the harm that comes to fisheries habitats from damming rivers.

One of the dams Chris was to encounter later in life was on the Clyde River in Vermont's Northeast Kingdom. The Clyde runs through some of the wildest lands in Vermont, roughly thirty-four miles from Island Pond to Lake Memphremagog. Home to native brook trout, the Clyde once boasted a wild landlocked salmon run each fall and spring. But the Citizens United Power Company put an end to that in 1957 when it dammed up the river to produce hydroelectric power. By 1994, Newport No.11 Dam on the Clyde River was due for its license review. But on the first day of May 1994, "The river decided its own fate," notes Chris. Heavy spring rains cut into the bank that abutted the dam, compromising the dam and allowing the river to flow naturally for the first time in thirty-seven years. Seizing the advantage Mother Nature had provided, Chris

argued successfully at the FERC hearing, on behalf of VNRC and a group of citizens in the region, to remove what was left of the dam and restore the native fisheries to the river.

Chris remembers driving to the hearing in Island Pond in the midst of a blinding snowstorm, expecting that there would be light citizen participation and that the hearing would end early. To his surprise, he discovered the hearing room packed with citizens, who were now releasing some of the pent-up outrage they had held for decades over the loss of their fabled river. The atmosphere was tense, and the Louisiana company that owned the dam was well lawyered-up, but Chris stood his ground: "that the dam should not ever be rebuilt." He later joked of "a gigantic spool of red tape" that he was prepared to "wrap them up in" if the dam didn't come out. The hearing carried well on into the night.

With a dynamite blast in June of 1996, FERC executed—for the first time in the nation's history—a dam removal for environmental reasons.

Paul Burns's initiation into advocacy came early in his life when he learned, as a teenager, that his mother had taken diethylstilbestrol (DES) during her pregnancies, putting at risk the reproductive capabilities of his sisters. This troubling realization galvanized his sense of outrage at the lack of government oversight and regulation to protect the public from corporate greed and indifference.

This sense of injustice led him to his work with the "PIRGs" in several New England states before settling in Vermont. As the executive director of Vermont Public Interest Research Group, Paul headed up VPIRG's campaign to shut down Vermont Yankee as scheduled in 2012. It was a massive undertaking involving extensive outreach to many communities around the state. The organization conducted a statewide survey to determine the optimal messaging for the campaign. "Closing Vermont Yankee as scheduled is the safe and responsible thing to do" would be the message.

With the fall of a cooling tower at the Yankee facility on August 12, 2007, the proverbial "floodgates" were opened, and the beginning of a series of revelations about the management of the facility ensued. Then came the news of groundwater contamination and the Entergy management team's false claim under oath that the plant had no underground pipes. All this

Above: (l. to r.) Paul Burns and Chris Kilian

reduced the public's confidence in Entergy's ability to manage the aging facility. Alone among the states, Vermont had established an unusual condition for allowing a license extension. According to the agreement with the power producer, the threshold issue would be the reliability of the facility to produce power. The 2010 Senate vote on whether or not to shut down Yankee at the end of its license was scheduled for February 24.

"There were literally thousands of protesters in Montpelier that day," recalls Paul. "We had been working tirelessly on organizing citizens for this day. And there were the folks who had been fighting this plant from the 1960s to today, like Ginny Callan and Cort Richardson. In the Senate chambers, you could hear a pin drop." When the vote was called and the tally was four against closure and twenty-six for closing Yankee at the end of its license, "There were a lot of tears, hugs, and cries of joy in that chamber and around the state. It was the most gratifying moment of my career."

"After Yankee, what can we expect? We need to make it happen on the ground," says Paul. "We have a monumental challenge in meeting our energy needs with clean renewable sources."

Both Chris and Paul agree that the solutions to the big energy puzzles ahead lie in our ability to get a new green energy infrastructure up and running, and in order to succeed, we'll need new regulations, financial incentives, and an engaged and active public.

"Vermont is on the right path now," says Paul. "By the end of 2012, Vermont will get 10 percent of our electricity from clean, local wind power, helping Vermonters take control of our energy future, keeping our money working in our state, and ensuring a positive legacy for future generations. We need to continue building clean energy, like wind, in Vermont today."

Two Legislative Successes and Some Effects

Nationwide, public surface waters have been considered public trust resources since 1896. If you own all the land around a pond, you own the pond but not the water in it. Subsurface water is equally important—two-thirds of Vermonters get their drinking water from underground aquifers—yet it wasn't treated similarly. In nature, the one kind of water very regularly becomes the other, making the legal difference between them unsupportable. In 2008, the Vermont legislature passed, and Governor Douglas signed, the Groundwater Protection Act, which declared groundwater to be a public trust resource. Inspired in part by Maude Barlow and Tony Clarke's 2003 book, *Blue Gold: The Fight to Stop*

Above: Author Maude Barlow, r., with Republican state senator Diane Snelling, both instrumental in the passage of the Groundwater Protection Act of 2008.

the Corporate Theft of the World's Water, the four-year lobbying-and-information campaign that led to the law benefited from the work of John Groveman of the VNRC, Annette Smith of Vermonters for a Clean Environment, and David Mears of the Vermont Law School. Concerned citizens in Bakersfield, East Montpelier, Randolph, Stockbridge, and Williston played a strong role, as well; some of those towns had seen or were facing the prospect of major commercial groundwater withdrawals. Wells of several homeowners had gone dry or had their productivity reduced. The new law called for the mapping and monitoring of groundwater resources, and it established regulatory control of extractions of groundwater in excess of 57,600 gallons a day, a cap low enough to discourage large-scale commercial extraction for bottling and sale. Vermont had not been in the forefront of this movement—Maine, New Hampshire, Massachusetts, and Michigan had had similar legislation on the books for

years—but Vermont took advantage of their good work and advanced it, and the state has avoided a crisis.

There were immediate applications of the law. In East Montpelier, town residents had resisted the plans of one part-time resident to extract and bottle 250,000 gallons of water a day for sale and profit. The new law gave direct and statuatory support to that effort, for it required that operations like that be reviewed for their environmental impacts and consequences for others. No longer would this public resource lie both unseen and undefended, available for the taking by anyone who could drill a well and install a pump.

And the law gave an additional legal argument to those seeking to close Vermont Yankee, the nuclear plant on the Connecticut River. Their efforts received new and sad support from Vermont Yankee itself when Entergy, the plant's owners, revealed that underground cooling pipes—whose very existence they had for a time denied—were leaking radioactive titrium into groundwater. Prior to the passage of the bill the contamination would have been bad news, "a regrettable incident," but not automatically a factor in deliberations over the plant's Certificate of Public Good from the state, which is required for its operation. The federal Nuclear Regulatory Commission reserves to itself all concerns about the safety of nuclear power, which means states can resist licensing and relicensing only on the narrower ground of whether or not the plant brings public benefits. Release of radiation has been defined as a safety

issue. The Groundwater Protection Act gave Vermont's Public Service Board additional legal grounds on which to define the release of radioactivity into water as a violation of a public trust rather than purely a safety issue. "The state must live up to its obligation under the 2008 law to manage groundwater in the interest of all Vermonters and follow through on its investigation of this contamination," said the VNRC's general counsel Jon Groveman in an op-ed that drew the connection between the release of radioactivity into groundwater and the new law. "It's no longer an under-the-radar issue. There is now a sense that groundwater is finite and needs to be protected."

In February of 2010 the Vermont State Senate heard testimony on closing the Vermont Yankee Nuclear Power Plant. Bottom: Cort Richardson, l., former executive director of VPIRG, awaits word of a Senate vote with James Moore, VPIRG's then clean energy advocate.

At Long Last, Smart Growth

The other major legislative victory for the environmental movement during the Douglas administration was one that sought to bring progress in concentrating development in growth centers. In 2006, the legislature passed and Governor Douglas signed a law to create the Vermont Growth Centers Program. Jointly administered by the Natural Resources Board and the Department of Housing and Community Affairs, the law codified smart growth principles and established incentives for municipalities to designate growth centers and limit development outside of them. Environmental organizations actively supported the bill. Some, however, soon expressed concern about its administration.

The growth center legislation came some twenty years after Governor Kunin's Growth Commission published its report calling for land use planning

in order to encourage the development of a better (we'd say sustainable) balance between culture and nature, economic development and ecosystem conservation. In the interim, Vermonters' attitudes—the social capital necessary to support land use planning—had changed, no doubt in considerable measure because the landscape itself had changed as well: in some areas the problem of sprawl had become more obvious with every passing year. Proposed by a consortium of interest groups including the VNRC, the Conservation Law Foundation, the Preservation Trust of Vermont, and Smart Growth Vermont, the law offered tax benefits and Act 250 allowances as incentives to build in areas designated for growth by local authorities with state board approval.

The first municipality to receive growth center designation was the town of Williston—site of big-box development close to its interstate exchange. The town had sought to define its growth

Smart Growth principles ask Vermonters to imagine a Vermont less dependent on the private auto.

center in an expansive way. Members of the smart growth collaborative worked with town planners to change the boundaries to better comply with statutory requirements. But after that agreement, the Downtown Board (a body identified under the existing Vermont Downtown Program and expanded to serve as the designator of growth centers), acting at the urging of board chair and secretary of Commerce and Community Affairs Kevin Dorn, expanded the boundaries beyond those the town had originally requested. The new boundaries included Williston's existing big-box stores and some adjacent lands—development that represents the antithesis of the smart growth the law was meant to encourage. When the VNRC and others sought to litigate the change, the Vermont Supreme Court ruled that the statute didn't allow such a case to be appealed. The law, as interpreted by the court,

didn't allow for any appeal of decisions by the Downtown Board—which gave the board an unprecedented insulation from review and accountability.

Seen one way, the law represented a significant step toward implementing the fundamental principles of smart growth. Seen another, it revealed a fundamental weakness: absent any mechanism of appeal, the effectiveness of the legislation would depend entirely on the manner and means of administration.

Thus, this effort to protect compact village centers and downtowns (and the quality of Vermonters' lives) from the debilitating effects of sprawl still depended on laws that offered mostly carrot and lacked stick and that were subject to "gaming" by interests antagonistic to the precepts that development-control law encodes.

While the law augmented programs aimed at preserving the working landscape, such as the Current Use Property Tax Relief program, it didn't specifically address preservation of the working landscape as such—it didn't give incentives to keep farmland in farming or forestland in forest. Still absent in this approach was any direct effort, such as added regulation to guide development outside the growth center. Nor did the law implement a coherent land use plan of the sort that will be necessary to achieve maximum sustainable well-being for Vermonters, a plan that would acknowledge ecological limits and apportion economic development and activity under them, assigning use of scarce ecosystem "sink" services regionally for maximum benefit to Vermonters.

The experience in Williston showed that Act 250 administration and smart growth legislation—especially as re-engineered by an administration that was less than supportive of the underlying principles of both—wouldn't necessarily halt the incremental loss of Vermont's landscape and ecosystem values.

If prohibition and penalty were themselves prohibited, then the movement toward sustainable development patterns and landscape use would have to be accomplished through laws and efforts that are limited to use of positive incentives. And if the incentives that are offered are insufficient to the task, then perhaps they could be augmented by other action and activity. One possibility: growth could be contained by assuring that designated growth centers are attractive areas to live and work, filled with economic vitality and offering the pleasures and benefits of prosperous communities. Environmental protection and with it further progress toward achieving sustainability might be achieved through economic health. This was the work to which many in the environmental movement turned in the latter years of the 2000s and into the next decade.

CHAPTER 6

The 2010s

Localization

Vermonters respond to the realities of climate change and work to develop the economic, social, and political capital needed to achieve a sustainable state.

"Are we there yet?" You've heard the question from youngsters strapped into the backseat of the car, and no doubt have asked it yourself a few times. If we ask it about the progress Vermont has made toward achieving a sustainable state, the answer has to be the one that parents so often give: "no, not yet; but we're getting closer." From that ribbon-cutting ceremony in Guilford that marked the start of Vermont's full-fledged entry into the modern petroleum economy just a half-century ago, we've traveled an enormous distance. But there is still more ground to cover in the effort to achieve a sustainable state, and the magnitude of the challenge has grown dramatically. Collectively, we've become increasingly aware that the planet has limits that we are capable of violating, and climate change is no longer a theoretical possibility but an accomplished fact, one that is already transforming our lives and livelihoods.

In the story we've told, the way humans live their lives in Vermont was revolutionized by changes released into the state by the arrival of the Interstate. That highway and the thousands and thousands of miles of highways just like it around the globe have led us to a changed world—one that puts civilization itself on a collision course with ecological limits. We all know what is needed now. And as we learn to wean ourselves from oil (and learn to thrive in compact, walkable communities), it is possible that the cars-and-concrete superhighways we have now will look—and be—as old-fashioned as the horse-drawn tedder that Romain Tenney refused to give up when the bulldozers and sheriff arrived on his farm to clear the way for the Interstate.

A new highway has entered Vermont in the past few decades: the information superhighway, which gives

VERMONT BY THE NUMBERS:

2010

- Population: 625,741
- Percent born in state: 52.2
- Cows: 135,000
- Farms (2007): 6,984
- Total farm acreage (2007): 1,233,313
- Registered motor vehicles: 557,370
- Percent of seasonal homes: 16
- Percent of homes with Internet access: 51.2

fingertip access to a wealth of information and a profusion of connection in nearly every remote town and village in Vermont. Some of the changes that this new technology will bring are fairly easy to foresee, and many are not. Some of the changes will point us toward a sustainable state, and some won't. Telecommuting may encourage us to reduce our fuel use and our need for highways, but it could also bring additional pressure on the state's working landscape as more people seek to escape urban life with a rural retreat in the woods of Vermont. It may give us better access to quality information about threats to ecosystems and rapid, effective ways to organize to resist them, but it may also encourage more and more Vermonters to live their lives virtually, disconnected from nature, diminishing their personal connection to the land, diminishing the love of place that has always been the foundation of environmental engagement and care. It may give us real-time information about such things as energy use and agricultural developments that will allow us to make

better progress toward a sustainable society, or it may help fragment the public wisdom and shared perception of reality that is the basis for any effective social action. The eventual effect this tool will have will depend on our choices about how and for what purposes we use it.

But even as the new information economy is layered on top of the old economy, a basic truth endures: culture has a root in nature. Humans can't live and an economy of any sort can't function without extracting matter and energy from the planet and emitting degraded matter and energy back into it. At a basic level, "all flesh is grass," as the Old Testament prophet Isaiah put it, and all grass is made of sunlight, water, and soil. Agriculture will always be the foundation of civilization, as it has been ever since its invention allowed the development of the first civilizations ten thousand years ago. Everything else an economy accomplishes, even the invention and construction of an information superhighway, is built on it. As George Perkins Marsh showed us, a civilization can't endure if its agriculture isn't sustainable.

Also durable is this truth: the planet is finite. It has a finite capacity to absorb greenhouse gas emissions, yet we continue to act as though that capacity is infinite. Climate change threatens to render nearly useless every achievement that the environmental movement has worked so hard to accomplish. The magnitude of the environmental damage and social dislocations that a rising global temperature will bring is barely comprehensible. The changes we have

unleashed on ourselves will tax our ability to cope to a degree that humans have never experienced.

There are, however, grounds for hope. Humans will eventually achieve a sustainable balance with the planet that supports them—unsustainable systems simply do not last. Rather than despairing in the face of a problem that seems too large to solve, we should keep in mind this empowering thought: any and everything we can do to build the systems that a sustainable human society needs will count as a positive contribution.

In closing, we present five hopeful stories drawn from current local initiatives in Vermont. Each offers a glimpse into the human spirit, which longs for connection to community and the beauty and bounty of the natural world. Each is about a grassroots response to the very complex global challenges we face in the twenty-first century. These aren't the only answers, and they aren't by themselves sufficient to solve the problems associated with global climate change and securing our energy future. Yet they represent important models, for they testify to the willingness of Vermonters to address, as directly and effectively as possible, the gaps and shortcomings left by the failure of state and federal governments to establish the policies we need to move us toward a sustainable state. Collectively, these good works inspire hope—and they show that the power of local, hands-on initiatives can carry us to a greener Vermont.

The Hardwick Renaissance
How will we feed ourselves?

The Center for an Agricultural Economy is located in the middle of Hardwick, at the epicenter of what people have begun calling Vermont's agricultural renaissance. It's a new role for this town of 3,500 people, which a decade ago was a worn-out, economically depressed town whose major industry—granite extraction— could no longer support the lives and life standards that had evolved in its heyday. Income in the town fell 25 percent below the Vermont average, and unemployment was high.

But a rebirth of farming activity has revitalized this small town, giving it a sustainable base while also stimulating a broader and renewed interest in maintaining Vermont's agricultural heritage. Scattered across the rolling hills that surround the village are more than one hundred small farms and several dozen food-producing operations that are pioneering a new path for agriculture: farm-based, value-added production. From the hills around Hardwick come cheeses and maple products, beer, organic tofu, even toasted crispy kale chips.

From its downtown offices, the Center for an Agricultural Economy has functioned as the nerve center, cheerleader, and brain trust for the new farming and food enterprises in the area. Its aim is to build a thriving "locally-based, 21st century healthy food system." And if that sounds ambitious and abstract, Program Director Elena Gustafson is clear that the organizational mission is as specific as dinner and as local as the Buffalo Mountain Co-op, a food co-operative in the walkable downtown, where many of the ideas behind the renaissance were first articulated.

"Our focus will always be on this area," she recently told a dozen visitors from a co-op in White River Junction who had come to listen, see, and learn. They and a handful of other interested people were preparing for a tour of several of the area's farms and businesses. Visitors from as far away as the Midwest and California have come to Hardwick to glean ideas for fomenting a new kind of agriculture—local, small-scale, organic, entrepreneurial, sustainable—in their own home regions. And there are regularly visitors from other parts of Vermont.

"There's this desire in Vermont to have a vibrant, local food economy," Andrew Meyer told the group. He's head of Vermont Soy, which contracts with area farmers to grow soybeans and then uses those beans to make soy milk, tofu, and other soy products. When he started, soybean fields were unknown in Vermont. It took Meyer and his assistants five years to develop a strain of soybean that

The farmers' market, as traditional as it is contemporary, is one of many year-round options for Vermonters to find fresh local produce.

Above right: Monty Fischer, director, The Center for an Agricultural Economy. Left: Preparing cheeses for aging in the cellars at the Kehler Brothers' Jasper Hill Farm, in Greensboro, Vermont.

would grow in Vermont's cool climate and yield the quality and quantity they needed. Now there are sixty acres of the beans growing on farms around the area.

Meyer worked on Capitol Hill in Washington, D.C., for a decade. His work there, like his work in Vermont today, focused on reforming what he and others see as a broken national food system—one that has become centralized, industrialized, vulnerable to fuel shortages and terrorist attacks, and plagued by food-borne diseases. Worst of all, Meyer and others suggest, it is driving small farmers out of business while producing food that is less than optimal and even unhealthy because of its heavy dependence on chemical fertilizers and pesticides.

How do you fix a national problem? If national policy won't do it—and

the agricultural policies written in Washington have been shaped by large agribusiness interests that define their problems quite differently—you tackle it one town, one field, one harvest at a time.

The innovative approach being developed in Hardwick is building a comprehensive food system that encourages farmers to grow crops and sell them locally. Even as it inspires entrepreneurs to find new ways of using those crops, it is finding new regional and world markets. The "eat locally" movement doesn't preclude export to other regions—as long as consumers in other places can't or won't always eat locally, the Vermont brand will continue to satisfy demand for pure, high-quality food products from the state. And shipping value-added, farm-

based products (cheese, beer, tofu) from Hardwick keeps food-chain work, with its jobs and dollars, closer to home.

Pete's Greens, a large vegetable farm ten miles north of Hardwick in Craftsbury, grows acres of everything from asparagus to zucchini. It cleans and packages the produce on site and sells it in a variety of farmers' markets, co-ops, small groceries, and supermarkets all over central Vermont. Pete's produce is so regionally famous and widely beloved that when one of his barns burned down in an accidental fire, the mourning was general—and was quickly organized into a relief effort that helped him restore the lost capacity. The Vermont Food Venture Center is a cluster of industrial-scale kitchens next door to Vermont Soy, and it offers rentable facilities to home producers

Steve Wright

TIME OUT

A native of Georgia, Steve Wright came to Vermont with his family in the summer of 1968 to the Northeast Kingdom's village of Craftsbury. A man of eclectic interests and talents, he's held a variety of notable positions over the decades since, from serving as president of Sterling College to being a public advocate for the disabled. He served as Vermont Commissioner of Fish and Wildlife under Governor Madeleine Kunin, who also appointed him to Act 250's Environmental Board in 1990 where he served for seven years, the last three under Governor Howard Dean. In 2009 he retired, after eight years with the National Wildlife Federation, where he helped develop and implement climate change education programs for hunting and fishing groups.

Steve was a vocal critic of the 1994 tie-breaking decision by then Lieutenant Governor Barbara Snelling to not renew the appointment of several members of the Environmental Board. Today, in his current volunteer efforts opposing wind energy development on Vermont's ridgelines and mountains, he works daily with Lukas Snelling, the grandson of the former lieutenant governor—"a delightful and talented young man," Steve says.

Steve is emphatic about his current work: "We desperately need a time out before making more bad decisions as in the Lowell Mountain Wind project. We are considering major surgery on our landscape, and many of the owners of the resource are calling for a second opinion. Unfortunately, we have lost our collective voice regarding the importance of the Vermont landscape to our daily lives."

Steve shakes his head at what he sees as a failed opportunity to unite the hunting and fishing community with what can be called the "non-game" environmental community. "Sometimes in step, more often not, or just not stepping at all, these two communities gave away a priceless opportunity to become political and intellectual powerhouses in Vermont," he says. "The so-called 'hook and bullet' folks disappeared into the

maw of the NRA and property rights fanatics. There they continue to hide from any important role in the state's conservation future. The 'tree-huggers' have done the same thing—grabbed their binoculars and run away—especially from working with the hook and bullet folk." What's at stake is more than a coherent, collaborative voice in policy, he says. "This loss, within our political and social process, of the connections to our landscape as experienced by these two groups may be the most significant social loss in our history—potentially giving away the opportunity to help future generations understand the importance of keeping our landscape healthy."

Asked about the environmental movement's future, he has a sharp observation to offer: "A new environmentalism is emerging with values having little or no connection to a healthy landscape. Their reality seems to relate more to rules and regulations than to an environmentally educated society. If you lack some basic understanding of natural processes, you cannot make effective decisions affecting those elements."

Steve adds one final thought. "There are two kinds of people: those who believe the earth belongs to them and those who believe they belong to the earth. We really need to get that right, and soon."

who, having cooked up a marketable food item in their kitchen, want to test out a scale-up. They can make the leap to a larger volume without taking on the risk of a huge capital expenditure until they get the income stream to support it. And in the hills above nearby Greensboro is Hill Farmstead Brewery, where a variety of tangy amber ales and dark porters and stouts are made.

Conventional dairying tied to the Boston milk market is still a mainstay of the farm economy in Hardwick. But several of those farms have either turned to organic dairying or have become cheese-makers, producing a value-added product that yields more

Below: Home and community gardens are increasingly popular as a source of locally grown foods. Below, right: Pete Johnson's farm in Hardwick, Vermont is the home of Pete's Greens.

reliable income than bulk milk sold under the federal milk-pricing system. Farming, long celebrated as a way of life in Vermont, has suffered at times from being not enough of a business. And the standard business models that have been offered to farmers ("grow, expand, use chemicals to increase output, sell more and more primary product") have also worked to winnow the number of farms ever downward, even as increased output depresses prices, making the larger, more "efficient" operations less and less economic. The innovative models being offered in Hardwick propose a different solution: Increase value added by going organic. Combine farming with entrepreneurial savvy. Export value added products—cheese, beer, tofu—rather than raw material. Keep the jobs and money here.

This approach has had what economists call a multiplier effect, attracting

new residents and businesses to the town and surrounding area. "These are real places with real jobs hiring more and more local people," says Monty Fischer, director of the center for an Agricultural Economy. And while he's proud of the role the center has played in promoting the increased vitality, the credit, he says, really goes to the community members and entrepreneurs who have believed in Hardwick and have invested time and energy in rebuilding and expanding its farming economy.

With that new energy and innovative thinking, one positive effect is no change at all, but something that is remaining the same: open land. While in other parts of Vermont (and indeed, the entire Northeast region of the United States) productive agricultural land is being lost to housing and urban development, the fields around Hardwick, Greensboro, and Craftsbury remain

green and productive. The rural culture of the Northeast Kingdom has been at least partially stabilized in this area, and that seems to be a fact that pleases just about everyone. If you make the trip to Hardwick, Meyer says, "What you'll see here is a collaborative effort of businesses and farms working together, revitalizing the agricultural economy."

"Eating is an agricultural act," writer Wendell Berry has told us. Since agriculture preserves a working landscape with its environmental and social values, how we eat is also a choice about how we participate in the movement toward a sustainable state. "The same is true of choosing local wood and wood products," says Kate McCarthy, VNRC's Sustainable Communities program director. "With our everyday choices about what we eat, where we live, and how we get around, we have the chance to choose the future of our state."

Ask environmentalists to imagine the world they want to see, and chances are their thoughts will turn to natural scenes: mountainscapes, forests, woodland lakes, and well-farmed fields. Gleaming stainless steel surfaces in an industrial kitchen aren't likely to be part of the vision. But processing facilities like those of the Vermont Food Venture Center and dozens of value-adding operations in Hardwick are playing a strong role in the conservation of agriculture and a way of life that is a crucial part of the movement toward a sustainable state.

The Vermont Energy and Climate Action Network
How will we secure the energy to power our lives?

On a warm day in June in 2010, the Middlesex Energy Committee hosted an energy efficiency overhaul of the local elementary school. Committee members were joined by teachers, school officials, energy professionals, and a dedicated group of volunteers for what they called a "21st Century Barn Raising." Like the literal barn raisings of days gone by, many hands not only made light work but were absolutely essential to accomplishing what got done; two or three workers working alone wouldn't have had the same result. That's because the event not only retrofitted the school but strengthened community ties, built camaraderie, and gave participants a shared sense of purpose and achievement. All told, the two-day, largely volunteer-driven Rumney Elementary School community weatherization project was no small feat.

"You're in the attic, on your belly, on your shoulders, with nails poking into your head. It's claustrophobic, it's hot, it's hard work," said energy committee member Paul Zabriskie, whose day job with EnergySmart of Vermont—a program operated through

Above: The dollar bill test: if you can pull it out, your windows are costing you money.

VNRC Energy program director Johanna Miller with U.S. senator Bernie Sanders at the first 350.org Rally at Green Mountain Coffee Roasters in Waterbury, Vermont.

the Central Vermont Community Action Council—positioned him as the crew leader of the project.

"With seven attics at Rumney, a traditional weatherization project would have been a huge cost," said Zabriskie, noting that what the group did will save the school between 2,000 to 2,500 gallons of fuel oil a year—at a cost of just twenty-five cents for every dollar saved. (For those interested in investment math: that's a return of 300 percent, far better than you get on Wall Street.) "The town also gets a school with improved air quality [and] warmer classrooms, [along with] lower heating costs."

Behind this scene and a myriad of others in communities around the state is the Vermont Energy and Climate Action Network (VECAN), a largely unseen but highly effective umbrella group that supports communities looking to reduce energy costs and their carbon footprint through conservation, increased energy efficiency, and conversion to renewable energy sources. The VECAN team, coordinated by VNRC Energy program director Johanna Miller, gathers on a regular basis to review and set priorities for providing services to a growing number of town energy committees. "Most challenging yet gratifying," Miller says of her work. "There is so much desire for a unified response to energy needs and climate challenges, it's hard to keep up with these incredibly energetic and dedicated Vermonters."

VECAN was founded by a partnership of five organizations—the 10 percent Challenge, the New England Grassroots Environment Fund, the Sustainable Energy Resource Group, the Vermont Energy Investment Corporation, and the Vermont Natural Resources Council—and it exists to form partnerships with town energy committees. These have grown in number from fifty in 2008 to about one hundred in 2012—one of the few instances in which exponential growth is definitely an environmentally sound strategy. (Vermont has 251 towns, so coverage is not yet halfway.) In the absence of a firm and far-reaching sustainable energy policy from Washington, D.C., and impatient with the lack of results on the ground in their homes and lives, "Vermonters are eager to get on with swift, meaningful efforts to cut energy costs, foster renewable energy generation, and lessen the state's contribution to global warming," says Ginny Callan of the New England Grassroots Environmental Fund, which makes small grants to citizen groups. The consensus on the need to act now to secure a sustainable energy future is growing, as more towns join the list by creating energy committees. Working with local officials, business leaders, friends, and neighbors, these community groups are not only saving energy and reducing greenhouse gas emissions, they're building social capital—the mutual trust and shared knowledge that will be needed to achieve a sustainable state.

Kathryn Blume

CHAMPIONING THE HEALTH OF THE PLANET

On December fourth, 2011, Vermont actor and activist Kathryn Blume gave a keynote speech to the Vermont Energy and Climate Action Network (VECAN). Her talk, entitled "Dancing to the Beat of the Great Green Heart" and excerpted here, tackled the tough issues Vermont faces on the road to a sustainable future—and tells us what we've got to do.

I submit to you that we need to draw a line in the sand and say we will not derive our energy from anything that adversely impacts the human or natural communities from which it's extracted, or that releases particulates, greenhouse gases, and other toxins into our environment.

I challenge us to say no—even if it threatens a short-term gap. In fact precisely if it threatens a short-term gap, because that gap can serve as a potent motivator for finding truly green, truly sustainable solutions. That gap can be a creative gap, a highly pressurized crucible for innovation. That gap is part of our moral obligation to—for once—champion the health of the planet over our own sense of entitled need.

Basically, it's time to move from incremental, predictable change to fundamental, breathtaking change, and you, each and every one of you, are fundamental change agents. Each and every one of you has the power to make an enormous impact on the long-term well-being of the places and the people you care about.

Really, there is no more waiting. This is the moment, a time when, all over the world, folks just like us are reinventing the democratic process. They're building community and fostering widespread participation. They believe that true power comes from the will of the people, and their job is to bring enough people to the table to have an impact.

They're teaching us about determination and commitment, and they're proving the truth of Paul Hawken's statement that, "If you look at the science about what is happening on earth and aren't pessimistic, you don't understand the data. But if you meet the people who are working to restore this earth and the lives of the poor, and you aren't optimistic, you haven't got a pulse."

Vermont exists in the real world—a world with powerful forces which operate in direct opposition to what we're trying to accomplish, and which work vigorously to undermine our campaign for wholeness, for survival.

Which means your job is to say to your leaders, "We've got your back. We'll hold strong and help you push forward." But you also have to say to your leaders, "We've got your feet—and we've got 'em in the fire. We're going to remind you—and keep reminding you—of the urgency of these times, the intensity of our aspirations and the uncompromising rigor of our goals. We're going to hold you to your highest ideals because nothing less will do."

The combination of high fuel costs and old housing stock makes home weatherization an area where Vermonters can achieve big savings for the environment as well as their pocketbooks.

The work of the town energy committees has been made easier by state adoption of an innovative program pioneered in California. Called Property Assessed Clean Energy—PACE for short—it's a financial tool to help homeowners install renewable energy systems or invest in weatherization. Very often, these investments save money, but homeowners often lack the up-front capital they need to implement them. The 2010 legislation adopted in Vermont enables municipalities to raise capital and then loan that money to homeowners to put toward energy retrofits. The loan is paid back with small mortgage-like payments added automatically to the structure's property tax assessment. The improvements stay with the structure, and so does the cost.

The road to securing this legislation wasn't a smooth one, and it wouldn't have come about without citizen advocacy. "Absolutely everything the legislature is able to do is a result of [pressure] coming from people, from the ground up," said Tony Klein, chair of the House Natural Resources and Energy Committee, who also represents two districts with very active energy committees—East Montpelier and Middlesex. "Town energy committees end up being the conscience of energy issues for local towns." The earlier passage of the "feed-in tariff"—a regulatory policy that implements net metering and that requires utilities to purchase home-made electricity at retail rates, making solar retrofitting more economically viable—played a role. That success, and willing participants calling for the new program, were crucial. Sometimes elected officials are wary of going out on a limb. As Klein noted, "I think the legislature was a little less risk averse [on this program]. It's the boots on the ground that help the lawmakers be more bold."

Thus, while much of the world waits on leaders to wake up to the need for—and the opportunities offered by—making the transition to a post-carbon economy, Vermonters are taking direct action through town energy committees. Their beneficial effect is amplified by the cooperation they seek and receive from state and local officials, businesses, non-profits, church leaders, and other organizational nodes within communities.

"Being on a town energy committee is a good way to help raise consciousness, spread the word about solutions, and help to avert global climate catastrophe," is how Putney's Daniel Hoviss put it. And he articulated a sobering truth about the vulnerability of nature when it has been too much bound and sectioned by the works and acts of humans: "Everything we do is critical; every tree and every fish matters. Being on an energy committee is just one small way of helping to change the world."

Above, right: At times necessary work in the rivers sparked tension between short term needs and long term river management goals.

Lessons in the Wake of Irene
How will we develop resilience to a changing climate?

Author Hunter Lovins calls it "global weirding" instead of global warming, to emphasize that with climate change, historical experience of weather will no longer be a guide to the present and the future. Rising sea levels; severe weather events throughout the world, from extreme heat and drought to record rainfall amounts; melting ice caps and glaciers; larger and larger floods and wildfires—all of these challenge our ability to adapt. We are becoming painfully aware that the temperate zones of the planet used to offer us a happy medium: neither too hot nor too cold, but comfortably in between. Vermont, with latitudes and altitudes higher than much of the country, was at the colder end of the American experience. Suffering through the deepness of a Vermont winter was not only a point of pride for its residents, it made the bursting of life every spring and the mild warmth of summer especially delightful. But temperate zones are migrating northward as levels of greenhouse gases rise in our atmosphere. In the 1980s, some Vermonters proudly wore T-shirts that proclaimed "Vermont is what America was," a celebration of the state's retention of its agricultural base, working landscapes, and village life. Today, that same slogan could be taken as an ironic reference to the changes that global warming is bringing to the country.

In the spring of 2011, Hurricane Irene left New York City relatively undisturbed and headed inland, where it could have been expected to lose its energy and gradually peter out. New York media reported that the city had dodged a bullet, and then they moved on to other stories. But Irene's skirting of Manhattan didn't mean there would be no damage. While its wind speeds did diminish, reducing it to the status of a tropical storm, Irene had most of its impact far from the sea. When its spiraling clouds swept up against the ridgeline of the Green Mountains they dropped their moisture, hammering Vermont with a very sudden six inches of rain. The water fell on soils already laden by a wet summer and ran quickly into brooks and streams and rivers. Like humans everywhere, Vermonters had long since adapted their built environment to "normal" rainfall, and roads, culverts, and houses were washed out, swamped, or simply destroyed by the abnormal load. Streams and rivers, too, adapt to normal conditions, which include occasional and irregular deluges that are far larger than normal. But prior to Irene, 75 percent of Vermont streams were already in some form of channel adjustment—they'd been altered by human activity, including gravel mining, rerouting, bank encroachment, and armoring. These unstable streams couldn't handle the deluge either. The damage was devastating. Major east–west highways in the southern part of the state follow rivers, naturally enough, as they are the flattest

The damage wrought in Brandon, Vermont, from Tropical Storm Irene.

path up and into the mountains; major portions of every east–west route south of Bethel were washed away. Some towns were left stranded, with no entrance or egress possible at all—a life-threatening situation for communities located far from medical care, medicines, and stores of water; without electricity; with scant food.

Vermont's experience of Tropical Storm Irene helped to demonstrate the reality and the power of climate change and visited heartbreaking (and very expensive) damage on the state. But it also demonstrated two qualities that are hopeful portents: the resilience of Vermont's communities and the ability of its relatively intact landscapes to absorb the power of raging storms. The flooding would have been unimaginably worse if the hillsides had been as bare as they had been in George Perkins Marsh's day. And efforts to preserve the historic settlement pattern of compact town centers had also preserved forest and open countryside, retaining their valuable water-management function. Unfortunately, preservation of historical settlement patterns didn't keep town centers and housing out of harm's way. Historically, rivers were conduits of travel and sources of power, and it made sense to build right next to them— and the settlers who laid out Vermont's villages saw the landscape through the lens of their urgent need for power and transport, not their knowledge of what a hundred-year flood might do.

As the state dealt with the aftermath of Irene, its long tradition of civil equality, mutual respect, and mutual aid, nurtured by centuries of town meetings, was readily apparent. Town meeting and village life gave Vermonters a heritage of facing problems—even crises—together. "Vermont Strong" soon became the unofficial then official motto of the relief and rebuilding efforts. Both its relatively intact landscape and the strength of its community spirit will help Vermont make its transition as it adapts to the sometimes brutal realities of a changing climate.

The damage done by Irene also prompted efforts at broad-ranging public education about natural systems. One of the lessons was that water driven by gravity has great force and will demand its way. Historically, humans have built dams and roads with little regard for what rivers themselves might be said to want or need. The desire lines of the rivers and the realities of the human infrastructures come into conflict in the flooding that comes with large storms—and climate change will give us more of them. While many in Vermont wanted roads and structures put back just the way they were as quickly as possible, no discussion needed, others saw the opportunity to build smarter and better.

How do you foster the shared understanding we need if we're to build smarter and better than the way we've built before? One good answer: you share information and knowledge and nurture ecological understanding among the general public. Vermonters, long used to thinking for themselves at town meetings, know that good thinking requires good information. So it was

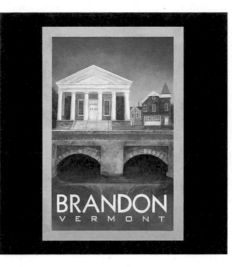

Above, left: A Warren Kimble painting of a peaceful Brandon. Right: VNRC Water program director Kim Greenwood

not at all unusual that on a cool day in May 2012 more than 220 people—a capacity crowd—attended a conference at the Capitol Plaza in Montpelier to learn what they could about "living with our rivers." Organized by Kim Greenwood, director of the water program at the VNRC, the conference featured speakers from the Agency of Natural Resources and from non-profit environmental organizations. To those prepared to learn, the storm taught that cutting a river off from its floodplain by raising its bank heights, armoring those banks, or deepening its channel is typically not a wise thing to do. Each of those strategies seems to solve a problem, but each simply helps retain a larger volumetric flow of water in the channel, increasing the sum total of the weight of water that must cascade downhill, crashing into the channel boundaries—the rocks, soil, vegetation, or man-made structures that make up the bed and banks of the river. Irene demonstrated that when the perceived solution to flooding is channelization,

constraint, and armoring, too often success simply means greater damage—downstream immediately and later in larger storms. "We have to learn to think about rivers and floodplains as a unit, a dynamic system with a function to perform," says Greenwood. "We have to design for that, and not just see the river as a scenic ribbon of water that wends its way through our landscapes but makes trouble sometimes. It's a living thing, and it's going to have its cycles. The more space we can leave for that to happen, the safer we'll all be."

Years ago, Aldo Leopold helped invent ecology by calling on us to "think like a mountain." When we build near watercourses, we'd be wise to "think like a river"—a river that will sometimes find itself larger and more powerful than it has ever been before.

Staying Connected
How will we manage growth to keep our forests intact?

The great Northern Forest runs from Canada's Maritime Provinces to Lake Ontario and the St. Lawrence River in New York, covering twenty-six million acres. In it a temperate zone, hardwood forest (mostly maple, birch, and beech) meets and mingles with northern boreal forest (spruce and balsam fir). Just a few centuries ago—an instant in geological history, the time scheme in which ecosystems evolve and adapt—it was a great, unbroken swath of wilderness. Vermonters, like Mainers and New Hampshirites, live in clearings

within it. In previous centuries, the economic value of the forest was clear: it offered the opportunity to extract timber, fuel, and game in quantities that seemed infinite. More recently, we've come to appreciate that this forest has other economic values. They include moderation of local and regional climate, absorption of rainwater, purification and replenishment of aquifers, flood control, cycling of nutrients, soil construction, and habitat for millions of species—some of them (like natural pollinators and insectivores)

of great importance to our agriculture, economy, and quality of life.

Much of Vermont lies in this Northern Forest, making the state an important transition corridor between the forested habitat to the west in New York and to the northeast in New Hampshire, Maine, and Canada. "One of the largest contiguously forested expanses in the nation," as David Dobbs and Richard Ober described it in their book *The Northern Forest*, the forest has been broken by clearing for habitation and agriculture. Within Vermont, areas of forested, unfragmented wildlife habitat are interspersed with field, farm, and pavement: towns and human works. If a hundred years ago Vermonters lived in clearings in the forest, in some areas of Vermont that relationship has been reversed: the forest exists as pockets in a cleared landscape, surrounded by development and farming. A copse of trees surrounded by plowed land is obviously an isolated ecosystem; but other forms of isolation aren't so obvious. For some species, the installation of a road or the cutting of a swath for a power line can set boundaries to territorial movement.

Animal species require access to ranges of varying size to find food and to mate, and the larger the territory,

Several Forest Roundtable participants. From l. to r.: Ann Ingerson, resource economist with the Wilderness Society; Put Blodgett, president of the Vermont Woodlands Association; Deb Brighton, fiscal analyst; Jamey Fidel, forest and wildlife program director for VNRC; Michael Snyder, commissioner of the Department of Forest, Parks and Recreation; John Meyer, consulting forester.

Bill "Rope" Roper

HEART AND SOUL

For Bill Roper, life consists of a series of decisions. "It is never easy for a town to decide against development; however when they say no to something (and there are times when they must say no) they are actually saying yes to something else. The trick is to identify and articulate what it is they are saying yes to. I tried to impress this on towns and non-profits throughout my career, helping them to find the courage to say no while stating it in a positive and productive way." Rope's commitment to land use planning and the environment solidified when he returned from travels around the world right after college. After gaining a very hands-on, experiential, global perspective, his impression was that the country he was returning to—unlike the many he had visited, both developed and underdeveloped—was "a young, healthy country, wasting its social and natural potential." He aimed to do what he could to change that. He studied environmental law and settled in Vermont.

In his work as an attorney in Vermont, he represented citizens and land trusts in Act 250 cases such as the first St. Albans's Walmart, the Parkers Gore bear habitat case at Killington, a Stowe Mountain Resort project that impacted the Long Trail, and the Northshore Partnership development that threatened Burlington aesthetics, particularly from the lake. From this work, Rope developed an abiding frustration. "These were high-profile cases, with statewide impacts. You'd think that developers and host communities could have worked out their differences ahead of time. But with high stakes and the lack of a statewide framework, many times folks just didn't know how to begin or how seriously to take Vermont's environmental protections. They also couldn't see how one proposal or set of impacts fit into the larger, statewide picture." This coupled with a lack of strong state leadership on planning matters made for a free-for-all time in Vermont's environmental history often pitting small towns and organizations such as

VNRC with community and/or environmental interests against developers with self-interest."

His desire to work at the "proactive front end" of development and land use issues brought Rope to the Orton Family Foundation where he served as program director for eight years and then as president and CEO for six.

Rope helped create a "heart and soul process, which broadens and deepens citizen engagement and makes community discussions and decisions relevant to peoples' lives." He explains, "It's very hard to solve land use problems when there is an emergency. It's even harder if there is no urgency in the neighborhood, no big changes or immediate threats even with changes on the horizon. So what do you do? You discard the traditional models of public meetings; you make it fun, relevant, and easy to participate in. You make sure everyone feels that they have been listened to, and you include them in the decision process. Community residents are the experts on the place they call home, and they are ready to pitch in if you give them a meaningful opportunity." And Rope adds, "Defining what you are saying no and yes to takes on a whole new meaning and power with the help of this approach."

the more numerous and secure the food sources and the more diverse and varied the gene pool of potential mates will be. In some places, the patches of suitable habitat that are left are insufficient to provide either element—food security or genetic diversity—in amounts that allow a species to thrive. This makes connection between these areas a matter of survival for some species.

The Staying Connected Initiative is a program built by a partnership among state fish and wildlife departments, state transportation agencies, and a host of non-governmental groups in New York, Vermont, New Hampshire, Maine, and southeastern Canada. Headed up, in part, by the Vermont Chapter of The Nature Conservancy, it coordinates state and private efforts to manage forested and other habitat areas to secure a goal that is beyond the reach of any single entity: the assurance of contiguous habitat sufficient to meet the needs of the region's wildlife. Local decisions affect land use, so part of the Staying Connected Initiative is to work with local governments, offering communities the best available science and technical assistance to help them participate in the mission of linking habitat areas by wildlife-friendly corridors. This mission is supported by other technical assistance partnerships as well, such as the one between the VNRC and the Community Wildlife Program at the Vermont Fish and Wildlife Department that produced an analysis and report with recommendations for town action titled *Wildlife Considerations in Local Planning*.

Since 80 percent of the forested lands in Vermont are privately owned, the Staying Connected project and other conservation efforts must enlist the cooperation of many landowners. Dave Marvin is one of the many informed and active landowners in the stretch of forest that runs unbroken from the Worcester Range eastward fifty miles to Essex County and the mostly intact forests of the Nulhegan Basin. A forester by training, Dave runs a consulting firm that advises some three hundred clients. He sees the Northern Forest as resilient but stressed. "There's not just one threat to the forest, there are several." Among the problems is a historical shift in ownership patterns throughout the region. Large, single-owner tracts have been broken up and sold. As the property-tax cost of holding forestland has increased, population has grown, and more and more people are looking to

Communities can plan for healthy wildlife populations by identifying and conserving large blocks of habitat and critical areas of connectivity.

own a bit of forest—or to clear it to build a house or camp. This phenomenon was documented in a 2010 VNRC report which showed that over a seven-year study period, 47,000 more acres of forestland had new dwellings associated with them, and larger parcels of forestland were being replaced with smaller parcel sizes.

While the economic and ecological health of existing forest is diminished by this "silent sprawl," the absolute amount of forest is also in decline. For the first time in 150 years, Vermont is seeing a net loss of forestland, as are all the other New England states.

In recognition of the ongoing problem of securing forestland from the forces that are diminishing it, in June of 2006 the VNRC convened the first meeting of its Forest Roundtable, an arena in which interested parties could exchange information, develop a shared understanding of the issues, and, when appropriate, recommend policies. The first meeting drew about 30 people; by 2012, 180 people were tracking its progress and participating. Chaired by Jamey Fidel, the VNRC's Forest and Wildlife program director, the Roundtable's members include consulting foresters, professional planners, government officials, land-owners, sportsmen, representatives from the forest products industry, conservation groups, biomass energy organizations, and public and private universities and colleges. Its meet-ings have addressed multiple topics, including trends in Vermont's real estate market, rising forestland values, property tax policy, land use and con-servation planning, estate planning, landowner incentive programs such as the Current-Use Program, and the long-term sustainability of the forest products industry.

Beyond fostering dialogue, Round-table meetings have produced tangible results, including a strong stakeholder consensus about the value of Vermont's Current Use Property Tax program; the convening of a Landowner Summit to teach about trends in forest ownership; and development of a statewide database for tracking land use, and subdivision rates in Vermont. In addition, in May of 2007, the Roundtable issued a report outlining policy suggestions to curtail the rate and mitigate the effects of parcelization and forest fragmentation.

Reflecting on the Roundtable's work, Fidel emphasizes that the dynamics that threaten the state's for-ests can be varied and complicated to deal with, ranging from impacts from land use development and invasive pests, to stresses from climate change. "It's important to look at Vermont's forests in the larger context of where we have come from and where we are going," Fidel says. In general, Vermont's forests have been recovering from heavy land clearing at the turn of the last century. The revitalized for-est ecosystems of the twentieth century have been one of Vermont's environ-mental success stories, but here too, because of new challenges, the success has to be seen as only temporary. The work is ongoing.

To assist the cause, Vermont's current use property tax program has promoted forests that provide Vermonters with jobs and ecosystem services. The state funds the program, compensating towns for lost tax reve-nue, as is appropriate, since the benefits of the forested landscape accrue to all Vermonters, not just individual land-owners or the towns in which the forest stands. Approximately half of Vermont's eligible forestland is currently enrolled. "This is an amazing success story," Fidel says "but we need to be thinking ahead to ensure that more land can be enrolled." In general, conserved land usually costs communities less than developed land, but towns see upfront costs and don't always see that future benefit. Forestland conservation programs are underfunded and face competition from other demands on limited state and federal funding.

Another challenge facing Vermont is the fact that participation in current use is voluntary and is only open to owners of forested parcels of twenty-five acres or more. When too many parcels

Ellen Kahler, Chuck Ross, and Brian Shupe

GENUINE PROGRESS

Vermont has a stable, small population and responsible government. "How do we take advantage of these characteristics in a way that will move us in an orderly transition to live within our means?"

Ellen Kahler heard her environmental wake-up call in 1986 at Bucknell University, when she listened to Dr. Helen Caldicott talk about the possibility of nuclear annihilation; Ellen was soon involved in social causes on campus. After settling in Vermont in 1989, she led a statewide conversation about the need for livable wages while directing the Peace and Justice Center during the late 1990s. She earned a master's in public administration from the Harvard Kennedy School of Government in 2003, and then returned to Vermont to create and direct the Peer to Peer Collaborative, which links entrepreneurs with experienced mentors in order to find ways to improve their operations—including ways to pay their employees a livable wage. "I really enjoy designing and creating opportunities for people to become aware of how systems work—whether it's our economic system, our food system, our education system, our ecosystem, or any kind of system." Ellen became the executive director of the Vermont Sustainable Jobs Fund in late 2005 and most recently has been developing a program to encourage local production of bioenergy for local use.

Chuck Ross was "born in Vermont to a Vermonter." His father raised him to appreciate the landscape in which he lived, and together they couldn't help but notice the dramatic changes that came to the area between Hinesburg and Burlington in the 1960s and 1970s, as farmland was lost to development. In the 1970s, influenced by the growing environmental movement, Chuck pursued environmental studies, ecology, and geography in college. Donella Meadows's 1972 book, Limits to Growth, was a major influence, as was his father, who, as a member of the Federal Power Commission (now known as the Federal Energy Regulatory Commission), had a professional knowledge of the role that energy plays in society—and a knowledge that energy is a critical system upon which we depend, but with profound impacts on our lives and environment.

Once he was out of school, Chuck got involved in politics. He has served as a representative in the Vermont legislature, where he chaired the House Natural Resources and Energy Committee during the early 1990s. He was U.S. senator Patrick Leahy's state director for over sixteen years, leaving that post in 2010 to become Governor Peter Shumlin's head of the Vermont Agency of Agriculture, Food and Markets.

To all those experiences, Chuck brought what he'd learned from geography and ecology about culture's relationship to its home in a generous but finite environment. "We're not managing it well in relation to ecological limits," he says pointedly.

Brian Shupe still finds himself surprised to be a "professional environmentalist." He grew up in rapidly suburbanizing Virginia where "every patch of woods seemed to be disappearing." He soon realized that nature needed protection, and this propelled him into the study of public lands and their management at Florida State University, where he received a master's of science degree in urban and regional planning.

In 1988, he arrived in Vermont, "sight unseen," mostly because friends told him it would be a "good fit." He has served as executive director of the Mad River Valley Planning District and director of planning and zoning for the town of Stowe, and for nearly ten years he was a partner with Burnt Rock Inc., Associates in Community Planning. Brian went from there to Smart Growth Vermont, where he served as director of programs. Soon he was serving as the sustainable communities program director at VNRC, and he became executive director of the organization in September 2011.

Chuck asks, "When we talk about sustainability, what form of humanity are we trying to sustain? What do we want to look like, what is our ecology in relation to the three systems that we influence—education, governance, economy—and the three resources that we depend upon—food, water, and energy?" They're all interrelated, but "with billions of decisions being made daily, the economic system is the only one complex enough" to be the vehicle for putting our answers into effect. "Our choices have gotten us here. We've reached the limits of our non-sustainable, growth-at-any-cost way of relating to the planet," says Chuck. "Now we need a whole new set of incentives to move into a different direction."

If our choices had been based on an ecologically realistic model (instead of an infinite-planet one), our world would look very different today. In the fields of government, energy, and education, for instance, we would take advantage of tapping into everyone's strengths by using dispersed and diverse networks, rather than concentrating and consolidating the means of production into a few thousand corporations, says Ellen.

Brian believes that the power of the economy and economics are not to be underestimated. "We've got to work with the communities' economic interests if we're to achieve a sustainable society." In essence, we've been shaping our ecological systems to reflect the demands we make on our economic system; this has given us monocultures, loss of ecosystem diversity, and centralized power. We need to reverse that relationship, he says, and shape our economy to fit our shared ecology. As part of that change, we'll need to invent a better system to measure the well-being we expect our economy to produce.

Below: (l. to r.) Chuck Ross, Ellen Kahler, and Brian Shupe

Chuck asks, "Will we move towards the future using an orderly process or a chaotic process? Historically, it has been chaotic." Brian suggests that we have opportunities in Vermont that don't exist elsewhere. A small scale entrepreneurial ethos, face-to-face democracy, a working landscape of farms and forests, vital communities, and caring Vermonters all contribute to a culture of innovation.

Ellen hopes that in twenty years Vermonters will have a different sense of how we define our quality of life—that we'll judge it by the quality of our relationships and not by the amount of stuff we have.

Brian thinks that soon, out of necessity, we'll be doing less with less, but with a relatively high quality of life. We'll use less energy and generally lower our consumption. We'll buy more of our food, fiber, and power locally. Our natural resources will be the basis of a strong economy, as Vermont adapts to the reality ahead.

fall below that size, the management of much of the forest is subject to individual, uncoordinated decisions. And even when there is a management plan in effect, often there is little coordination between adjacent land owners to manage large areas of forest as an integral whole. Land trusts have helped counter this effect with specific, well-placed projects, but across Vermont, the lack of a coherent conservation or management plan for an area can weaken the integrity of the forest as development and other impacts fragment the landscape. This in turn has consequences for the human civilization that depends on forest ecosystems for valuable, even crucial services.

This is why Fidel thinks Vermont needs to focus on a complementary suite of strategies that can be accomplished without large amounts of money. One is proactive planning at the municipal level. Through planning processes already in place through Vermont's planning enabling law, towns have the authority to plan the future of their natural resource assets. As development continues, towns can be mindful about where houses and related infrastructure are placed. Towns could adopt best-practice zoning and subdivision policies that guide development while conserving our forest resources, working lands, and their ecosystem services. Communities can plan for healthy wildlife populations by identifying and conserving large blocks of habitat and critical areas of connectivity—corridors that allow animals to travel safely from one area of habitat to

another. "Helping communities plan for a healthy future is where VNRC is putting a lot of stock right now," says Fidel.

Another strategy for conserving the economic and ecological value of forests and working landscape is suggested by this insight: One reason that ecosystems

and landscapes are under threat of degradation from piecemeal development is that we have neglected to value them sufficiently in our decision making. And that's the path that another group of environmentalists have pursued, giving us our fifth story.

Measuring What Matters
How will we measure well-being?

A healthy environment is a key element in the quality of life for all Vermonters, but its benefits aren't properly counted within our basic measurements of economic well-being. Both Gross Domestic Product (GDP) and its derivative, Gross State Product (GSP) measure the sum total of all commercial transactions in an economy —the commotion of money, nothing

more. And that's not a good measure of economic well-being, let alone of our overall quality of life.

Realizing this, in 2011 the board of the VNRC passed a resolution calling on state and other public officials

One of the benefits of the GPI (General Progress Indicator) is that it includes ecosystems services such as the wetlands seen here along the Connecticut River.

to develop and compile a better, more comprehensive set of indicators of economic well-being. As an affiliate of the National Wildlife Federation (NWF), the VNRC sent the resolution on to the NWF annual meeting for consideration, where it was unanimously endorsed. The resolution, instigated by board member Eric Zencey, pointed out the flaws in using GDP as our main measure of how well-off we are (or aren't). Nearly a century ago, when the planet seemed infinite, this gross measure of economic activity seemed to be a good indicator of economic well-being, and economic well-being seemed like the only kind that economic policy had to deal with. We had so many of the other elements of well-being in such abundance that we could take them for granted. But today the costs of environmentally damaging development looms larger, and the non-economic aspects of our well-being can no longer be taken for granted; GDP is no longer a good measure of what matters to us.

Influenced in part by the VNRC and those connected with it, and by others who are active in the alternative-indicators movement, in the 2012 legislative session Senator Anthony Pollina and Representative Suzy Wizowaty introduced bills calling on the state to develop an improved set of economic indicators. Signed into law by Governor Shumlin, the bill calls on the University of Vermont's Gund Institute for Ecological Economics to compile a Genuine Progress Indicator (GPI) for Vermont. The GPI is an emergent standard in the international alternative-indicators move-

ment and has roots that reach back several decades. It corrects GDP figures by subtracting costs that GDP doesn't count and adding benefits it ignores. The costs it counts include loss of leisure time; the expense, in both money and time, of commuting; net loss of farmlands and wetlands and air and water quality; loss or depreciation of infrastructure and existing consumer durables (like cars, appliances, and computers and roads washed away in tropical storms); and use of non-renewable resources. The benefits that GPI aims to measure include the services of things we already have and the value of volunteer work and domestic production like cooking, cleaning, and maintenance, along with child care and elder care.

Because it deducts environmental losses from economic gains, and because it counts goods and services that GDP doesn't count, GPI will be a better, more effective measure of the sustainable, delivered well-being Vermonters enjoy.

Kate McCarthy, VNRC Sustainable Communities program director, helped to usher in the GPI Bill.

Vermont Ranks

6th	"Kids Count" list
1st	United Health Foundation state rankings
1st	Health Care State Rankings (2003)
4th	Immunization rates
2nd	Prenatal care
50th	Auto fatalities per miles driven
5th	Adults registered to vote
2nd	Fewest bankruptcies filed per capita
4th	Percentage of self-employed
1st	Maple syrup production
14th	Dairy production
7th	Cleanliness of public waters
2nd	Clean air
1st	Least toxic chemicals released per capita

Maryland was the first state to compile a GPI officially, but Vermont has the opportunity to become a leader of the movement with the addition of two innovations. The law directs the Gund Institute to make recommendations for additional indicators that will measure other aspects of well-being that matter to Vermonters, such as access to health care, access to affordable housing, and percentage of jobs that pay a livable wage. And it encourages the executive branch to use the indicator set in evaluating the outcomes and costs of government programs and services, an effort that will complement the "dashboard" of indicators that is being separately developed by the Shumlin administration. No other state or country has yet integrated a broad-ranging measure of sustainable, delivered well-being into its policy planning and budgeting processes in this way. The result will be greater efficiency in achieving the goal of a sustainable state: the delivery of the maximum possible sustainable well-being to Vermont's citizens.

The passage of the GPI bill doesn't guarantee that policy makers will work to improve the conditions it measures. But you can't even aim at a target you can't see. The GPI will give state officials and citizens a better sense of our progress toward achieving the goal that the environmental movement has always pursued: a sustainable balance between humans and nature, a balance that gives us the highest possible quality of life.

The Work Ahead

Throughout its history, a strong part of the Vermont environmental movement sought to protect natural resources *from* people, as did John Muir, and an equally strong part of the movement has also strived to conserve resources *for* people, as did George Perkins Marsh and Gifford Pinchot. Increasingly, we are coming to understand that these two approaches are one—and that achieving either will require thinking in new, more encompassing ways.

As the VNRC saw in adopting its resolution for better, more comprehensive indicators of economic well-being, the work of the Vermont environmental movement will be easier when the environment's contribution to our collective well-being is officially counted. It will also be easier when every Vermont town has an energy committee that helps its neighbors find their way to a sustainable energy future; when thriving local economies are built on jobs and businesses that depend on healthy, working landscapes; when those landscapes offer sufficient habitat to the species with whom we share our home; and when the lessons of the state's recovery from Tropical Storm Irene are widely understood and broadly applied.

But even then, there will be work for the environmental movement. Infinite-planet thinking and infinite-planet behavior are firmly rooted in American culture, and resisting and transforming them won't be accomplished overnight. New pressures on the landscape will be loosed by such large dynamics as population growth, climate change, the migration of ecological refugees worldwide, and the withdrawal symptoms of a civilization addicted to oil. These will bring unprecedented challenges to Vermont, some of them far beyond the purview of the environmental movement as traditionally understood. The movement must, and we think will, rise to that challenge.

One of the fundamental principles of ecology was offered by John Muir

Angella Gibbons and the EarthWalk School

GIVING EVERY CHILD AN OPPORTUNITY TO FALL IN LOVE WITH THE EARTH

Angella Gibbons and her EarthWalk students have no building to call a school. Instead, their classroom is a quiet woodland adjacent to the Goddard College campus in Plainfield, Vermont.

The students of EarthWalk are building long-term relationships with the land and with each other, learning within a culture of "nature mentoring" based on the educational philosophy of Jon Young and the Wilderness Awareness School of Duvall, Washington. EarthWalk is one of over one hundred nationally and internationally affiliated schools founded on principles of nature connection as the foundation for all learning.

Angella quotes David Orr, who cautions that "all education is environmental education; by what is included or excluded we teach the young that they are part of or apart from the natural world."

Angella says, "I learned at a very young age that I am an integral part of the natural world. What a gift I was given. And what I'm doing now has everything to do with how I grew up."

A childhood love of being outdoors was only the beginning. After graduating from the University of Vermont, Angella did a stint with MASSPIRG canvassing door-to-door to try to "save the earth." Though she was talking about the earth she loved and helping to educate people, she was feeling completely ineffective. She realized what was missing: active engagement with learners in direct contact with what she loved—the natural world.

In 1987, she accepted a job as a naturalist at a residential environmental education program in the coastal redwood forest of California. She has been passionately mentoring young people ever since in nature connection. After returning to Vermont in 1993, Angella founded Lotus Lake Discovery Center, which had worked with over 15,000 students and teachers in Central Vermont by 2003. She moved on to create a long-term nature mentoring school in 2005 called EarthWalk Vermont, with the mission of inspiring and empowering children, families, and communities to reconnect with and care for one another and the earth.

It seems so simple; we take care of what we love. So, when asked, What is the most important thing? Angella responds: "Go fall in love with the earth, and if you can, take a child with you."

Below: (l. to r.) Angella with EarthWalk students: Tristan Brown, Cedar and Marguarite Souligny, Liam Walker, Lila Humphries-LePage, and Sadie Fischbeck

Deb Markowitz

VERMONT, A MODEL OF RESILIENCE

In 2010, Deb Markowitz ran for governor on her record of outstanding leadership and the managerial experience gained in the twelve years she served as secretary of state. She is a powerhouse, but her formidable record complements a light-hearted and happy nature, based in her firmly rooted optimism about the future. The winner of the gubernatorial race—Peter Shumlin—wisely chose several of his opponents for his cabinet. He tapped Deb for the position of secretary of the Agency of Natural Resources, and now she plays a key role in determining Vermont's response to climate change and in assessing the effects of renewable energy options on the state's natural resources. She chairs the governor's Climate Cabinet.

The cabinet brings together senior officials from eight state agencies to catalyze and coordinate climate change work across state government. The work is directed in large part by the Comprehensive Energy Plan prepared by the Shumlin administration, which calls for the state to obtain 90 percent of its total energy from renewable sources by 2050. Meeting that goal will require rethinking and reengineering the economy: electrical generation, home heating, industrial processes, transportation, even land use decisions will be affected. It won't be easy. Getting there, Deb says, "will require Vermonters to virtually eliminate their reliance on fossil fuels." But the goal is within reach: "The administration believes it can be done through enhanced efficiency and greater use of clean, renewable sources for electricity, heating and transportation." The administration realizes that renewable energy has to be brought online responsibly, ensuring that overall energy costs for businesses and residents remain regionally competitive. If and when the price of carbon fuel starts to reflect the social costs it imposes on us, this transition will become easier. And as oil production peaks and declines, the development of a sustainably fueled economy will ensure Vermont's economic health in the decades to come. The two goals are compatible:

"We must act boldly to protect both our environment and our economic security," Deb emphasizes. To this end, she is a leading voice in the statewide conversation about how we must balance the costs and benefits—environmental, social, and economic—of renewable energy sources in an age of global climate change, from wind to biomass and from solar to methane.

The devastation wrought by increased precipitation, such as we saw with Tropical Storm Irene, demands that we maintain and develop a deeper resilience in our built systems. Our energy economy needs to be resilient, with many diverse sources of renewable energy flowing through systems that use the latest technologies to be maximally efficient. Our infrastructure needs to be resilient, to meet the challenge of unpredictable weather and climate change. And our communities need to remain resilient. "Research shows that people with strong social networks are more resilient than those without them," Deb notes.

decades ago: "If you try to pick one thing out by itself, you find it hitched to everything else in the universe"—everything is connected, and a change anywhere in a complex system tends to reverberate through the whole. Our environmental problems are themselves like an ecosystem, a complex web of interconnection and relation that we don't completely and may never fully understand. To address them effectively, the environmental movement will have to "think like an ecosystem"—see, conceptualize, and deal with the problematic system as a whole. Climate change is upon us, and its magnitude is barely comprehensible. Tropical Storm Irene came from a place far from the state, but its causes have roots that extend into our lives and homes. As long as Vermonters burn fossil fuels as if the planet's capacity to absorb greenhouse gases were infinite, we contribute to the problem. And doing our part to solve the problem will not be enough.

The task can seem daunting. The infinite-planet system has enormous inertia, and like a healthy ecosystem, it is resilient and tends to "heal" itself, absorbing change, adapting, maintaining its status quo. This means that many of the victories of the environmental movement are, indeed, all too temporary. But there is also an advantage offered by the complexity of the problem: any action, anywhere, that begins to transform that system will have an effect on the whole. It has leverage points (food, water, energy, transportation, waste streams, economic indicators) at which concerted effort

can bring amplified results. And action can be taken in the assurance that the alternative system of practice—sustainable communities—will eventually outcompete the unsustainable system it seeks to replace. It's definitional: an unsustainable system cannot last.

Until its ultimate goal is reached, the environmental movement in Vermont, as elsewhere, will play a much-needed role as it embraces and defines and works for that vision of sustainable communities. This is the high purpose of civilization in the twenty-first century, and until that goal is achieved, the main task of the environmental movement will be to ensure that our progress toward it is steady and certain.

In this, the movement will simply be doing what it has always done. The purpose evident in its work—to ensure that Vermonters live within and make use of nature's infrastructure wisely, sustainably—is as old as the movement itself and yet as new as the challenge of fully greening Vermont.

In 1970, as the Gibb Commission produced what would become Act 250, its report warned that what was at stake wasn't just a way of life for a small, rural corner of the United States but nothing less than the survival of mankind. Action resulting from this report was swift. Forty years later, as we endure the consequences of our irresistible addiction to oil, it has become increasingly clear that the Gibb Commission's warning was not overstated. Whether we can respond as wisely and swiftly to the challenge of climate change remains an open question.

Jeff Danziger's cartoon sums up the work ahead: bringing the old and new technologies together and the energy of community initiatives to move us to a new clean energy future.

The Search for a Sustainable State

by Bill McKibben

If anyone thought
they could hole up in
a bucolic Vermont and
avoid the woes of a
warming earth, Irene
was the final proof that
was folly.

By the start of the current decade, Vermont was environmentally schizophrenic. Within its borders the state was as green as any spot in the nation: for instance, the local food movement, a novelty five or six years earlier, was a fixture. The state led all comers in green jobs per capita; hardly a week went by without a dedication ceremony for some new "solar farm." Even advising the rest of the world on how to go green had become a growth industry: traveling to China, say, I'd invariably come across mayors of huge cities who'd just been consulting with alumni of Efficiency Vermont about how to use their utility rates to drive conservation. (In fact, these guys had usually heard of precisely two American states, California and Vermont, and in their minds they were roughly equal in size and import.) As one place after another worked on transition town initiatives, as the fight to close Vermont Yankee slowly gained ground, as the state became the first in the nation to ban fracking for oil and gas—it was possible to imagine that the Green Mountain State was on a path to meet its environmental challenges. Even endemic troubles like the nutrients pouring into Lake Champlain seemed potentially surmountable as big dairies began to understand that manure was a profitable new source of power. In his inaugural speech after the 2010 election, new governor Peter Shumlin said Vermont would "provide the brainpower, make the products, and seize the job opportunities a lower carbon economy requires." A few months later, still in his first term, he was named green governor of the year. "You're going to see an economic revival for the people who get this right," he told reporters.

Hooray and huzzah. The problem, however, is that the state is no longer in control of its environmental destiny—the biggest problems now are coming from a distance. Which became clear to pretty much everyone in the last week of August 2011. On the 24th, Matt Sutkoski, in the Free Press weather blog, told boat owners that they might want to batten down; a hurricane named Irene, slowly working its way up the East Coast, might blow this way. Oh, and if it dumped five inches of rain "we would have some wicked serious flooding." Three days later, Irene wandered over the warmest seas ever recorded off New York and New Jersey, and since warm air holds more water vapor than cold, it picked up moisture like a sponge. On the night of August 28, that sponge got wrung out along the eastern spine of the Greens: in places, ten inches of rain came down, and "wicked serious flooding" was upgraded to "Oh my God." Everyone knows the story, at least in outline: Vermont's most expensive disaster, people swept away downstream, eerie YouTube shots of covered bridges falling into raging creeks. Some towns were cut off for days, with helicopters dropping food and medicine to survivors. For weeks, getting east or west across the center of the state was an adventure; despite yeoman work by the agency of transportation, it wasn't until January that all the major roads were more or less reopened.

The morning after Irene, with the rain stopped but waters still rising, the governor stepped off a helicopter long enough to give an interview to Amy Goodman on Democracy Now. After reporting on the emergency response, he added, "I find it extraordinary that so many political leaders won't actually talk about the relationship between climate change, fossil fuels, our continuing irrational exuberance about burning fossil fuels, in light of these storm patterns that we've been experiencing. Listen, since I've been sworn in as governor just

seven months ago, I have dealt with—this is the second major disaster as a result of storms. We had storms this spring that flooded our downtowns and put us through many of the same exercises that we're going through right now. We didn't used to get weather patterns like this in Vermont. We didn't get tropical storms. We didn't get flash flooding. It wasn't—you know, our storm patterns weren't like Costa Rica; they were like Vermont." And in that short outburst, he nailed our future: ever less Vermont, ever more tropics.

If anyone thought they could hole up in a bucolic Vermont and avoid the woes of a warming earth, Irene was the final proof that was folly. Farmers in the Intervale, arguably the show-piece of the state's local agriculture movement, were finally preparing for a harvest after spring floods had delayed planting. But in a matter of minutes, the Winooski rose over the crops—growers in canoes tried to evacuate bee hives, while others just watched stunned as a season's labor was covered in mud. Across the state, beautiful organic farms turned into piles of silt and gravel. In Cuttingsville, Ryan Wood-Beauchamp and Kara Fitzgerald watched the water rise above Evening Song Farm, a CSA feeding fifty families. Ryan: "There's

Above: Vermonters gathered on the statehouse steps to demand action on climate change. Below: At the culmination of a walk from Ripton to Burlington, VNRC executive director Elizabeth Courtney and Vermont climate change activist Bill McKibben addressed a large rally in Battery Park.

rocks, river rocks, debris, forest debris, the remains of our greenhouse and that's it. There's no vegetables, there's no soil, there's no subsoil, it's the river that goes through here now." Fitzgerald: "You can't actually get worse than this, you can't. There's no land. I know a lot of people we've talked to and I've even seen pictures are like, the waters will recede, we'll come help you, we'll bring our excavators, we'll re-divert the river, but it's not going to change." As it happens, the farmers found three acres of borrowed land the next summer to keep the CSA alive and reported that they were looking for new land to buy—but maybe not along a river.

So now the challenge is twofold, both hard. One is to keep building a resilient Vermont, one prepared for a planet emerging from the stability of the Holocene to the chaotic turbulence of whatever comes next. As rising temperatures bring more turbulent weather, fortune will likely favor the squat, the hardy, the durable, the small and spread out. Vermont—despite a mountain and valley topography that makes water hard to deal with—boasts the right mindset and institutions for survival in turbulent times. Above all, as the aftermath of Irene proved, the state's powerful sense of community is an asset hard to measure but impossible to overlook. "Vermont Strong," Governor Shumlin called it.

But even community resilience only goes so far. There's a limit to how many times one state can rebuild. So the other half of the equation, even harder, is that in self-defense Vermont has to help take

the lead in getting the whole planet off the fossil fuels that cause climate change and toward some kind of reasonably soft landing. Given Vermont's tiny size, that seems laughable. Except that the biggest grassroots climate change movement began in the state in 2008, when a small team of Middlebury students and faculty launched 350.org, taking its name from what scientists said was the most carbon we could safely have in the atmosphere. (We're currently at 393 parts million and rising two parts per year; hence Irene). From small beginnings in Addison County, the organization grew to encompass every nation but North Korea by 2011 and led the largest civil disobedience campaign in thirty years in this country in late summer of that year, a fight to stop construction of a pipeline to Canada's tar sands, a vast pool of carbon.

In fact, those sit-ins in front of the White House were in full swing when Irene slammed into Vermont. On August 30, a busload of Vermonters piled out on Lafayette Plaza, ready to take their place in the demonstration. They'd had an odyssey just getting out of the state, hard-pressed to find an open bridge in the wake of the flooding. But as one woman explained as she was being put into handcuffs, "There's nothing we can do to stop Irene now. But we need to make sure there's not another one."

Writ large, that's Vermont's challenge for the half-century to come.

GET INVOLVED!

What can you do to help achieve a sustainable state? Here's a partial list:

• Inform and educate yourself and others.

• Do an energy audit of your house—and your whole life.

• Walk, bike or take a bus instead of a car.

• Move closer to work or to a walkable village center.

• Buy local so that your purchases help create a resilient local economy.

• Attend school board meetings to ensure that the curriculum includes ecological literacy, the cafeteria serves healthy, locally sourced food, and that the school has a plan for adapting its taxpayer-supported facilities to the post-petroleum economy.

• Join a CSA.

• Join the VNRC and 350.org

• Contact your local energy committee. If your town doesn't have one, start it.

• Contact the Transition Town Movement in your area, and start a chapter if there isn't one near you.

• Join the movement to get state governments, pension funds, colleges and universities to disinvest in the carbon economy.

• Support a Green Tax Shift—the effort to tax throughput of raw materials instead of the value we add to those materials with our labor.

• Write a letter to the editor or an op-ed. Start a neighborhood group to help and join you.

• Throw a neighborhood party for no better reason than to connect with neighbors and friends.

• Measure and minimize your ecological footprint.

• Be the change you want to see—and then work to change your community so that it's easier to be the person you want to be.

• Grab whatever levers of power and influence are within your grasp, including participating in town and village and local governments, including joining with others to demonstrate in person when and where it will help.

• Remember that, as Woody Allen said, "eighty percent of success is just showing up."

For further information on these and other acts of constructive sustainability, see the web page for this book, accessible through the VNRC website at VNRC.org.

For an index to *Greening Vermont* and a list of sources and further readings, please visit the book's website at VNRC.org/ GreeningVermont.

ART AND PHOTO CREDITS

*Special thanks to all the photographers
and other artists for their work.*

PRODUCTION NOTES:

Design/production: Laughing Bear Associates, Montpelier, VT

Printing: Villanti, Milton, VT (an FSC® certified company)

This publication was manufactured with electricity that was offset with Green-e® certified renewable energy credits and high-solid, soy-based, VOC-free inks.

Text paper is 80# Cascades Enviro 100 Satin Text which is manufactured using Bio-Gas and is 100# post-consumer waste.

Cover paper is 100# Sappi Galerie Art Silk Cover which is produced using Green-e® certified energy.

More information and an Environmental Calculator are available online at **vnrc.org/greeningvermont.**